Hollows, Peepers, and Highlanders

An Appalachian Mountain Ecology

George Constantz

Mountain Press Publishing Co.
Missoula, Montana
1994

Copyright © 1994
George Constantz

Second Printing, March 1995

Illustrations © Peggy Kochanoff
Cover Painting © Dorothy Sigler Norton

Grateful acknowledgement is made for permission to quote
"Fireflies in the Garden" by Robert Frost,
from *The Poetry of Robert Frost* edited by Edward Connery Lathem.
Copyright © 1956 by Robert Frost.
Copyright 1928, © 1969 by Henry Holt and Company, Inc.
Reprinted by permission of Henry Holt and Company, Inc..

Library of Congress Cataloging-in-Publication Data

Constantz, George, 1947-
    Hollows, peepers, and highlanders: an Appalachian Mountain ecology / George
Constantz
        p. cm.
    Includes bibliographical references (p.   ) and index.
    ISBN 0-87842-263 (paper) : $14.00
    1. Natural history—Appalachian Region.   2. Forest fauna—Adaptation—
Appalachian Region.   3. Forest plants—Adaptation—Appalachian Region.
4. Forest ecology—Appalachian Region.   5. Appalachian Region.   I. Title.
QH104.5.A6C65 1994
508.74—dc20   94-2315
                                                                                                    CIP

Printed in the U.S.A. on acid-free, recycled paper.

A portion of the proceeds from this book
supports the conservation of Appalachian rivers.

Mountain Press Publishing Company
P.O. Box 2399 • Missoula, Montana 59806
406-728-1900 • 800-234-5308

This book is dedicated to the wolf spiders and white-footed mice that share my study. Their reproductive success, despite my efforts to the contrary, has earned my grudging admiration.

Contents

Acknowledgments

I owe a great deal to many generous people. John Ailes, Maurice Donohue, Marshall Sprague, and David Vis encouraged me to make the commitment. The following highlanders provided literature: Jerry Atkins, Russell LaFollette, Gerald Lewis, Harold Parsons, Andy Rogers, Bob Smith, Gary Strawn, Charlie Streisel, Roger Thomas, Dr. Randy Thornhill, Ro Wauer, and Dr. Peter White. Dr. Quinn Constantz and Gary Wilson helped with the field work. For word processing help, I thank Tammy Barnes, Mary Kay Clem, Carol Fultz, Beth and Betty Loy, Jo Ann Shepherd, Jane Small, Bill and Dan Snyder, and Robby Pyles. Several chapters were critically reviewed by Dr. George Bunting, Dr. Stephen Fretwell, Phil Gallery, Bob Groves, Mode Johnson, Jim Matheson, Philip Nixon, Tom Stump, and Dave Trimmier. The following people read and criticized the entire manuscript: Sylvia Donohue, Dr. Ed Flaccus, Eric Patterson, Dr. Gary Evans, and several classes of biology students. Although their contributions do not fit neatly into a single category, I appreciate the help of the following mountaineers: Rodney Bartgis, Wes Bicha, Dr. George Byers, Grey Cassell, Kathy Emerson, Bob Faulkner, Dr. Ross Kiester, Gary Morfoot, Robin Pancake, Shirley Parsons, Dr. Thomas Pauley, Arlene Saville, Charlie See, Phyllis Starkey, Harold Smallwood, and Linda Ullery. For her mastery of carrot-and-stick, I appreciate Kat Ort, my editor at Mountain Press.

Peggy Kochanoff's sensitive drawings grace the chapter heads. Jim Holmes' photograph of a spring peeper was the model for Dorothy Sigler Norton's cover painting.

My wife, Nancy, helped me every step of the way.

Thanks to all.

1

Modus

I AM AN UNABASHED PARTISAN of the Appalachian Mountains. It is not that there are rocky, majestic peaks here; quite the contrary: Eons of erosion have delivered rounded highlands that are approachable and gentle on the eye. But beneath Appalachia's soft exterior run myriad short-lived scenes, each being played out by an individual organism competing for its part in the evolutionary play. No play runs in a vacuum, though. As G. Evelyn Hutchinson, the intellectual grandfather of many contemporary ecologists, put it, the long-term evolutionary drama can be appreciated only within the context of its environmental theater.

The play is complex, showcasing a tremendous diversity of actors. Appalachia hosts more species of deciduous trees, salamanders, darters, and shrews than any other region of North America. Mosses, ferns, sedges, and heaths also abound. This huge variety of living things is due in large part to the highlands' antiquity and convoluted topography. Appalachia's beauty is dynamic and every walk unique. Autumn colors, wing prints in snow, spring wildflowers, and a stream of tiger swallowtails punctuate my year. If you are open to it, every day will reveal a new sight, sound, or smell. Even in the dead of winter I can detect change in the tufted titmouse's call, a shifting to the serious song of spring.

I have written this book for three reasons. First, I want to share my excitement for viewing Appalachian plants and animals from an evolutionary perspective. Contemplating a leaf or laughing at a squirrel, friends often ask me, "What good is it?" or "Why does it do that?" Such prodding questions provide this book's thread: *Most* traits of a living thing exist because they have contributed to the reproductive success of that individual's ancestors; therefore, the ultimate function of most traits we see in contemporary organisms is to promote the reproduction of the individual. According to this view, survival of the species is merely an incidental, statistical by-product of the behavior of many individuals, each selfishly pursuing its own reproduction. The essay "Autumn Leaves" registers my caveat on why I emphasize "most".

I interpret the existence of an organism's traits in terms of "why" questions in addition to "what" or "how" questions. That is, I try to maintain an explicit distinction between what historical, evolutionary causes may account for the traits of an organism compared to how that trait develops and functions in an individual. The foundation for many of the following chapters, then, is the critical application of the theory of natural selection. This theory embraces some of the most basic concepts of evolutionary biology, such as adaptation, trade-offs, and sexual selection.

Grappling with such questions is called "selection thinking," a type of logic introduced by Charles Darwin and reinforced more recently by George C. Williams, a contemporary synthesizer of evolutionary biology. Over the last 20 years, I have been applying the theory of natural selection to interpret the lives of organisms in my local environment. Viewed through this neo-Darwinian paradigm, I see individuals as life-long reproductive competitors and have come to appreciate the role of conflict in shaping the daily routines of plants and animals. One of my priorities is to expose the conflicts that underlie the beauty and mystery of Appalachian life: violence among fireflies, sexual parasitism within frog choruses, deception by flowers. The bottom line is that natural selection has led to traits that best contribute to individual reproductive success, not necessarily to characteristics we would judge as generous or ethical.

The second reason for writing this book stems from my experience as a teacher: I want to see people do more "backyard biology." Even though the processes of photosynthesis and meiosis are crucial to living systems, we cannot readily experience these concepts firsthand. We can, however, peer out a frosted window, identify a northern junco, and based on its size and color, predict whether it will drive off another flock-mate to steal its food or whether it is subordinate and will be displaced.

Most of Appalachia's living wealth is within a day's drive of half the people in North America, an association that brings both advantages and disadvantages. On the positive side, our hills are close to long-standing centers of scientific research, so we have been able to learn a great deal of their natural history. However, on the negative side, growing demands for minerals and timber, fish and game, and open space have led to major environmental changes. Thus, my third motive is to stimulate preservation through appreciation.

This is not a broad survey of Appalachian natural history—other books, such as Maurice Brooks' *The Appalachians*, do that very well. Instead, I paint specific vignettes that residents, summer campers, and lost travelers can reflect on as they bump into Appalachian organisms. Although a few of the chapters deal with topics I have personally researched, most are stories that have piqued my curiosity via the labors of other biologists. For most of the essays, I gathered the data from research journals and recast the stories in less technical language.

I will lead you through the following drama. "Stage and Theater" traces the geological origins of the Appalachian Mountains, sketches the processes by which many species evolved in isolated hollows and mountaintops, and presents several views of the structure and function of today's forest. "The Players" is a series of essays on the unique, even quirky, adaptations of selected species. We explore why jack-in-the-pulpits undergo sex changes and how box turtles seem to live in the past. The third section, "Seasonal Acts," takes you through the Appalachian year, examining topics such as how an animal's body shape affects its chances of coping with winter and what, if any, are the reasons for fall colors. In a reflective "Epilogue," I look at the biological consequences of dissecting the forest and register my views on Appalachia's most pressing environmental problems.

Because I love living in a little hollow in the Ridge and Valley province of central Appalachia and because my writing teachers have exhorted me to write about what I know, many of my examples may strike you as parochial. I assure you, though, that the concepts engage not only the full range of Appalachia but the entire eastern deciduous forest, which covers half of the United States.

A note about jargon. I have tried to avoid technical words wherever possible, but I have also not been afraid to jump right in where precision, efficiency, and color may reward a curious reader. I have settled on the following compromise: In each chapter, I define the technical words on first use; thereafter, I hold you to remembering the definition or using the glossary.

Hollows, Peepers, and Highlanders, then, is a collection of narratives and essays about some of my favorite natural events in Appalachia and their evolutionary interpretations. In setting the tone for this trip, I'd like to borrow the ideas from two earlier travelers. In *Life on a Little-Known Planet*, entomologist Howard Ensign Evans felt awe when he discovered another new detail about the life of a little insect. In *Pilgrim at Tinker Creek*, essayist Annie Dillard stressed the importance of practice in sensing the moods of nature. As you move through the book, consider this blend: We have the power to see wonder in the common-place, but only with a little practice.

Stage and Theater

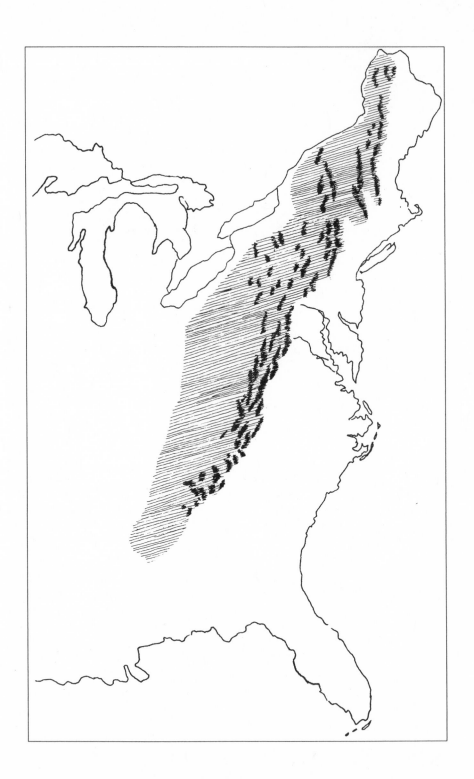

2

Origins

O<small>N THE SURFACE</small>, defining this mountain range appears a straightforward proposition. Most authorities agree that the Appalachian Mountains are a loose group of peaks and ridges that form the sinuous axis of eastern North America, that they roughly parallel the Atlantic coast, and that they stretch about 1,100 miles as the raven flies. We also agree that the chain's southern limit extends into northern Georgia and Alabama, where the highlands abruptly give way to coastal plain. Here, however, the consensus ends. For example, we disagree about Appalachia's northern limit. Some stretch the Appalachians northward onto the Gaspé Peninsula of Quebec; others draw the line at the Hudson River in eastern New York. The southern limit of the last glacial advance, located in southern Pennsylvania, yields a neat and, as we shall see, biologically relevant southern border for northern Appalachia. But here again, we disagree on how to divide the remainder. For our purposes, let us consider central Appalachia as gradually merging into a southern section centered in the Great Smoky Mountains. Central Appalachia consists of low ridges of 4,000 feet, while the other two sections top 6,000 feet.

The eastern half of North America consists of several geographic regions, called physiographic provinces, each featuring a distinct topography. Although again lacking a professional consensus, I consider the

9

core of Appalachia as, from east to west, the Blue Ridge, Ridge and Valley, and Appalachian Plateau physiographic provinces. The two flanking provinces—the Piedmont to the east and the Interior Plateau to the west—lack a mountain flavor and, more importantly, have presented organisms with different evolutionary pressures than those enforced by the mountains.

The Blue Ridge, the easternmost zone of Appalachia, runs from Carlisle, Pennsylvania, southward into Georgia as a single ridge averaging 3,000 feet in elevation. This narrow belt, 14 miles wide in the north and 70 miles wide in the south, includes the Great Smoky Mountains in Tennessee and North Carolina. For a while the Blue Ridge escarpment penned European colonists along the East Coast.

Between the Blue Ridge and the Ridge and Valley provinces lies the Great Valley, which some geographers place within the Ridge and Valley. Varying in width from 2 to 50 miles, this giant trough stretches almost the entire length of the Appalachians. As the Great Valley extends southward, its name changes from Cumberland Valley to Shenandoah Valley and ultimately becomes the Tennessee Valley. Overflowing from Pennsylvania, settlers finally colonized areas west of the Blue Ridge by streaming southward through the Great Valley.

West of the Great Valley lies the Ridge and Valley province, also called the Folded Appalachians because of its corrugated topography. Here, even-crested, roughly parallel mountain ridges alternate with valleys. The Ridge and Valley stretches the entire length of the Appalachians and varies in width from 14 to 80 miles. Where I live, this zone cuts a 46-mile-wide swath from Winchester, Virginia, to Keyser, West Virginia. Throughout the Ridge and Valley, erosion-prone rocks, such as limestone, underlie the valleys, and erosion-resistant strata, such as sandstone and conglomerate, form the ridges. Amazingly, even though the province narrows by half as it stretches southward, the number of ridges and valleys remains constant. This squeeze is accommodated by steeper strata and more deep fractures in the narrow portions than in the wide zones.

I will never forget my first view of the Ridge and Valley—from an airplane in early spring. The skinny, brown, forested ridges alternated with valleys of bright green cover crops. It seemed so uniform, so perfect.

For a moment I was incredulous—the scene could have been a painting. It's no wonder that some geographers have called our Ridge and Valley the most elegant folded mountain belt on earth.

To the west of the Ridge and Valley lies the Appalachian Plateau province—mildly folded strata and plateaulike mountains dissected by deep valleys. In general, the Plateau was uplifted less and the strata left less deformed than was the Ridge and Valley. The Plateau's dissected surface causes streams to branch randomly in all directions and at almost any angle, a condition called dendritic drainage. On a topographic map, dendritic streams contrast strikingly with the parallel, or trellised, drainage typical of the Ridge and Valley. The highest Appalachian province, the Plateau gradually loses altitude westward.

The highlands and their green blanket have undergone a long and complex evolution. In fact, scientists are still coaxing the stories out of the rocks and trees—today's theories may be superseded tomorrow. In Appalachia, older strata overlie younger layers, pieces of Africa cling to North America, and geologic forces have shoved surface layers many miles westward. A series of collisions of drifting continental plates folded, faulted, and metamorphosed the geologic terrain, eventually uniting North America with Africa and raising the Appalachians during Paleozoic time, 570 to 248 million years ago. A period of deep erosion followed each episode of mountain building. The degree of deformation of strata decreases away from the front of tectonic collision: greatest corrugation in the Piedmont, moderate in the Ridge and Valley, least in the Appalachian Plateau. The Andes and Alps display a similar pattern relative to their zones of geologic upheaval.

The early Appalachians, then, rose as the first primitive fishes appeared over 500 million years ago. Here's a telling comparison: Appalachia existed for 200 million years before terrestrial organisms evolved to occupy it. Today, the seaward portion of the Appalachian belt includes large and small blocks of distinctive rocks, called terranes. These terranes were welded onto North America. The suture of the two megacontinents that collided to raise our Appalachians forms the Brevard zone, a long fault trending northeast-southwest through Brevard, North Carolina, and connecting Atlanta, Asheville, and Roanoke. Terranes of foreign rocks lie east of the Brevard zone. Discontinuous

extensions of the Brevard zone even reach Staten Island, making part of the Big Apple a piece of the Old World.

While reptiles appeared during Carboniferous time, 360 to 286 million years ago, the North American and African plates began to rift apart, forming the present Atlantic Ocean. Since then, eastern North America has remained tectonically quiet, while the North American plate has drifted west-southwest about one inch per year.

We can also view Appalachian origins from a local perspective. Rather than immersing yourself in the technical details of the entire mountain chain, I encourage you to explore via hikes and geological maps the peaks, rocks, and folds in your own Appalachian neighborhood.

A local set of corrugated strata often remind me of the the power of tectonic collision. Two road cuts between Gore, Virginia, and Capon Bridge, West Virginia, expose layers of folded Devonian shale so severe, elegant, and compelling that at times I am hard-pressed to keep the old truck on the road—even though I steer by that spot at least once a month.

I live alongside Pine Cabin Run, a creek flowing over sedimentary rocks of the Devonian Chewing series laid down about 400 million years ago. Chewing rocks are part of the western half of the Meadow Branch syncline, a group of strata bent into a U. In order to visit my friends Mike and Annette at their cabin, I wind halfway up the North Mountain anticline, a set of strata bent into an upside-down U. Flanking this anticline are Silurian White Medina and Red Medina sandstones deposited 420 million years ago. Ordovician Martinsburg shale, a fine-grained sedimentary rock formed 500 million years ago, tops North Mountain. My westward drive to Romney, the county seat, passes over an unnamed anticline that forms Cacapon Mountain and then over a syncline underlying Cooper Mountain, both of which expose Oriskany sandstone from the Silurian (all of which you are now equipped to interpret). On behalf of my old truck, I thank our erosive water for delivering today's gentle highlands; they are much kinder on the transmission than the original rugged landscape would have been.

The Appalachian Mountains began to rise about 600 million years ago and reached their maximum height about 300 million years ago. Our mountains have been steadily eroding since Triassic time. Altogether, the Appalachian Mountains have been uplifted out of the ocean for more than 500 million years, making Appalachia one of the oldest terrestrial environments on earth. By comparison, today's great mountain ranges—the Andes, Himalayas, and Alps—are infants, a mere 50 million years old. Recognizing Appalachia's antiquity is crucial to understanding the range's biological diversity.

At the beginning of Mesozoic time about 248 million years ago, the formerly joined ancestral continents of Laurentia and Gondwanaland went separate ways. Their resident land-dwelling animals became geographically isolated and began to follow different evolutionary paths. Most of the modern vertebrates of North America evolved from the primitive Laurasian faunal element: they are animals that arose in proto-North America. A few representatives of the Gondwanaland fauna, such as the catfishes and toads, colonized North America much later.

The Pleistocene period, 1.8 million to 5,000 years ago, brought heavy rains and erosion to warm, southern areas and continental glaciation to cold, northern zones. The last two million years may have seen 18 to 20 glaciations, each glacial cycle lasting about 100,000 years. Typically, brief (15,000 years) warming phases, called interstadials, alternated with long (85,000 years) glacial conditions. The last glacial period, called the Wisconsin, began 30,000 years ago and reached a glacial maximum 18,000 years ago. This last cooling saw the vigorous, 2,000-foot-thick Laurentide ice sheet polish rocks, excavate lake basins, and scrape away soils before it ground to a halt in southern Pennsylvania.

The ice front stood at its southernmost extension for about 4,000 years. During this period the species composition of plant communities beyond the ice sheet was stable. Within 40 miles of the ice front, grasses and shrubs grew; farther south, throughout central and southern Appalachia, pine and spruce boreal forests dominated the landscape. At the height of the Wisconsin glaciation, deciduous flowering plants completely disappeared from the Appalachian Mountains, possibly surviving in small populations in the lower Mississippi Valley and southern coastal plains.

The Wisconsin ice margin, which I use to separate northern and central Appalachia, began retreating about 14,000 years ago and receded into Maine 12,000 years ago. Only in the last 10,000 years have soils developed in many glaciated areas of northern Appalachia. As the ice retreated, deciduous plants slowly recolonized northern Appalachia, and the coniferous boreal forest shrank to one-third its former size.

Throughout the last 5,000 years, the Appalachian forest presented a loose, changing assemblage of tree species dispersing northward and dissolving the Pleistocene flora. Each plant species advanced northward in response to changes in its own environment, at a rate independent of that of other species. Jack pine spread north just behind the melting ice, eastern hemlock invaded central and northern Appalachia somewhat more slowly, and the American chestnut reoccupied New England just 2,000 years ago. All this geologic and climatic history presents us with an interesting irony: Appalachia is an extremely old mountain range that has accumulated a great variety of species, many of which are ancient. But the species comprising any particular community may have only a short shared evolutionary history. Thus, mutually complementary adaptations, the sorts of traits that result from long-term, shared coevolution, may be rare among Appalachian plants and animals. Biologically, Appalachia is more tossed salad than long-simmered stew.

3

Forest Design

ON THE HILL ABOVE MY LAB, a pine thicket senesces. Interspersed among the pines are some young maples and oaks, signs that this woodlot is changing from a coniferous to a broad-leaved stand. In fact, in this part of Appalachia, this particular replacement is predictable.

The structure of a forest—both the three-dimensional architecture and the kinds of species that comprise the forest community—changes through time. Through ecological time, often measured in terms of several years or a few generations, new plant assemblages replace old ones in a process called succession. Within limits and in a given region, the timing and sequence of the turnover of plant species are more or less predictable. In central Appalachia, a simplified succession might include the following stages, each named for its dominant species: lichens, mosses, grasses-ferns, blackberry-black locust, pines, oaks-hickories, and hemlock.

Classical succession theory holds that the end product of this process is the climax plant community, in which the numbers and types of plants do not change over the long term. In this view, successional change eventually yields a self-reproducing, stable community because until climax is attained, superior competitors displace species of the previous stage. Some plant ecologists estimate that it takes 200 to 1,000 years for succession to achieve climax in Appalachia. Others wonder whether

17

succession ever really leads to complete stasis because neither biologists nor their funding lives long enough to determine the significance of subtle long-term changes.

For all practical purposes, modern ecologists have abandoned the classical theory of succession. In lieu, one current hypothesis states that succession is a result of evolution for avoiding competition between species. In essence, some plant species colonize new habitats because they tolerate environmental extremes but thereafter are excluded from later stages by competition from other plant species. In another modern hypothesis, environmental catastrophes play a dominant role. Disturbances such as forest fires, windthrows, and rock slides set succession back to early stages and thereby help maintain biological differences among patches of vegetation. Frequent disturbance produces a flora rich in disturbance-adapted species. Such plant species possess traits such as high tolerance of environmental extremes, low tolerance of competition, fast growth rates, high reproductive potential, and short life span.

If we look even closer, climax becomes a heuristic device only arbitrarily distinguishable from early stages. The composition of an apparent climax community may be influenced more by the frequency of disturbance than by inexorable laws of species replacement. Frequent disruptions result in mixes of species that are fleeting in time and space. If the interval between disturbances is short enough, the landscape will never host a climax community. Even relatively undisturbed communities lack complete predictability of their climax communities because seemingly minor historical events, such as the type of seed trees in an area, greatly influence present composition. In general, plants shift through succession from primarily herbs to trees, from annuals to perennials, and from synchronized to widely timed reproduction.

Species vary in how they colonize disturbed habitats. American beech, a climax species that grows slowly and waits persistently for an opening in the canopy, produces large seeds that germinate in shaded litter. Yellow birch annually broadcasts lightweight, winged nutlets that succeed only if they land in a canopy gap, a disturbed site where they face little competition from other plants. Moderately moist forests, with low frequency of fire and long intervals between disturbances, may be the only plant community where the shade tolerance exhibited by beech is a characteristic strategy.

Not only do the species of plants and their life histories change with succession, but the three-dimensional structure of the plant community changes as well. I am reminded of this as I walk across our lower field and enter the forest. The forest edge is thick with stems and leaves from ground to canopy. After I scramble through the brambles and vines, though, the inner forest opens up. Once inside, my shoulders brush against leaves of dogwood and witch hazel, trees that seldom exceed about 15 feet in height. But few leaves hit my waist. This experience reminds me that the eastern deciduous forest has a definite spatial structure.

After about thirty years of succession, the leaves within a forest concentrate in definite horizontal strata. To understand what causes this layered look, we must imagine a forest near climax. Before Europeans settled in North America, the eastern deciduous forest was a nearly unbroken expanse of trees. Interrupted only by occasional burned sites, windthrows, and rivers, the forest probably approached climax more closely than we allow it to today. In that natural state, the mature deciduous forest took on a layered constitution: a bunch of tall trees with a dense layer of leaves at the top called the canopy, a haphazard carpet of green plants on the ground called the ground cover, and a sparse layer of leaves on short trees and shrubs between the two called the understory.

The canopy, some 15 to 50 yards high, forms a continuous ceiling of sun-adapted leaves of the largest trees. The canopy includes the leaves of trees such as oaks, hickories, maples, white ash, black walnut, American beech, basswood, tulip poplar, eastern hemlock, and, formerly, American chestnut.

Understory shrubs and trees, which may be 6 to 15 feet tall, intercept flecks of light penetrating the canopy. Never growing high enough to join the canopy, the understory includes woody plants such as flowering dogwood, maple leaf viburnum, common witch hazel, redbud, sassafras, and American hornbeam. These plants form a scattered, rather continuous, layer.

Understory trees and shrubs depend on sunflecks, patches of direct sunshine that contribute up to 80 percent of the light penetrating the

19

forest interior. Immediately beneath the canopy, a point can be either in a gap and illuminated or under a leaf and shaded. At this level, light intensity varies greatly across the horizontal plane. As the streams of light approach the ground, the light diffuses and coalesces, creating a horizontally uniform layer of light. One theory suggests that plants of the understory have evolved to grow up to, but not exceed, this intermediate horizon of consistent light. A competing hypothesis calls on a flush of germination following a disturbance such as a forest fire to yield a stand of trees of similar height. A forest disturbed in the last 30 years or so would have an evident understory stratum because of the synchronized growth of such a community.

The forest's bottom layer, the ground cover, consists of short, shade-tolerant plants that grow to about three feet tall. Common plants of the ground cover include mosses, fungi, ferns, grasses, and herbaceous wildflowers.

Within the soil of a forest, fungi, algae, and even the trees themselves play hidden roles. In the Appalachian Mountains and probably in forests throughout the world, trees have benefited from a subtle ally—an underground forest. We have only recently come to appreciate that most higher plants have evolved an obligatory intimate relationship with fungi, an association called mycorrhiza, or fungus root.

Mycorrhiza is the "organ" through which many plants absorb water and nutrients. This union is especially important for the uptake of certain insoluble nutrients, such as phosphorus. In poor soils, mycorrhizae solve the nutritional deficiencies of their hosts. Mycorrhizal plants grow satisfactorily on soils with low concentrations of zinc and phosphorus, conditions that stunt the growth of noninfected plants. The fungus colonizes the outer layer of young roots, and its hyphae, or fungal threads, grow out into the soil. Because hyphae contact a greater volume of soil than do the plant's roots alone, they increase the absorptive capacity of the root system. In return, the plant transfers to the fungus some of the carbohydrate it produces. In this relationship, both parties benefit.

In addition to mycorrhizae, a complex community of free-living fungi reside in the forest's soil. The greatest diversity of fungal species inhabits the organic upper layer of soil, especially the surface litter and the horizons of decomposing organic matter. Down through the under-lying mineralized soil, the diversity of fungi decreases rapidly. Most species of free-living fungi achieve their maximum density in only one horizon, suggesting that competition between species has segregated the various species of soil fungi.

Even though little light penetrates the forest's soil, it hosts a teeming algal community. Forest soils contain up to 136,000 cells of algae per gram of soil. Closer inspection reveals two categories of algae within the forest's soil: ephemeral species, which appear suddenly, multiply rapidly, then disappear, and perennials, which persist through all the extreme conditions of the soil environment. Algae contribute organic forms of carbon and nitrogen to the soil and even stabilize soil against erosion.

Slime molds in the forest's soil accelerate decay, thereby recycling nutrients. A field study of five species of soil-dwelling slime molds found that each species existed in patches, suggesting that, as with fungi, competition between species has shaped the structure of the slime mold community. Alas, it seems that no group of organisms, even in the forest's soil, is immune to interspecific competition.

Some ecologists have suggested that trees influence each other underground. Each tree species produces its own unique blend of root exudates, substances that healthy plant roots release into the sur-rounding soil. Exudates contain carbohydrates, amino acids, organic acids, and inorganic ions. Some chemical exudates seem to inhibit the growth of other plants; others may nourish neighboring trees. The evolutionary question begged by this latter possibility is, "Who is feeding whom, and what is their genetic relationship?"

The idea that ties together such diverse topics as vertical stratifi-cation, mycorrhizae, and communities of soil slime molds is the concept of succession. As the woody plants in my field shift from blackberries to black locust and red cedar, to oaks and hickories, so does the three-dimensional structure of the forest change from dense and uniform to open and layered. Likewise, the ground cover changes from grasses and annual weeds to perennial wildflowers and ferns. As I wander through the woods trying to understand the design of Appalachian plant com-munities, I grow increasingly impressed by the power of the concept of ecological succession to explain a good chunk of it.

4

Creating Diversity

Within the borders of Great Smoky Mountains National Park grow 1,400 species of wildflowers. Thirty species of birds breed in one spruce-fir woodlot in Maine. At least 21 species of lungless salamanders (not just any type, but terrestrial vertebrates without lungs!) prowl the hollows of West Virginia. If you look, you will find similar diversity in deciduous trees, ferns, shrews, and darters. Why is it that no other region in North America hosts so much living diversity?

A new species arises when one group of interbreeding individuals, a population, becomes physically isolated from the rest of the group, impairing reproduction between individuals of the two groups. Over many generations, the separate populations accumulate observable differences. Should the two groups reestablish contact, the odds of interbreeding would depend on how much they had diverged during the schism. Evolutionary biologists think it usually takes hundreds or thousands of generations before divergence precludes interbreeding. Called allopatric speciation, this process is thought to be the primary force in the creation of new species.

Assuming allopatric speciation, a landscape that offers more opportunities to fracture populations should host more speciations than an environment that allows the free mingling of individuals. For complementary reasons, species whose individuals disperse poorly become subdivided more readily into isolated populations. In other words, all else being equal, slow, plodding organisms yield new species faster than ones that move quickly over vast distances. Birds have speciated more slowly than sala-manders in part because flight thwarts reproductive isolation.

A habitat's antiquity also promotes biological diversity. Old areas have been available for colonization by immigrating species for a longer time than new sites, and more species evolve over a vast stretch of time than over a short period. Worldwide, centers of great biological diversity are often topographically complex and very old: mountains, coral reefs, and tropical jungles. Northern Appalachia is both ecologically younger and biologically less diverse than more southerly zones. With land masses uplifted long ago from marine waters and unscoured by continental glaciation, central and southern Appalachia offer the longest continuously available terrestrial habitat in North America. The past 600 million years have provided more than enough time for the evolution of many new species.

We can explore such an adaptive radiation in perch, fishes of the family Percidae. Perch dispersed to North America from Asia via Beringia, a land bridge that connected Siberia and Alaska during the Pleistocene epoch, one million years ago. Darters, a branch of that original colonization, arose in and are still naturally restricted, or endemic, to North America. Darters are small, two- to three-inch fishes that rest on the bottoms of streams. The approximately 145 species of modern darters evolved relatively recently, probably no earlier than the late Pleistocene, one million years ago. The Tennessee River basin, which is the theater of greatest explosion of darter species, currently sustains 52 species. Within the basin, the largest concentration of extant darters resides in the Appalachian regions of eastern Tennessee and northern Alabama. By contrast, the much larger Missouri River system has only 19 darter species.

On any given day, darters swim only a short distance. Their broad-bottomed shape, supportive ventral fins, and lack of a swim bladder complement their sedentary life on the stream bottom. Members of the darter genus *Etheostoma* have adapted to upland streams with hard substrates and fast flows. Because of their limited power of dispersal and restriction to headwaters, individuals of the same *Etheostoma* species that live in different streams seldom interbreed. Consequently, marked genetic differences accumulate between headwater populations even within small geographic areas.

Two *Etheostoma* species illustrate this ongoing evolution. The orange-throat darter is restricted to headwaters by downstream competition with the orangebelly darter, a situation that severely curtails the flow of genes among populations of orangethroats. This isolation has allowed significant genetic differences to accumulate in the populations of orangethroat darters.

The story of speciation in lungless salamanders (family Plethodontidae) is more complex. Although sparse in northern Appalachia, salamanders appear to have evolved relatively undisturbed for millions of years south of the Pleistocene ice front. As was the case for darters, topographic diversity and limited mobility have combined to catalyze the formation of new species of lungless salamanders. The landscape of central and southern Appalachia—numerous disconnected mountains separated by narrow, often river-filled valleys—has enforced genetic isolation among populations restricted to different mountains, allowed divergent evolution, and led to today's high endemism of plethodontid species. Let us focus on one such species swarm.

In the Great Smoky and nearby mountains, Jordan's salamander exhibits different color patterns on different peaks and has thereby earned different names: Metcalf's salamander has a black back and gray underside; the red-cheeked salamander is black with bright red patches on its cheeks; the red-legged salamander has black flecks and gray patches; and so on.

All of these salamander populations live primarily in spruce-fir forests, which, in southern Appalachia, exist as isolated islands at high elevations. Perhaps as recently as the retreat of the last glacier, populations of Jordan's salamander became isolated on separate mountains. While the climate remained cool and their habitat was at low elevations and probably continuous, Jordan's salamanders may have looked alike everywhere. As the climate warmed, the spruce-fir forests and their salamander associates dispersed up the mountains, until each fir-salamander community became trapped in the unique habitat of a single peak. Adaptation to the singular environment of that peak plus a possible contribution by random genetic changes unrelated to the environment presumably have led to divergent forms in isolated populations. From one ancestral species, Jordan's salamander, many new species of woodland salamanders are just now evolving. The high number (about 25) of salamander subspecies endemic to southern Appalachia reflects this ongoing speciation.

The darter and lungless salamander stories are relatively well known, but the speciation of many other Appalachian organisms reflects the same constraints of physical barriers, limited movement, and the evolutionary divergence of populations that have become reproductively incompatible. The snowshoe hare, which seems to require the shelter of dense stands of red spruce, does not venture below the 3,000-foot elevation. Its southernmost population, located in West Virginia, is 200 miles from the nearest neighboring hares in eastern Pennsylvania. Because of their reproductive isolation, the West Virginia hares may be on their way to becoming a new species. Hares at this southern outpost not only change color at the same time as northern individuals, but also exhibit explosive population cycles with periods of 9 to 11 years that coincide almost exactly with those exhibited by populations in New England and eastern Canada. The latter are 600 miles away! What causal connection could possibly exist between populations separated by such a vast distance? Here we face yet another mystery.

Allopatric speciation—which includes roles for antiquity, topographic diversity, physical isolation, limited movement, genetic and morphological divergence, and finally reproductive incompatibility—can result in high diversity only over a vast geographic area. This process by itself would yield just one or a few species per taxonomic group in each habitat island. The hallmark of Appalachia, however, is that many species exist at each site. Therefore, sometime after new species arise in isolation, they must come together and occupy the same piece of ground. Recurrent continental cooling and stream capture appear to have contributed to the overlapping ranges of salamander and darter species, respectively.

In the Pleistocene, salamanders were forced down from the uplands by cold temperatures. When the climate warmed and the glacier retreated, the salamanders followed their thermal limits upward. Each species colonized several hills, mixing several species on each hilltop. Here, in turn, they underwent a round of isolation and speciation.

Climatic change has also induced species mixing among plants. The boreal coniferous forest, dominated by spruce and fir, extends southward along the frigid crest of the Appalachians into North Carolina. The boreal islands in the Great Smoky Mountains, rich in endemic plants and animals, are surrounded by a sea of deciduous trees growing at lower elevations. Some tree species typical of northern Appalachia—common juniper, spruce, gray birch, and quaking aspen—have representatives in the region's southern reaches. These trees apparently dispersed into central and southern Appalachia during the Pleistocene and have persisted ever since as isolated colonies in high, favorable sites. In this way, within a fairly small area, boreal and temperate species mixed.

The bunchberry is my favorite local example of glacially induced plant species mixing. This miniature member of the dogwood family grows in such diverse locations as Admiralty Island in southeast Alaska and Ice Mountain, a site at less than 1,000-foot elevation in eastern West Virginia. On Ice Mountain's steep, north-facing hillside, cold drafts issuing from the gaps among sandstone boulders create a series of cool microsites. Here, bunchberry and a few other species have persisted unchanged from their boreal ancestors since the Ice Age.

In contrast, some tree species show significant evolutionary changes down the Appalachian backbone. Normally a boreal species, balsam fir (*Abies balsamea*) extends southward through the Appalachians. On some peaks in Virginia and West Virginia, another species of fir (*Abies intermedia*) differs only slightly from northern balsam firs. Farther south, firs in the Great Smoky Mountains show even greater differences and are called Fraser fir. During glaciation, the balsam fir presumably dispersed southward and during interglacials dispersed upward, leaving isolated populations on cool, southern peaks. Thus, Fraser fir appears to be a young species endemic to southern Appalachia. Derived via an intermediate step from the boreal balsam fir, Fraser fir now grows mixed with trees of the eastern deciduous forest.

Because the high-altitude habitats of southern Appalachia resemble those of the boreal north, the two areas continue to share a large proportion of species. On the basis of overall appearance and species composition, the spruce-fir forests of southern Appalachia are part of, yet distinct from, the great northern boreal forest. Stated from a different point of view, the coniferous forests of today's high Appalachian peaks are somewhat altered relicts of the widespread boreal forests of the past.

Possibly because of such climatically induced mixing, the southern Appalachians are poor in endemic tree species. No tree genus is endemic to southern Appalachia, and only ten species are endemic to southern Appalachia: Fraser fir, Carolina hemlock, Table Mountain pine, yellow buckeye, cinnamon clethra, Fraser magnolia, Catawba rhododendron, kelsey locust, clammy locust, and mountain stewartia. Thus, trees of northern and southern origins are neighbors along the Appalachian continuum.

If we turn from Appalachia's forests to its streams, we find many fish species endemic to only a single drainage. Consequently, the southern Appalachians harbor an extremely diverse fish fauna: One recent list totaled 398 species, the most common fish families being minnows, suckers, catfishes, sunfishes, and perches (including darters). The high species diversity of Appalachian fishes results from two phenomena: dispersal between bordering drainages and stream capture.

During the Pleistocene, headwater tributaries lying farther from the ice were less severely affected by faunal extinction than were streams closer to the glacier. The more distant streams served as refugia, areas where organisms persisted until the climate returned to favorable status. When the climate warmed, species moved among subbasins, enabling species exchanges among the Tennessee, Cumberland, and Mississippi River basins. The Mississippi River basin was probably the site of origin of most of the freshwater fishes east of the Rocky Mountains.

Stream capture also contributed to high fish diversity. Two headwater streams cutting toward a common divide will eventually meet, breaking down the ridge and forcing one stream to yield its water and fishes to the other. The Greenbrier River, a tributary of the New River in West Virginia, expanded north at the expense of some southern tributaries of the Monongahela system. Specifically, multiple piracies beheaded Glady, Laurel, Dry, and Gandy forks of Shavers Fork along Lynn Divide. By stealing the tributaries' flows and species, the Greenbrier has come to host a grand variety of fishes.

Central and southern Appalachia support a huge number of plant and animal species. The ridges and hollows split populations of slow-moving organisms, allow biological differences between populations to accumulate over many generations, and encourage the evolution of new species. Organisms from more northerly climes were forced southward during the last glaciation and dispersed upward as the climate warmed, becoming stranded on mountaintops. Whether created in situ or accumulated from without, different kinds of living things became close neighbors by processes such as glacier-induced migrations and stream captures.

My half-day hikes often pass through several sets of hollows and peaks. The tulip poplars and black walnuts of the hollows grade into the oaks and hickories of the slopes, then into the firs on the peaks. Many a time I have forgotten about my sore feet while concentrating on the changing plants, conjecturing about the roles of allopatric speciation and glacially induced mixing, and wondering how close I am to the truth.

5

Catastrophe and the Appalachian Quilt

I**N ECOLOGY**, as in other areas of inquiry, the problem of scale thwarts our understanding of fundamental processes. Answers to even the most elementary questions hinge on the breadth of the observer's vision. Take, for example, the question of how the males of a territorial bird distribute themselves across a landscape. They could appear uniformly distributed when viewed on the small scale, being spaced evenly by their mutual repulsion. Since the birds' territories occupy only certain habitats, the individuals could also appear clumped in discrete groups if viewed at an intermediate scale covering several hills. Finally, the birds could appear randomly dispersed across a large geographic region where the habitat blocks are scattered haphazardly.

To understand why the Appalachian Mountains continue to host so many species, we must view the forest at several scales. Observing through a continuum of scales provides the most realistic impression, but also proves unmanageable. We will simply examine the extremes: viewing some of the broad causes of biological diversity, such as environmental gradients and ecological disturbances, and then narrowing our scope to explore small-scale factors, such as canopy gaps.

As you climb a mountain, the temperature gradually cools. This thermal gradient helps determine which plants grow where on the slope. Moisture gradients similarly influence plant communities. In the oak

31

forests of Virginia, several trends become obvious as you move from moderately moist to dry sites: the canopy coverage, stand height, and stem basal area decrease, while these features in the shrub level increase.

At the continental scale, environmental gradients contribute to the maintenance of plant diversity. The boreal forest covers a huge area across southern Canada and southward along the high ridges of Appalachia. Dominant boreal trees include balsam fir, black and white spruces, red, white, and jack pines, quaking and bigtooth aspens, paper birch, and balsam poplar. Farther south, the broad-leaved trees of the mixed deciduous forest, the heartland of eastern North America, take over as the dominant species. The mixed deciduous forest may assume several forms, including northern hardwood, oak-chestnut, oak-pine, mixed mesophytic, and cove hardwood forests. Mesophytic refers to a medium level of moisture. A cove is a bowl-shaped valley with rich, damp soil. One way of appreciating the great diversity of communities within the mixed deciduous forest is to compare three of its subtypes: the northern hardwood forests of New England, the mixed mesophytic forest of central Appalachia, and the cove hardwood forests of southern Appalachia.

The northern hardwood, or transition forest, combines features of the boreal woodland and the deciduous forest of southern Appalachia. Northern hardwood forests, common in New England and at high elevations in the southern Appalachians, contain only a few dominant species: yellow buckeye in wet spots, beech in drier conditions, and yellow birch on rock slides.

The mixed mesophytic forest of central Appalachia supports a marvelous diversity of tree species. Commonly, three dozen species are prominent in a climax community. Canopy trees include white basswood, beech, sugar maple, tulip poplar, red and white oak, hemlock, magnolia, white ash, and black cherry. Tulip poplars inhabit lowlands, hemlocks can monopolize ravines, and oaks dominate drier ridge tops.

The cove hardwood forests of southern Appalachia exhibit the greatest diversity of tree species in North America. Within a single stand, 8 to 10 tree species may share dominance in a total assemblage of 40 species. Trees common in southern cove forests include tulip poplar, sugar maple, yellow buckeye, basswood, beech, yellow birch, red oak, black cherry, and Carolina silverbell.

In addition to the contributions of altitude and latitude, ecological disturbance and the introduction of exotic species contribute to biotic diversity. Episodes of fire and windstorm may actually be more important in determining species composition than long stretches of tranquility.

Fire, so important in conifer-dominated systems such as boreal forests and southern Appalachian pine forests, also plays a role in the drier parts of deciduous forests. Fire alters light intensity, water and nutrient contents of the soil, microclimate at the soil's surface, and reseeding sources. Repeated fires favor species with fire-adaptive traits (such as serotinous cones that release seeds when stimulated by the heat of a fire), resprouting by roots, and even increased flammability of the plant community as a whole.

At first glance, fire appears to be a force imposed from without. However, the quick buildup of highly combustible organic matter and the fire-dependent reproductive strategies of some species suggest that some plant species actually encourage fire. For example, fire aids reproduction of Table Mountain pine by destroying competing vegetation and forest litter while releasing seeds from the pine's serotinous cones. Without fire, the cones of Table Mountain pine (which adorn these pages) remain closed for two years. At two years, 40 percent proceed to open even without fire; the rest stay closed on the parent tree, holding viable seeds for up to ten years. The serotinous cone is designed to release seeds into habitat cleared of competitors.

From an ecological point of view, fires truncate succession, restarting it at an earlier stage. From a landscape perspective, small, localized fires create forests composed of many stands at various stages of succession. In presettlement Wisconsin, forest fires recurred at intervals ranging from several decades to a century, apparently precluding a widespread climax forest. In contrast, New England forests burned less frequently, allowing large areas to approach climax. In the Great Smoky Mountains, a natural fire-return interval of ten years favored fast-growing, thick-barked tree species over slow-growing, thin-barked ones. Apparently, thick bark enhanced survival. With the advent of fire suppression in the 1940s, thin-barked species were suddenly allowed to grow large enough to resist fires. The longer the period of fire suppression, the greater the proportion of the forest claimed by thin-barked, slow-growing trees.

Fires scattered through time and space create a diversity of habitats for other organisms. A succession of animals depends on the succession of plants that follow fire. Deer mice are common for about seven years following a burn but decrease thereafter, whereas moles increase in number as the plant community continues to mature.

Windstorms, occasionally blowing down large expanses of temperate and boreal forests, also help maintain biological diversity. Waves of collapsing trees contribute to soil mixing and create pit-and-mound relief, which provides a variety of microenvironments for seedlings of various species. In southern Wisconsin, severe thunderstorms cause catastrophic windthrow, toppling more susceptible trees that fall domino-style. Since a return to climax takes 200 to 300 years, 17 to 25 percent of this forest remains in subclimax stages, with each stage supporting its own characteristic species of plants and animals.

The invasion of exotic species provides another type of large-scale disturbance that contributes to biotic diversity. Until the early 1900s, the American chestnut was the most common tree species in many parts of Appalachia, often forming 40 to 60 percent of the canopy. Chestnuts fed squirrels, bear, deer, wild turkey, and people. Chestnut logs, almost impervious to rot, were used to construct homesteads. Old chestnut split-rail fencing graces our farm in West Virginia, and chestnut joists support our cabin's flooring—all still going strong. Chestnut blight, first detected in 1904 in New York City, swept through the northeastern forests, then southward through Appalachia. First noted in West Virginia in 1912, the blight appeared in the southern Appalachians by 1925. By 1930, the disease infected 80 to 90 percent of the American chestnuts in North Carolina. The blight's spores, carried by breezes, birds, and insects, enter healthy trees through wounds in the bark. The fungus then clogs the plant's vascular tissues. Although some roots survive, the blight kills most shoots before they are large enough to bear nuts.

Before the blight, the oak-chestnut forests—composed of several species of oaks, American chestnut, red maple, and black cherry—were extensive. After the blight, native species of oaks (chestnut, red, white) and hickories (pignut, shagbark) partially filled the canopy gaps. Acorns replaced chestnuts as the major food for wildlife. Within half a century, the great mixed deciduous forest of eastern North America changed from oak-chestnut to the present oak-hickory forest.

Each of the many large-scale disturbances varies in frequency, predictability, area, and severity. As if that is not complex enough, the type and frequency of disturbance gradients often parallel environmental gradients. For example, the severity of windthrow is greater at high, wet sites than at low, dry ones. Such overlapping causes make accounting for biological diversity a huge challenge.

Think of our contemporary Appalachian forest as a patchwork quilt in which each section has a different disturbance history. A few rare patches have gone undisturbed for 1,000 years and host a climax forest; other stands have been disturbed every few years and support pioneer species; most patches, though, have been disturbed within the last 100 to 200 years and sustain an intermediate stage.

Biological diversity depends on the preservation of this heterogeneous matrix, not just the virgin old-aged communities. Successional patches of burns, fields, and brambles are important to animals such as white-tailed deer, red fox, and songbirds. Within limits, natural and human-caused disturbances contribute to the diversity of living things in Appalachia.

Tremendous diversity exists not only in large regions of Appalachia but within smaller areas as well—on a single hillside, along a stream, and even under a single tree. What maintains many species in small patches?

A temperate forest may contain more than 12 species of nonwoody plants, or herbs, per square yard. Subtle differences in topography, nearness to canopy openings, temperature, and sunlight account for much of the diversity of the ground cover. In the spring, shoots of many forest herbs expand and occupy the same layer. In the four to six weeks that pass between the last hard freeze and canopy leaf-out, the herb layer is richest in light, heat, moisture, and nutrients. Although their leaves may fill the ground cover, herbs apparently compete little for light because the shoots remain unfurled for different durations. If herbs competed heavily for light, strong selection should have caused them to deploy leaves higher than their lowly 4 to 40 inches.

When a tree falls, it leaves a mound formed by the roots and attached soil and a pit where the roots used to be. These local topographic differences contribute to herb diversity. Pit-and-mound microsites differ from the surrounding forest in moisture, pH, temperature, and litter depth. At an even smaller scale, characteristics of the mound differ from those of the pit. In one New England site, mounds and pits cover 20 to 50 percent of the forest floor. Such a mosaic maintains populations of mosses, ferns, wildflowers, and many other species of the ground cover.

Still-standing trees create still more microhabitats for plants of the understory and ground cover. The trees alter the amount of light and moisture reaching the soil, thereby determining the rate at which the soil dries out. Trees contribute minerals dissolved from the leaves and stems to the soil at the tree's base. By inhibiting young individuals of the same species, trees of the canopy contribute to biological diversity. Seedlings face stiffer competition beneath their own species than under other species, and fungi are more likely to kill or weaken seedlings that sprout under trees of the same species than under adults of different species. Further, the larger resistant trees may host diseases or pests that infect smaller individuals already weakened by competition.

Sassafras provides an excellent example of this growth suppression strategy. Sassafras invades abandoned fields, expands clonally from root sprouts, and persists as a relatively pure stand through various successional stages. Sassafras leaves, litter, and roots release a variety of plant poisons that exclude ten plant species, including several annual herbs. Seven other plant species thrive beneath the sassafras canopy. The latter seven appear to succeed because of their perennial growth cycle, which somehow makes them more resistant to the chemical interference. Plant poisons selectively harm some species, thus incidentally favoring others. One major drawback results from inhibiting growth of one's own species: dominant species may be unable to replace themselves. In this way, growth suppression may assure that climax is never reached.

Tree seedlings in mature southern Appalachian forests face the greatest chance of surviving if they sprout in small canopy gaps created by the death of one or a few trees. In cove hardwood forests, the species of the replacement tree usually bears no predictable relationship to the species of the fallen tree. Unpredictability rules because most tree species reproduce by mass seeding of light gaps, a roulette process. In virgin forests, one dead tree is usually replaced by a single successor that comes to occupy more or less the same space in the canopy. In this way, less tolerant species persist by opportunistically capturing some canopy gaps.

As I lumber up the hillside behind my cabin, I am impressed by the variety of ferns and wildflowers. I must typically take several steps along the slope before I come across a second individual of a just-sighted species. As I crest the ridge, my gaze sweeps across a broad landscape, an Appalachian patchwork quilt of forest stands, each at a different stage of succession. I revel in this diversity.

6

Balds

SCATTERED THROUGHOUT THE HIGHER REACHES of southern and central Appalachia lie discrete areas without trees called balds. From an ecological perspective, a bald is a patch of naturally treeless vegetation occupying a well-drained site below tree line in a predominantly forested region. At least eighty of these inexplicable breaks, ranging in area from 2 to 20 acres, are strewn from Virginia to Georgia, most at elevations above 4,000 feet. Similar treeless communities appear in the Ozarks, Nevada, and New Zealand, where they might be called slicks, glades, knobs, or barrens.

Balds take on a variety of forms. Grass balds, also called meadow balds, are devoid of shrubs and support herbaceous vegetation, such as mountain oat grass. Grass balds are common in sections of the Blue Ridge, particularly in North Carolina. In some places, grass balds merge into heath balds or barrens—mountaintops covered with a variety of densely growing heath shrubs and other low-growing plants, commonly huckleberry, blueberry, mountain laurel, and mountain azalea. In moist areas, alder balds support a tangled mess of thick, shrubby, green alders three to four feet tall.

No neat, widely accepted theory explains the origin of balds. When Europeans settled the Appalachians, at least some contemporary balds were bare of trees. Some ecologists propose that Native Americans cleared trees and then periodically burned the areas to encourage the growth of mountain oat grass. Others suggest that Indians, particularly Cherokees, cleared some sites as sacred places. A third hypothesis holds that early European settlers cleared balds to graze cattle. Even biotic causes, such as attacking insects and browsing native mammals, have been implicated. Climatic factors, such as injury due to winter ice, wind-throwing of trees, and drought, have all been suggested. These points of view are consistent with the fact that balds often occupy rounded summits exposed to desiccating southwesterly winds. Natural fire and specific soil types have been ruled out, though, because neither burn evidence nor a consistent pattern of soil types exists in the balds.

A more complex hypothesis posits that about 4,000 years ago a long period of hot, dry weather killed the spruces and firs near their lower limits, allowing beeches and maples to replace them. A cool trend, which continues to the present, caused these latter species to perish. Spruce and fir were unable to reestablish themselves in the clearings because their seedlings lacked the necessary protective canopy. Without competition from trees, grasses invaded most of these sites, producing grass balds. Rhododendrons from the forest understory invaded a few of the high-elevation grass balds, creating heath balds.

Some biologists have observed that, when plotted altitudinally, most balds occupy the border of two forest types. This suggests that balds develop along the tolerance limits of the dominant tree species. For example, in southern Appalachia, most balds lie near the upper limits of beech, buckeye, and red oak, and at the lower limits of red spruce and Fraser fir. If climate changed at this boundary, trees would reinvade the site very slowly because the wind, drought, and temperature extremes of the open bald would kill seedlings. Another possibility is that, as the climate cooled during the Pleistocene, balds grew larger because deciduous trees retreated downhill faster than spruce invaded the vacated sites.

One final possibility—and this is anathema to ecologists hungry for generalizations—is that different kinds of balds have different causes of origin, even that each individual bald has resulted from a unique combination of causes. The bottom line is that we don't know what causes balds, but all hypotheses share the idea that a disturbance has not been followed by succession.

What maintains balds? We are not even sure that they are being maintained. Although a few might be expanding, many seem to be shrinking. Our uncertain knowledge reflects the fact that the edge of a bald is constantly threatened by the invasion of woody plants. The war between the opening and its forest envelope keeps the size and species composition of a bald dynamic.

Several theories attempt to explain the persistence of apparently stable balds. The possibilities include that thick mountain oat grass prevents tree seedlings from getting a foothold, harsh weather prevents tree colonization, and the trampling and feeding of grazing animals, such as bison, cattle, and sheep, reinforced early successional communities. In heath balds, the dense network of rhododendrons' roots and leaves may exclude most herbaceous plants.

Some balds seem to be shrinking as herbaceous plants invade from cleared fields farther down slope. Such uphill immigrants include mountain oat grass, certain mosses, and bracken fern. Where seed sources are available, spruce is invading some grassy balds. Some balds seem to have begun to shrink when livestock ceased grazing on mountain summits. If this last observation is true, some balds will vanish during the next century.

So, here is a mysterious Appalachian scene that embraces everything from archeology to zoology, with healthy doses of botany, geology, and meteorology thrown in. The exceptional nature of balds underscores the importance of identifying what creates and sustains them. Comprehending treelessness will help us understand the existence of our dense, diverse eastern deciduous forest. What fascinates me is the possibility that each bald may have been created and is currently being maintained by a unique mix of causes—and therefore is following its own successional path.

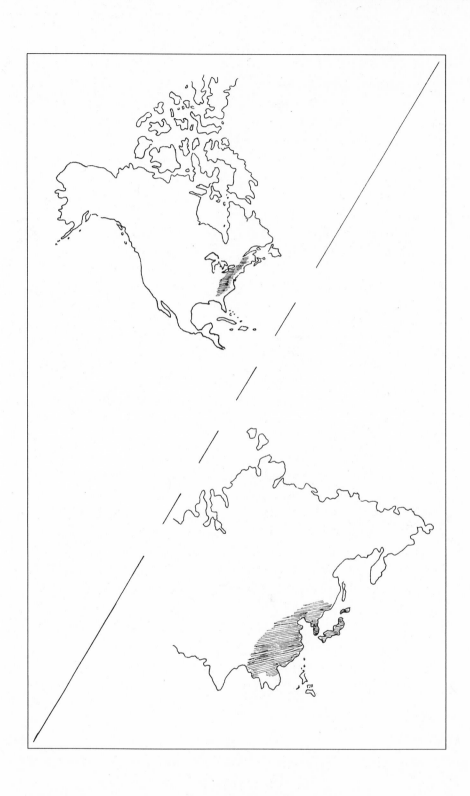

7

The Asian Connection

HERE'S A CLAIM that may surprise you: The forests of eastern Asia and southern Appalachia are so similar that if you were swept from one to the other you would be hard pressed to tell them apart. These regions share many similar plants and some animals, even though intervening areas host vastly different organisms. Living things with fractured geographical distributions are termed disjunct. In this chapter we will explore this unexpected connection: the Asia-North America disjunction.

The disjunction, usually at the genus and species levels, involves more than 50 genera of Appalachian plants—plants that are restricted to eastern North America and eastern Asia and, except in fossil form, are absent in between. Among some genera, several Appalachian species are separated from Asian relatives: hickory, tulip poplar, sassafras, yellowwood, coffee-tree, silverbell, witch hazel, and stewartia. Within other tree groups, such as the maples, dogwoods, persimmons, hollies, sumacs, snowbells, Hercules-clubs, and sweetleafs, the disjunctions affect only certain pairs of related species. Many disjunct genera contain few species, and all are confined exclusively to eastern North America and eastern Asia. If not for these two facts, we might have dismissed the separations on the basis of random chance alone. This frees us to pursue a more interesting explanation.

Among trees, two pairs of related species, tulip poplar and Carolina hemlock, present particularly striking disjunctions. There are only two species of tulip poplars, one in China and one in the United States. Likewise, the closest relative of Carolina hemlock, a local tree peculiar to the southern Appalachians, is in eastern Asia. In both the tulip poplar and hemlock genera, each North American species differs only slightly from its Asian twin.

The understory and ground cover of the two regions also share many plants. More than two-thirds of the total orchid genera of temperate North America are related to orchid species in eastern Asia, and of these, at least eight genera consist of disjunct species pairs. In contrast, not a single orchid genus grows exclusively in North America and Europe. Similar Asia-North America disjunctions are also known for some ferns, ginseng, mayapple, jack-in-the-pulpit, skunk cabbage, lichens, and mosses.

If we focus on even smaller regions of China and North America, we find that the eastern Chinese province of Hubei and our Carolinas share many plant families and genera. About 75 percent of their plant families are represented by at least one species in each region. Mimicking the continental pattern, many of the provincial and state disjunct species are closely related. The floras of these two areas differ in that each has evolved some of its own endemic plants.

Although less common, some animal distributions are also disjunct. The copperhead has a species in the same genus in southeastern Asia. The paddlefish, hellbender, and alligator also have disjunct Asian relatives.

So, here we have a provocative observation and an apparent conflict: Eastern North America was most recently continuous with the continents of Europe and Africa, yet Appalachia is botanically more similar to eastern Asia.

The most widely accepted theory to explain this paradox suggests that the isolated plants remain as survivors of an ancient circumpolar plant community that died out in Europe, western Asia, and western North America. A land bridge called Beringia linked Russia and Alaska beginning in the Miocene epoch, about 9.25 million years ago. Could this have been the connection? No. One-half to two-thirds of the Chinese plant species originating in the late Cretaceous, 70 million years ago, and one-fourth to one-half of the plants arising in the late Eocene, 40 million years ago, are nearly identical to their nearest relatives in North America. The fossil record shows only a few Chinese species similar to those of North America after the Eocene. Therefore, today's disjunct plants must have been continuous between eastern Asia and eastern North America long before land connected Russia and Alaska. These floras must have been connected via Europe.

The disjunct genera of eastern Asia and eastern North America must represent remnants of ancient plants that were once broadly distributed throughout the Northern Hemisphere. The two floras remain similar today presumably because neither site experienced extensive Pleistocene glaciation and both have shared a similar climate.

Not only do these two regions have similar plant genera, they also reveal four compelling ecological parallels. First, both are dominated by woody, broad-leaved, deciduous plants. Second, their nonwoody plants have underground storage organs and bloom in the spring. Third, herbs are either early-leafing ephemerals or shade-adapted perennials with buds that overwinter in the soil. Finally, in both areas the kinds of plants change predictably along environmental gradients.

The similarities in plant categories, life histories, and individual sizes and shapes reflect evolutionary descent in similar environments from a set of common ancestors, an evolutionary process called parallelism. The less-preferred, alternate theory in this case is evolutionary convergence, in which organisms with different ancestors evolve similar traits because they inhabit similar environments.

Today, eastern Asia is the foremost center of remnants from the widespread ancestral plant community that covered the northern hemisphere; eastern North America is second, featuring roughly half as many tree species from the ancestral community. By comparison, eastern Europe and western North America have about one-fourth as many remnant taxa as eastern Asia. Some tree genera are widespread in all four regions, but eastern North America and eastern Asia share the most tree genera, 16.

So Appalachia features blocks of African rock and hosts many plants of Asian connection—this is quite the cosmopolitan place.

The Players

8

The Improbable Lady's Slipper

STEALING THROUGH THE PINE THICKET to spy on the incubating broad-winged hawk, hiking up Pine Cabin Run to study nest-building chubs, and hunting for morels—all these activities have been interrupted, commandeered would be a better word, by a lady's slipper. That flash of pastel, which I usually detect peripherally, demands my focus. After an internal struggle to continue my rounds, I accede, take a seat, and at least for a while, babble to the flower about how pretty it is. After a few seconds of ogling, I realize that I am witness to a highly unlikely event, and this, in turn, usually triggers that smug satisfaction of being in the right place at the right time.

Although orchids may not abound at any one spot, around the world there are a great many species. In fact, Orchidaceae is probably the largest family of flowering plants in the world. With 25,000 species in 800 genera, the family boasts fully 10 percent of all species of flowering plants, a whopping share of the modern plant world. With all these species to draw from, it is no surprise that the orchid family has evolved the most varied floral structure in the plant kingdom. And orchids continue to evolve today.

Orchids arose in the tropics after Gondwanaland—a land area thought to have contained the landmasses of the Southern Hemisphere—broke up in the early Cretaceous, 120 million years ago. West

Gondwanaland, which later split into South America and Africa, became the center of flowering plant evolution. Although orchids are cosmopolitan, they remain most diverse in the tropics. Most orchid evolution took place after the Paleocene, 55 million years ago, when lush blankets of vegetation encircled the northern hemisphere. That relatively continuous environment allowed some species of orchids to take on a circumpolar distribution.

Although many tropical species grow upon plants, especially trees, all northern temperate orchid species root in the ground. About 100 species, of which half are relatively recent immigrants from the tropics, live in the continental United States. Most native North American orchid species grow in the rich, shaded humus of the eastern deciduous forest; there are 30 species along the Blue Ridge Parkway alone. As with trees, a few orchid species clinging to the high peaks of southern Appalachia are relics of the boreal forest.

Appalachia hosts three subfamilies of orchids: the Spiranthoideae, which includes downy rattlesnake plantain and nodding ladies tresses; the Orchidoideae, which is basically an African group and includes showy orchis; and the Cypripedioideae, which includes the subjects of this essay, the lady's slippers.

The lady's slippers' genus, which contains at least 110 species worldwide, is not ancestral to any other group of living orchids, but instead went off on an evolutionary tangent that preserved its own unique features. Allow me to introduce several Appalachian lady's slippers. The pink lady's slipper, also called pink moccasin-flower and stemless lady's slipper, dwells in high, dry woods. Early in the spring, each plant produces two large, light green leaves, and a leafless flowering stalk that emerges rapidly from between the paired leaves. Sometime between April and July, depending on elevation and latitude, the plant produces one flower with purplish petals and a pink labellum, the lower lip that extends into a saclike pouch.

Yellow lady's slippers, or yellow moccasin-flowers, grow as clones, which are groups of asexually produced, genetically identical individuals. As the most widespread species of the genus, the yellow lady's slipper ranges throughout the eastern United States except the southeastern coastal plain. A crab spider in matching yellow hunts on these flowers. Frozen and camouflaged, the predator grabs visiting would-be pollinators.

The showy, or queen's, lady's slipper is our largest and most spectacular native orchid. Its white sepals and petals contrast with a pink-mouthed labellum. It grows from New England southward through the Appalachian Mountains.

All Appalachian species of lady's slippers emit odors that attract insects. Sources of the essence include petals, sepals, and labella. Both the pink and showy lady's slippers release a sweet scent; the yellow smells strong and spicy. The former two species are visited by large, solitary bees; the latter by both social and solitary species.

With attractive colors and appealing fragrances, lady's slippers entice insects to enter their flowers in search of pollen or nectar. They find neither—here the plot thickens. After a nectar seeker enters the flower, the port's one-way funnel-like construction prevents a quick exit by the same route. Specifically, the margins and hairs of the aperture point inward and thwart the insect's escape. To egress, the insect must shove its way under the stigma, the female organ, where it will leave pollen grains from a previously visited flower. Then the insect must squeeze beneath an anther, the male organ, where it picks up clumps of sticky pollen grains on its back. Light penetrating a translucent patch on the back wall of the pouch draws the visitor to where the margins and hairs turn outward and allow it to escape. This order of events makes self-pollination unlikely.

Although scientists knew as early as 1793 that some species in the orchid genus *Orchis* do not reward pollinators, biologists have only recently explained how the system works. Bumblebees visiting orchids expend time and energy but gain nothing for their efforts. Only bees that twice fall into the same unrewarding trap will transfer pollen between flowers. All else being equal, individuals that avoid orchids should have more time and energy available for their own reproductive activities and, thus, produce more offspring than tricked bees. It seems that the pollination of today's orchids depends on insects whose ancestors were favored by natural selection to actually avoid orchids. Here is a paradox.

If natural selection favors individual bees that are not deceived, or deceived less frequently, bees should pollinate lady's slippers less with each passing bee generation. Although we know that in some areas pink

51

lady's slipper flowers go unpollinated, we do not have crucial long-term data on pollination frequency and cannot address this issue.

Using a different approach, let us examine this seemingly counter-productive pollination system from each party's perspective. From the insect's point of view, it is "mistaken pollination." Visits to a flower are mistakes by the pollinator caused by unrewarding flowers mimicking rewarding ones, in this case via colors and smells. From the plant's point of view, though, no mistake is involved. So-called "chance pollination" is an adaptation maintained by a low recurrence of fertilization.

A degree of naïveté by the insect is requisite for the pollination of nonrewarding flowers. After one or a few mistakes, though, many pollinators avoid such flowers. As a result, seed set is better when pollinators have just emerged from metamorphosis—while they are still naïve—than when they are experienced. The reproductive capacity, and thereby population density, of lady's slippers is limited by the pollinator's learning ability. For chance pollination to work, orchid densities must be low. If plants grow in a dense stand, there are more chances for negative reinforcement of the insect, leading to less efficient pollination, than if the orchids are sparse. This paradoxical pollination system is the first improbable scene in a lady's slipper's life.

The second oddity involves germination. The seed capsules of orchids contain thousands of tiny, dustlike seeds, a condition called microspermy. Orchid seeds, among the smallest produced by any flowering plant, rarely are longer than one-twelfth of an inch and may be as small as one-hundredth of an inch. Their tiny size allows orchid seeds to float through the atmosphere for vast distances, a peculiarity that may have contributed to the cosmopolitan distributions of some species.

Each seed, a small round mass of cells within an outer transparent coat, lacks endosperm, the food-storage tissue of common seeds like corn. How do tiny seeds with no food germinate successfully? They have help. Throughout the plant kingdom, microspermous plants are either mycorrhizal or parasitic. Orchids exemplify the former—they maintain a mutually beneficial relationship with a fungus. For a seed to find the correct fungus requires widespread dispersal, accomplished by legions of small, lightweight seeds.

North American lady's slipper seedlings lead subterranean lives for several years. The pink and showy lady's slippers do not produce a green leaf above the ground until their third year of life. Because an interred life precludes photosynthesis, lady's slippers seedlings are unable to grow without a fungal "infection."

In contrast, some other orchid species have seedlings that grow at the surface. Such seedlings can photosynthesize and may grow slowly without mycorrhiza, although even here at least some fungal participation seems to help. In general, species of sunny, wet habitats have green seedlings that grow rapidly; species of the forest, like our lady's slippers, produce slow-growing, subterranean seedlings.

The health of young orchids seems to depend on the mycorrhiza. The fungus invades the entire root system of its host. The host's roots digest part of the fungus and nutrients collected by the fungus. A hormonal feedback ensures that neither party dominates the relationship. Fungi secrete a substance that stimulates the orchid's root to produce orchinol, a compound that, in turn, inhibits fungal growth. The few individual lady's slippers that squeeze through the bottleneck of germinating with the proper mycorrhizal infection settle into a pattern of slow growth and long life.

Now when I trip over a pink lady's slipper in the woods, I feel awe over the sheer improbability of it all. First, bees have to be tricked into visiting nonrewarding flowers—not just once, but twice. And second, one of a million helpless, dustlike seeds must land by raw luck on a spot with not only the right conditions for germination, but the appropriate fungus for root infection and underground life. Although this sequence of events strikes me as colossally improbable, the roulette has obviously been working. The next time you bend down and mumble compliments to its pretty flower, think of the odds that plant beat. You might come to admire that lady's slipper for reasons more profound than its delicate pastel.

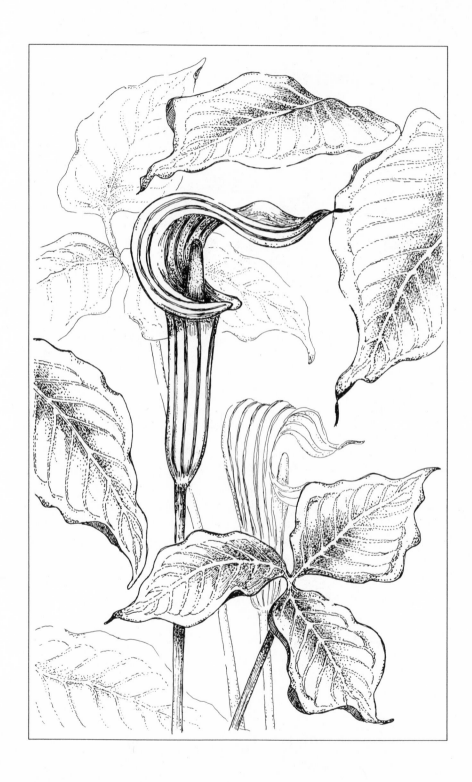

9

Sexual Decisions of Jack-in-the-Pulpit

JACK-IN-THE-PULPIT, a knee-high, deciduous, perennial herb of eastern North America, is one of over 100 related species found mainly in the temperate forests of China, Japan, and India. Only two species of this disjunct group inhabit North America. Widely distributed from Maine to Florida and west to the prairie's edge, jack-in-the-pulpit thrives in the moist, species-rich woods of Appalachia, in some places forming dense populations of up to five plants per square yard. This arum, a member of the plant family Araceae, is a typical forest herb in that it has an extended juvenile period and a long life span, low rates of growth and adult mortality, and clonal reproduction. Jack-in-the-pulpit survives the winter as a dormant corm, or underground stem, and as the canopy closes in the spring, a bud emerges from the soil, leaves expand, and a single unusual flower unfurls. A very unusual flower, indeed.

The flower develops at the end of a fleshy column and is surrounded by a modified leaf, or spathe, that wraps around and forms a hood over the bloom. The floral spike bears flowers with either anthers, the male organs, or stigmas, the female parts. During any given season each plant functions as either a male or as a female. A single individual plant can change sex from year to year—female one year, male the next.

Small flies, specifically several species of fungus gnats, are tricked into pollinating the flowers, apparently receiving no reward. As they look for mushrooms in which to lay their eggs, the flies are lured—probably by smell—into the flowers. Once inside, the fly is trapped and can move only downward. Pollen grains cling to the gnats' hairs and bristles, and pollination occurs when the gnat visits another flower. Flies can escape male flowers through a gap where the spathe folds over upon itself; female flowers lack this feature, so flies die within.

In some locations, female plants produce few seeds, a sign of inefficient or unreliable pollination. Due to forest fragmentation, fungus gnats may be less common today, and therefore less effective at pollination than in presettlement days.

The fruit takes most of the summer to mature, first enlarging and greening, then turning into a bright red berry by late summer. A fruit cluster may have one to many berries. The seeds within the berries disperse in the autumn when the stalk breaks or animals pick the berries. Seeds germinate the following year.

The plant stores food reserves in the thick corm, to be used for next year's leaves. Because reserves are not used for growth or repair of tissues in the current year, neither the plant nor its leaves grow after they develop in the spring. Possibly because these plants cannot repair themselves, the leaves, corm, and green berries are protected from herbivores by crystals of calcium oxalate, sharp little points that imbed themselves in mucous membranes of would-be grazers.

By first frost, the embryonic cells of next year's leaves and flower have formed within a bud at the top of the corm. Dormant corms reveal their future clearly: Large corms will produce two leaves and bear next year's female flower; smaller, one-leaved corms usually produce male flowers. The smallest corms will form no flowers at all. In essence, by late summer the plant has made a developmental decision about which sex to be the following year based on the level of its reserves. In the closely related Japanese species, corm weight is also strongly related to sex: 91 percent of corms weighing 0.5 to 0.8 ounce yield males, 65 percent of the corms weighing 0.9 to 1.2 ounces develop into females, and virtually all corms heavier than 1.3 ounces become female. Gender expression appears related to size or physiological condition, and since individuals grow with age, over a lifetime they tend to change sex from male to female.

In making its sexual changes, the plant's growth seems to follow an internal debate: "Should I produce one or two leaves? Should I produce a male or female flower, or none at all?" This mock monologue is laced with contingencies: "If I am a medium-sized plant and have had a good year, I will produce buds for two large leaves and a female flower, but if I have just barely replaced my reserves, I will again form just one leaf and a male flower bud. If I have had an outright bad year, I will not produce a flower at all."

Such fictional introspection also applies to the Japanese relative. When females of the Japanese species were transplanted to a site with poor growth conditions, most switched into males the following spring. When males were cultured under excellent growth conditions, most developed as females the next year.

In natural populations of jack-in-the-pulpit, individuals change sex frequently. At one site in New York, 8 percent of nonflowering plants, 64 percent of the males, and 63 percent of the females changed their sex from one season to the next. Thus, there are two patterns of sex change: going from no flower to male to female with steady growth, and changing back-and-forth between male and female with reversals in body size. Both of these patterns of sex change are called sequential hermaphroditism, one of the rarest sexual breeding systems in plants. Other than jack-in-the-pulpit, only a few species of orchids, the striped maple (another Appalachian species), and two species of juniper also practice sequential hermaphroditism.

Back at the New York site, 60 to 80 percent of the female plants failed to set seed. When these same plants were artificially pollinated, seed set increased by a factor of ten, suggesting that in this population seed production is limited by the availability of pollen rather than by the availability of nutrients. It is consistent that, in areas where jack-in-the-pulpit is not pollen limited, plants do display signs of nutrient limitation, such as smaller size and a shift to maleness.

With that bit of background, let us try to determine why jack-in-the-pulpits change sex. The most widely accepted hypothesis, called the size-advantage model, includes two general predictions. First, sex will change if the age- or size-specific expectations of reproductive success are different for males and females. For example, plants will change from male to female if larger plants are able to produce a greater number of successful offspring from seeds than smaller plants can by producing pollen. And second, sex will change at the size where the reproductive successes for the two sexes are equal. For example, plants will change sex at the size at which the number of seeds produced by females equals the number of seeds fertilized by males.

An important element of this theory is the idea that females allocate more of their resources to reproduction than males do. Regardless of the plant's size, male flowers represent about 8 percent of the plant's biomass. In contrast, female flowers represent 10 to 20 percent of the plant's biomass in large and medium-sized females, respectively. Simply put, the physiological costs of reproduction are greater for females than males. A small individual would have difficulty paying the cost of being female. By reproducing as a male when it is small, the plant avoids the prohibitive cost and frees resources for growth.

That makes good sense theoretically, but in some populations reproductive success appears linked less to plant size and limited more by available pollinators than the size-advantage hypothesis assumes. All jack-in-the-pulpit populations exhibit a minimum size below which female reproduction is prohibitively costly. This threshold creates selection for sex-changing. But because seed production and sex ratio vary from year to year, the strength of the selection pressures for maleness versus femaleness also fluctuate. Such variation makes it unlikely that in such areas jack-in-the-pulpit will ever attain the simple nonreproducing-to-male-to-female sex-changing sequence described by the size-advantage theory.

In a population near Concord, Massachusetts, female jack-in-the-pulpits do exhibit greater reproductive output with increasing plant size. This population conforms to the assumptions of the size-advantage model: it seems to be less pollinator-limited and more nutrient-limited. With this assumption of the theory met, ecologists calculated the theoretical size at which plants should sexually transform, the size at which 50 percent are of each sex. Sure enough, the optimal and observed switch points were similar: when a plant reached a height of about 15 inches. The size-advantage model had predictive power for this population.

Plants that alter their gender seem to do so in response to environmental factors that vary unpredictably. The general tendency among many animal and plant species, including jack-in-the-pulpit, is for stress to induce maleness, where stress is defined as conditions that reduce growth, survival, or ability to allocate resources to reproduction. Like jack-in-the-pulpit, some hermaphroditic orchid species also function as females in sunlight and males in shade—with shade and sunlight being transient features in the forest. When neighboring trees of equal height knock into one another, abrasion of buds, leaves, and branches create and maintain "crown shyness" gaps. Much of the light reaching the ground passes through such gaps, which seem to be unpredictable through space and time. Individual jack-in-the-pulpits root in spots that provide a variable and unpredictable energy supply.

Many ground cover herbs are in the same unpredictable ecological situation, and yet, sexual hermaphroditism is extremely rare. Why don't more Appalachian plants exhibit sex reversal? Three published hypotheses attempt to answer this question. It seems the energetic costs of making the sexual change—retooling, if you will—lead to increased mortality or time taken away from breeding. Further, anatomical constraints may hinder the evolution of sex reversal from individuals having separate sexes. Finally, opposite selection pressures—favoring male versus female functions—may cancel each other out. I would add that sex change could be more common than we are aware, just undetected.

In the last few years, biologists have discovered sex reversal in a wide variety of plants and animals. Wrasses on Caribbean coral reefs and snails in the Amazon also display reversible gender, apparently for the same size-based reasons. And here beneath the canopy of our Appalachian forest lives one of the stars of sex reversal, the jack-in-the-pulpit.

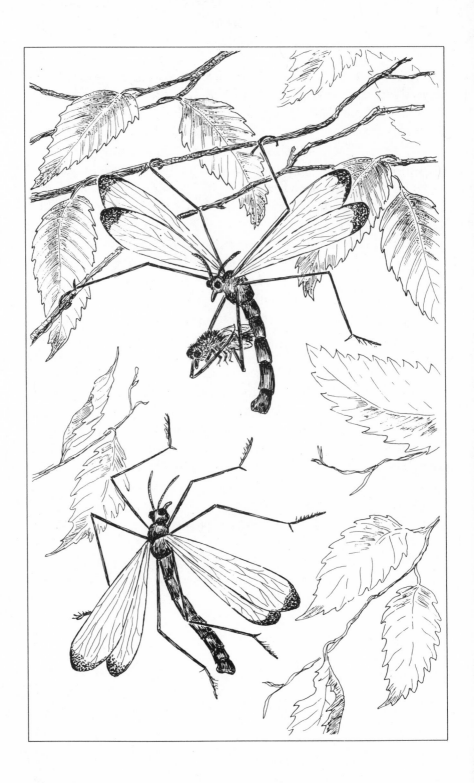

10

Nuptial Gift of the Hangingfly

HERBS TICKLE MY ARMS as I sit on the ground in a cove forest watching the sex life of the black-tipped hangingfly. I can see the medium-sized (0.8 inch), slim, brownish body, long thin legs, and four narrow, black-tipped wings of each hangingfly. Named for their habit of dangling from foliage by their front legs, they hang with wings outstretched rather than folded over their abdomens. Hangingflies superficially resemble long, slender, delicate flies but are not true flies, members of the order Diptera; they just look like them. In central and southern Appalachia, you will find the hangingflies' story easy to follow—they fly slowly over short distances, catching prey and mating throughout the day.

Research on the black-tipped hangingfly's behavior has revealed a complex blend of courtship, nuptial giving, thievery, and sexual prevarication. Although the male and female hangingflies look similar, their behaviors are markedly different—and therein lies the tale.

The male hangingfly uses his strong rear legs to capture houseflies, daddy longlegs, and other arthropods. While holding prey with the prehensile segment of his last leg, he catches on to a leaf or twig and prepares the meal. He pierces the prey with his needlelike snout and injects digestive juices that paralyze the insect and liquefy its innards. After a brief taste, the male hangingfly may discard the prey; if he retains it, he begins making short (less than 12 feet) flights through the ground cover. After each flight, he hangs from a leaf or twig and everts a pair of abdominal glands that release a pheromone, a specific molecule released by one individual that carries a message to a receiving individual. (Some biologists have suggested that a man's sweat contains a sexual pheromone that excites women. Not so in my experience.)

A female hangingfly responds to the male's pheromonal invitation by settling beside him, then hanging by her forelegs facing him. She signals sexual readiness by lowering her wings, which stimulates the male to present his gift of food. Both are initially hesitant and noncommittal: While the female evaluates the prey by feeding on it, she keeps her abdominal tip pulled away from the male. The male retains a firm grip on the prey with both hind legs and one or two middle legs.

Thus, each member of the consort pair has made a conditional contract: If the prey is unpalatable or too small, the female flies away unmated or after having allowed copulation for a short time, an average of only five minutes. If on the other hand, she finds the nuptial gift to be satisfactory, she allows a lengthy copulation. In this latter situation, mating lasts an average of 23 minutes, during which the female feeds on the offering. Female black-tipped hangingflies select or reject mates on the basis of their food offering—much like humans.

Dr. Randy Thornhill of the University of New Mexico has discovered a tense battle among selfish individuals underlying this apparent romance, each fly pursuing its own reproductive priorities. A closer look at the hangingfly's mating behavior reveals the brutal details.

Hunting is a dangerous activity for hangingflies. It not only costs time but exposes them to the webs of predatory spiders. Hangingflies have evolved several methods to reduce these costs. Female hangingflies do not hunt when their own predatory males are abundant. When they do hunt, they retain the prey items. In contrast, males discard about 32 percent of the prey items as unpalatable or too small. This intersexual difference suggests that females reduce their odds of falling prey by allowing copulation in exchange for food.

Trading a meal for sex makes the male more vulnerable than the female to predation by spiders. Males have evolved a strategy for reducing their risks during hunting. They may capture free-ranging arthropods, as reported above, or they may steal prey from other males. Although a male with prey is a potential theft victim while feeding, flying, and copulating, he is most vulnerable when releasing pheromone because at that particular moment he is physiologically programmed to receive a female.

Fully 50 percent of a male's time between copulations is spent searching for prey. Males that steal rather than hunt for themselves reduce that unproductive interval by 42 percent, thereby obtaining more copulations than do nonpirates. Further, because thieves move about less than hunters, they are less likely to get ensnared in a spider web. Thus, stealing food brings two benefits to a male: increasing the rate of mating and decreasing the odds of being eaten.

How a particular male obtains prey, by hunting or stealing, seems to depend on what he encounters first, a free-living arthropod or another male hangingfly carrying prey. This mixed hunting strategy may have evolved because the male's success at stealing depends on the density and sex ratio of fellow hangingflies, both of which seem to vary unpredictably through time and space.

The hangingflies employ two equally common styles of successful prey snatching. A male may fly forcefully into another male or into a mated pair, then grapple for the prey, or the male thief may behave like a typical female and deceive the male into giving up his prey. Transvestites fly up to a pheromone-releasing male and lower their wings, normally the female's signal that she is ready to copulate. About one-third of the time, the male with prey flies away undeceived, but in the rest of the bouts he presents his gift to the female-mimic. With both males gripping the prey, the mimic begins to feed. While the courting male attempts to copulate, the mimic keeps his abdomen out of range, just as a female would. This may continue for a couple of minutes before the owner tries to retrieve the prey from the mimic's grasp. In about one-third of these cases, the mimic successfully secures a hold on the prey and flies off with it. Like food thievery, female mimicry leads to more prey and mates, and lowers the odds of getting snared by a web. Female-mimics succeed because the sexes are similar in appearance, giving courting males few cues to warn them of impending theft.

The relationship *between* the sexes is also fraught with tension. After a successful copulation, the male normally terminates mating. In an ensuing struggle, the male tries to uncouple from the female and pull the food item from her grasp. After separating, the male feeds briefly on the prey, and if he finds that it is still satisfactory, he repeats the pheromone-emitting and mating sequence. In this fashion, a single prey item may yield up to three successive copulations. Prey items in the size range of 1.1 to 1.8 inches square are most frequently employed twice. Smaller prey do not offer enough nourishment for more than one meal, and larger food items are too difficult to hold during the postmating struggle. If the prey has little nutritive substance left, the male discards it and hunts for another. Males win 64 percent of the struggles for final possession of prey; females, only 8 percent. In the remaining 28 percent of the battles, prey drop onto the leaf litter.

Male-terminated copulations result in maximum insemination and turn off the female's sexual receptivity. A mated female hangs from vegetation for about three hours and drops an average of three eggs onto the ground. Thereafter, females are ready again to eat and copulate.

Females, then, discriminate among males at two levels. If the meal is inadequate, she may reject the male before copulation, or if the relationship proceeds, she may terminate coupling before the male transfers a full complement of sperm. The duration of copulation is important because of the positive correlation between the length of time coupled and the number of sperm transferred. Five minutes of copulation, which typically accompanies a small nuptial gift, must pass before any sperm are transferred and before the female is stimulated to lay any eggs. For matings 5 to 20 minutes long, the number of sperm transferred increases with time elapsed; after 20 minutes sperm delivery ceases. Males with small or unpalatable prey mate only briefly and transfer little or no sperm, whereas males offering large, tasty meals enjoy prolonged matings and maximum insemination. Natural selection favored males that offered large, nutritious prey because this superior resource fortified the eggs.

At first glance, the black-tipped hangingfly seems to be playing in a romance in which males sally forth to capture prey, court females by offering these nuptial gifts, and then mate blissfully. However, competition and tension between and within the sexes are the real forces that shape this Appalachian scene. Capturing the arthropod gift involves risks that males try to avoid by stealing from each other, either by direct assault or by mimicking females. On the other side of the relationship, a female will not accept a male's sperm until she is assured of a sufficiently nourishing meal. After mating, the conjugal partners even struggle over the leftovers. Although left feeling robbed of a romantic tale, I receive a deeper satisfaction from understanding how complex—dare I say humanlike?—a small Appalachian insect can be.

11

Femmes Fatales of Twilight

SUMMER IN APPALACHIA has its share of magical moments. For me such a time comes when I squeeze out through my second story window, settle on the porch roof, and survey the firefly meadow.

> Here come real stars to fill the upper skies,
> And here on earth come emulating flies
> That, though they never equal stars in size
> (And they were never really stars at heart),
> Achieve at times a very starlike start.
> Only, of course, they can't sustain the part.
>
> —Robert Frost, *Fireflies in the Garden*

In his poem "Fireflies in the Garden," Robert Frost is so taken by the spectacle that he flirts with equating fireflies and stars, but in a final line of reflection, demurs. Poetic license is fair, but he was wise to change his mind, for beneath the twinkling pageant is a society of liars and cannibals.

Fireflies are a family of beetles that emit light from specialized tissue in the ends of their abdomens. Male fireflies typically crisscross an area, flashing rhythmically. Females remain stationary on the ground or in a bush and respond to males with their own flashes. When a male receives an answer, he hovers and orients his lantern toward the female. Eventually, he lands near her, and they mate.

Each firefly species has its own unique male signal and female response. Between species the signals and responses vary in the color, number, duration, modulation, rate, and intensity of the light emissions, the rate of repetition of the pattern, and the speed, altitude, time, season, habitat, and maneuvers of flight. All this variety enables us human observers, with practice, to identify many species by their flashes alone.

It seems counterintuitive, then, that only the timing of the flash has been shown to play a role in a firefly's ability to identify a member of its species. For males, the parameters of timing involved in this communication include frequency, duration, and pause between flashes. The most critical characteristic of the female's response is her delay in answering the male's flash. The time lag preceding a female's response varies among species from three to nine seconds.

Before we allow this scene of firefly behavior to get complex, let's explore a basic, no-frills example: *Photinus pyralis*, the most widespread species of firefly in North America. Males of this species begin flashing at dusk, typically about three feet above the ground. Each flash lasts about one-half second, and the male repeats it about every seven seconds. Emitted during the upswing following a short swoop, the flash looks like an upward arc of light. On the ground, receptive females answer with a one-half-second flash three seconds after the male's. His visual display is not meant to attract a female of his own species, rather to persuade a receptive female to reveal her location.

Add the research findings of Dr. James E. Lloyd of the University of Florida and the plot thickens. In a firefly meadow, males greatly outnumber females. Because competition for mates is keen among males, a male spends much of his time searching for females. When answered, he must reach and mate the female before other males converge. Given this much, we could logically conclude that natural selection should favor males that locate, reach, and copulate with receptive females as soon as possible. The catch is that the male's bright advertisement and scramble for mates make him vulnerable to exploitation—by other fireflies.

Of the three major genera of fireflies in North America, two (*Photuris* and *Photinus*) carry on a complex, intriguing relationship. (A warning: Keep these two genera straight.) Let us first focus on the behavior of fireflies in the genus *Photuris*.

Prior to mating, a virgin *Photuris versicolor* female answers almost exclusively the triple-pulsed flash of males of the same species. About three days after mating, she takes a station on or near the ground, stands erect with her jaws open and begins to mimic the flash response characteristic of females of other species. She even imitates the latency credibly. No longer interested in mating, she is now a predator. When her successful flash response attracts a male of another species, she pounces on and devours him. In such femmes fatales, mating seems to induce the switch from receptive virgin to voracious predator. Apparently, something transferred with the sperm initiates the transformation.

This type of predation, called aggressive mimicry, has been reported for ten species of *Photuris* fireflies. At least three more species are suspect. In fact, further research will probably reveal that most species of the genus *Photuris* can switch on predatory behavior.

The females of some *Photuris* species prey on males of more than one species. So far, the extreme example of this type of versatility is *Photuris versicolor*, whose females prey on males of at least 11 other firefly species. These virtuosos readily adjust both the form and timing of their flashes in response to different male flash patterns.

Females of various *Photuris* species have been caught ambushing male fireflies in Appalachian locations from Massachusetts to Georgia. As this story continues to unfold, aggressive mimicry will almost surely be found throughout the entire Appalachian chain.

Why do *Photuris* females prey on other fireflies? Fireflies spend the first few years of life as larvae in the soil, then live as adults for only one to four weeks. Food acquired as larvae permits females to produce some eggs, but protein gained via predation augments their fecundity. Thus, through aggressive mimicry a female firefly increases the number, and possibly quality, of the eggs she produces.

The risk of falling prey to aggressive mimics has led to the evolution of counteradaptations in males. *Photinus* males (that's the other genus) do not just fly directly to a responding female; instead, they fly close, hover, back away, reapproach, and flash repeatedly. The male's ambivalence reflects a deep conflict. Should he pursue a seemingly receptive female and risk the predator's jaws, or dally and lose the copulation to another male? The male's compromise: if he lands, he does so several feet from the female and then approaches cautiously on foot.

For the male, the risk of being eaten is significant. In *Photinus collustrans*, for example, males are answered by up to five times as many predaceous *Photuris* females as by females of their own species. In one study, 16 percent of the males lured by females were duped and eaten.

Aggressive mimicry by *Photuris* females may have influenced another aspect of the evolution of firefly behavior: it may be the reason that males of most *Photinus* species fly at twilight rather than at dark. If a *Photinus* male can spy the silhouette of a larger *Photuris* female, with a shape and stance different from that of his own females, he can stop short of the poised jaws. *Photuris* females of several species have evolved another predatory tactic—aerial predation. Guided by their prey's luminescence, *Photuris* females attack flying male fireflies at night. These "sidewinder hawkers" sometimes use the aerial strategy together with aggressive signal mimicry.

And it gets even more bizarre. The males of one *Photinus* species display an alternate mating strategy that exploits aggressive mimicry. The normal flash pattern of *Photinus macdermotti* males is two short flashes two seconds apart. While he is on the ground courting a female, a male sometimes injects a flash into the last one-quarter of the interval between the flashes of an approaching rival male. The timing of these injections matches the flashes that the predaceous females of two *Photuris* species occasionally—and apparently by mistake—emit. Thus, the courting *Photinus* male appears to be mimicking the accidental injection flash of predatory *Photuris* females. Injected flashes slow the approach of converging males, thereby extending the first male's sexual monopoly of the female. This neat trick is an example of the mimicry of a mimicry.

Even the males of some *Photuris* species exhibit mimicry, although not for predatory purposes. Some *Photuris* males duplicate the male flash of species that may be prey of their own *Photuris* females. They restrict the decoy signals to the habitats, seasons, and daily periods of the prey. If a hunting *Photuris* female answers and approaches the imitating *Photuris* male, he quickly grabs and inseminates her. Thus, *Photuris* males exploit their own female's mimicry to increase the odds of gaining a copulation. Since mating causes *Photuris* females to change from male-seeking to prey-seeking, males pursuing this strategy run a serious risk of being cannibalized.

Variation exists here too. Males of *Photuris* species can mimic the male flash patterns of two or more *Photinus* species. Some *Photuris* males can shift back and forth between their own species' flash pattern and those of other simultaneously active species. This also seems to be a strategy for increasing the pool of potential mates.

Understanding the last layer of complexity requires Herculean concentration because it combines the ideas of injection flashes and males mimicking males. When a predatory *Photuris versicolor* female mimics the flash of *Photinus macdermotti* females, the predator may produce extra flashes that mimic the injected flashes used by males that are competing for females. Such injections are made during the last 0.6 second of the rival's flash pattern. By mimicking competition flashes, *Photuris* females draw more *Photinus* males to the general area and thereby improve their chances of a successful hunt. This is an example of a female mimicking a female mimicking a male that is mimicking a predaceous female.

How did such a complex, interdependent system of behavioral mimicry evolve? Apparently, a step-by-step evolutionary arms race is responsible. Initially *Photinus* may have produced only simple flashes of fixed duration, whereas *Photuris* may have shown variability. The latter presumably demanded a higher order of neural processing by the female, which in turn may have allowed the evolution of changeable female responses, the prerequisite for predation. Opportunistically, the males of some prey species may have incorporated deceit in their mating signals to maximize their own mating success.

We knew all along that fireflies were not very much like stars. But when I contemplate my firefly meadow now, my mind vacillates between the romance evoked by twinkling lights and the logical fatalism provoked by ambush. The bard was right in withdrawing the parity, but for reasons far more intricate than he may have suspected.

12

Small Fishes in Shallow Headwaters

As drivers of Appalachian dirt roads, we are at least subliminally aware of the schools of fish that dash madly about as we splash through a ford. The most common fishes flushed by our tires are members of the minnow, sucker, sunfish, and perch families. Within these comparatively few families, Appalachia's numerous small, steep streams have catalyzed the evolution of a great fish diversity.

Many fishes native to Appalachia live in the alternating pools and riffles of headwater streams. These habitats are shallow, subject to torrential spates and bone-dry droughts; the fish dwellers are exposed to predation by raccoons, snakes, and herons. How do small fish persist in shallow headwaters?

During spring and autumn, when streams flow abundantly, fish can move freely among pools before settling down for the season. Once established, fish seldom wander, even when moderate water levels allow them to explore other pools. One study found that after summer flash floods, 75 percent of the fish remained in their original, pre-flood locations. Darters and sunfishes in particular exhibit this kind of site loyalty.

If winters are so cold that fish risk being frozen in shallow water, they migrate from their springtime spawning grounds in shallow headwaters to deeper overwintering reaches farther downstream. Presumably, natural selection has favored young adults returning to breed in

73

their own home pool—one of the best indicators of future reproductive success is that one's parents successfully reproduced there. Each creek, even each pool in a single reach, probably holds a unique chemical odor that becomes indelibly imprinted in the memory of the juvenile fish during its first summer. We know that coho salmon imprint on naturally occurring chemical cues for homing. The salmon's homing response is highly specific: molecules with atomic structures that differ slightly from the stimulating molecule do not elicit the homing response.

If we assume that small fish in Appalachian streams use chemical cues to return to their home pool, an important part of the story remains a mystery—what molecules provide pool-specific cues? Root exudates, the organic molecules released by the roots of trees, are a possibility. The number of combinations of different organic molecules comprising the exudate constellation in soil and water must be enormous, and their tree sources remain stable over the long term.

In Pine Cabin Run and thousands of other Appalachian headwaters, adult creek chubs prey on blacknose dace and cannibalize juvenile creek chubs. Adult creek chubs themselves fall prey to belted kingfishers and green herons. How do small fish in shallow headwater pools escape predation?

Where shelter is limited, adult creek chubs aggregate under cover during the day. At night, when the birds are gone, they disperse to find their prey. Where shelter is plentiful, adult chubs do not aggregate. Young chubs employ a combination of camouflage and stillness, finding cover beneath leaves and other small objects. As you might expect, in pools that host predators, prey density increases with the complexity of cover provided by rocks, limbs, and overhangs. Both predator and prey choose pools that minimize their odds of falling prey.

Countershading, body coloration that combines a dark back and light belly, also reduces the odds of being eaten. Viewed from below, a fish with a pale belly presents less of a contrast against the sky than one with a dark underside. The dark back camouflages a fish from aerial fish-eating birds. A fish with a light back and dark belly would be obvious to predatory fishes from all directions.

Yet another way to avoid being eaten is to hide behind another individual. The random movements and indistinguishability of individuals within a school preclude the predator from fixing on one individual.

A fascinating adaptation for reducing the odds of being eaten is the alarm system, a method of communication in which a fish emits an alarm substance that elicits fright in pool mates. Two major groups of bony fishes—one including chubs, dace, and catfishes; the other contains perch and darters—rely on alarm systems. Large, specialized cells, called club cells, produce the alarm substance, rupturing and releasing their contents when the skin is injured. Nearby fish of the same species smell the alarm substance and display a fright reaction. Each species, even each developmental stage, exhibits a fright reaction suited to its own specific predators. A species that normally schools may tighten, flee, and avoid the site of the stimulus. Other species swim against the bottom and stir up a cloud of silt. Some freeze on the bottom and rely on camouflage for protection. Adult creek chubs sink to the bottom individually, but juveniles flee as a school. Although individuals respond most strongly to the alarm substance released by other members of their species, fright reaction is not completely species-specific. The alarm substance of some fishes may elicit fright reaction in members of other, closely related species.

The fright reaction may even visually signal other members of the same species. For example, when two aquaria are placed together, an alarm-substance-induced fright reaction in one tank will trigger a fright reaction in fish of the adjacent tank, even though there is no exchange of water between the two tanks. This strategy allows rapid chemical and visual communication of danger among the fish in a pool.

The individuals of some species lose their alarm substance cells, but not necessarily the fright reaction, during the breeding season. Seasonal loss of the ability to alarm has evolved to complement abrasive spawning habits. At the onset of the spring breeding season, male fathead minnows lose the cells that contain alarm substance. This allows males to clean a site and spawn by rubbing against pebbles without releasing alarm substance that would frighten away interested females. In the fall, males regain the ability to produce alarm substance.

The alarm signal system of fishes resembles warning signals of other animals—alarm calls of birds, tail flagging by deer, and alarm pheromones of tadpoles—in that they appear altruistic. Over the past twenty years, biologists have been trying to understand how such seemingly sacrificial signaling systems could have evolved. If there is an evolutionary cost to the sender, such as producing and maintaining alarm substance cells or putting the sender at risk of predation, the trait is called an adaptation. However, if the substance eliciting fright is merely a normal bodily fluid that leaks passively, it may not be eligible for the status. Because the club cells in the skin seem to have no function other than to synthesize and store alarm substance, warning others has a cost.

The most likely evolutionary explanation for this adaptation seems to be kin selection. Recall that young fish return to their natal pool. Although fish in a school may not be full siblings, their site loyalty suggests that they are related. Kin selection could operate in a straightforward manner: individuals releasing alarm substance may increase the odds that a nearby genetic relative will be aware of a predator. The alarm pheromone might even reduce cannibalism by inducing fright in a large fish of that species, thereby saving siblings.

Kin selection is easier to invoke if genetic relatives are spatially near each other. Even if kin disperse widely and non-relatives school together, kin still might be able to favor each other. Recent evidence suggests that fish can identify relatives through chemical cues. In fact, in a wide variety of animals, an individual's odor is in part determined by its genes. Small fish in Appalachian headwater pools may be able to identify kin solely through olfaction, and then favor them with alarm signals. It is awesome to consider the possibility that scattered throughout Appalachia's hollows are brothers, sisters, and first cousins clustered in pools reciprocating favors while slighting unrelated individuals in the same pool.

The other day as I drove my old truck through the ford of Pine Cabin Run, I tried to follow the streaking dace, my mind checking off the components of this intricate scene. It was daytime, so the dace were safe from predatory creek chubs who lurked under the rock ledge. Their countershading made them doubly hard to follow as they zig-zagged randomly within the school. I wondered whether any of them might have burst a few club cells and released a little alarm substance. It's getting harder all the time to simply splash through the ford and step on the gas.

13

Darter Daddies

DARTERS, AS BRIGHTLY COLORED as rain forest butterflies and coral reef fishes, are the fish analog to lungless salamanders—both have radiated extensively in the fractured landscape of Appalachia.

Darters in the genus *Etheostoma* draw my attention because of their multifarious forms of parental care. Males alone care for the eggs after the females deposit them. Some species lay their eggs on plants, logs, and other exposed substrates; others form a multi-layered cluster of eggs on the undersides of flat-bottomed rocks; the remainder deposit eggs in a single layer directly on the undersides of flat-bottomed rocks. A fish in the last category, the tessellated darter, has intrigued me for several years, especially after I observed in them an unusual behavior among animals: males caring for eggs that were fertilized by other males.

The tessellated darter lives throughout the Atlantic drainages of northern and central Appalachia. Male tessellated darters defend flat-bottomed rocks as spawning grounds. When a ripe female approaches a spawning rock, the territorial male flares his fins and quivers his body, then leads her to his rock. Just before she reaches the rock, he scoots under it, inverts belly-up, and begins wiggling across the ceiling. Through this behavior, he seems to be advertising his willingness and ability to clean eggs. In response, she swims under the rock, and inverts and wiggles across the ceiling, probably inspecting its quality. If the male's courtship is successful, the female may begin depositing eggs, one at a time, directly on the bare rock ceiling. As she attaches each egg, the male simultaneously fertilizes it. After the female deposits ten to fifty eggs in a loose two-dimensional cluster, the male chases her away and begins caring for the eggs. If still gravid, the female may approach another nest and mate again.

The male cleans the eggs with ventral fins while swimming upside down. To aerate the eggs, he maintains his position using his pectoral fins while he pushes water into the nest with his caudal fin. Both cleaning and aerating the eggs burn calories and preclude other activities, such as courting females. Thus, caring for one batch of eggs reduces the total number of eggs a male could potentially fertilize. So far, this scene does not challenge conventional evolutionary ideas. The quirk is that males routinely clean and aerate eggs fertilized by other males.

The first time I saw a male cleaning eggs that I knew had been fertilized by another male, I could feel Darwin's grip squeeze my Adam's apple. Weaned on neo-Darwinian paradigms, I started talking to myself on the stream bank, alternately feeling excited and confused. The male's behavior, if consistently displayed by other males of the population, could be an exciting exception to the dogma that the function of behavior is to promote individual reproductive success. Or it could be a distant outlier explainable by extending the concept of natural selection.

During the next three years I dissected the tessellated darter's social system, carrying out a series of experiments to uncover the causes of this altruism. I studied the tessellated darter in a small stream that offered only a few rocks suitable for spawning because of the heavy silt that smothers most rocks. The silt blanket and a dense population of darters meant there were more adult males than suitable breeding sites. Consequently, only a few large, dominant, territorial males were able to secure a spawning rock. This left smaller males, which composed the majority, without rocks. Small, subordinate males, or floaters, spent most of their time roaming the stream in search of suitable nest rocks.

During the first day of fatherhood, the male scrubs the ceiling, aerates eggs, and repulses potential egg predators. Quite the model parent, he swims only an inch or two from his brood. Mother, long gone, contributes nothing to embryonic survival. When the embryos reach two days of age, father begins to stray. During extended forays several times per hour, he visits a series of other nest rocks, bullies his way into occupied nests, chases off attendant males, and attempts to usurp fertilizations. Cruising male darters embody the tradeoff between monogamous commitment and promiscuous behavior, a conflict also felt by many humans.

What opens the door to daddy's profligate behavior? During the first few hours after fertilization, the egg membranes are pliable, and the eggs are only weakly attached to the ceiling. By one day of age, the eggs have become firmly glued to the rock, rigid, and resistant to puncture. Now the eggs are virtually invulnerable, and father can chase females elsewhere without risking his embryos to cannibalism.

After most cruises, father returns to his original nest rock within twenty minutes. Once every two or three days, a cruising male finds a receptive female and spawns again at another rock. Because this restarts his commitment clock with a new brood at a new nest, he abandons his previous clutch.

Father, however, could not stay away without harm befalling his eggs unless another process came into play. Within minutes after a territorial male leaves his nest rock, a floating male enters it, inverts, and begins wiggling over the ceiling. Floaters sometimes peck at attached eggs, appearing to test their edibility, but almost always give up after a few nibbles. Floating males that occupy newly vacated rocks achieve a remote chance of attracting a female and fertilizing a few eggs. From an evolutionary perspective, a little reproductive success is immensely better than none at all. Because the dominant male's eggs are arranged as a loose cluster in the middle of the ceiling, interstitial and peripheral space is available for the floater's spawning. Cleaning the first male's eggs is incidental to the second's cleaning the ceiling for his own spawning. Further, females are stimulated to spawn by a few healthy eggs. Caring for the first male's eggs, then, involves no obvious costs and significant benefits for the subordinate male.

Dominant males cruise because spawning at more than one rock leads to greater reproductive success than fertilizing a single clutch. In essence, large dominant males sequentially monopolize a series of spawning rocks that are temporarily most desirable to females. Father can get away with abandoning his offspring because of the ready availability of surrogate egg-sitters.

Floating males ensure the survival of eggs they did not fertilize because in the process of maintaining the ceiling for their own spawning, they incidentally clean and aerate the previously attached clutch. They clean unrelated eggs to advertise to females that they are effective fathers. Thus everybody wins. Although the behavior of small males initially appeared altruistic, a few critical experiments demonstrated it is consistent, albeit somewhat anomalous, with conventional evolutionary thought.

Let us look at this problem from a broader, comparative perspective. The mottled sculpin, like the tessellated darter, also defends nest rocks in Appalachian streams. The list of similarities between the two fishes is long: suitable breeding sites are limited; there are numerous egg predators and cannibals; males are larger than females; large males monopolize the most desirable nest rocks; small males are relegated to less desirable sites; and males mate with more than one female. The most frequent egg predators are female mottled sculpins, whose large mouths make them efficient cannibals. Unlike male tessellated darters, sculpin fathers remain with their own eggs until they hatch.

Large male sculpins obtain large spawning sites, and females choose to spawn with large males who are most effective at repelling potential cannibals and least likely to abandon the nest. This is important to the female because she deposits all of her eggs for that year in one discrete hemispherical mass. Field studies have confirmed that sculpin eggs are lost to predators and cannibals less frequently when they are guarded by large males than by small males.

Even though tessellated darters and mottled sculpins share a host of ecological and behavioral traits, the extent of their paternal loyalty differs because darter eggs scattered on the ceiling harden and adhere to the point of invulnerability, whereas the clump of sculpin eggs can be eaten in a single bite.

Through such experimental and comparative studies, small, easily overlooked fishes of Appalachian streams have stretched our concept of natural selection. Under unique conditions natural selection can even favor adults that care for genetically unrelated offspring if the behavior enhances their own reproductive opportunities and entails little cost. In his essay "Altruism," Lewis Thomas reasoned that sacrifice is our duty to each other because, compared to other organisms, we humans share much of our DNA. In contrast, the darter's act suggests a more realistic alternative: One human is more likely to help an unrelated human when the "altruist" gets something out of it, or at least when he loses nothing in the process.

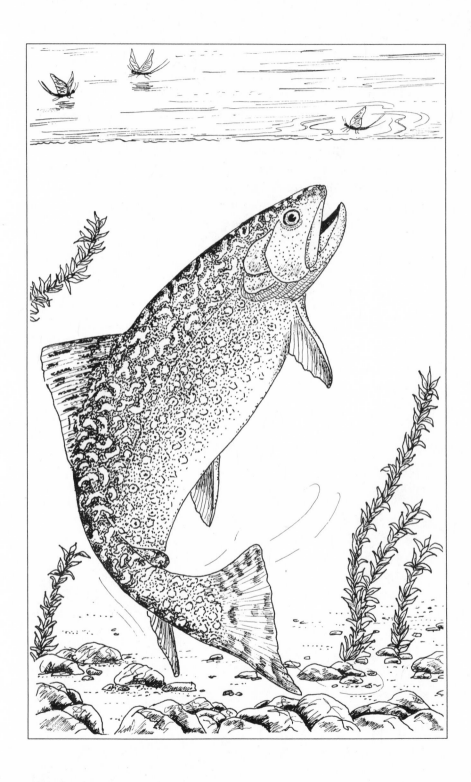

14

To The Brook Trout, with Esteem

I BOTH RESPECT AND PITY the brook trout. On the one hand, a stream-dwelling population of native brookies elicits admiration, even reverence, for these fish have been self-supporting since their origin—no hatchery-reared fish here. Painful to say, they seem to be losing the evolutionary battle. Brook trout live only in cool, clean water, and that kind of habitat is dwindling. Consider this essay first as a tribute, second as a natural history, and third as an expression of righteous indignation for the plight of a small, noble fish.

A male brook trout in breeding condition—its striking olive body streaked with iridescent red, blue, and white markings—is one of Appalachia's most beautiful fish. Light-colored, worm-like markings on the brook trout's dark green back, evoke a second name, speckled trout. I saw my first native, male brook trout decorated in breeding colors in Big Run near Spruce Knob, West Virginia. Viewed through binoculars from the bank he was elegant, even cocky, hovering assertively as he patrolled his pool.

Originally distributed throughout northeastern North America, westward through the Great Lakes, and southward along the Appalachian Mountains, brook trout have been transplanted broadly by conservation agencies. The fish has acclimated to numerous other areas, including the western United States. Like darters, brook trout

85

in Appalachian headwaters maintain separate and discrete populations. These populations probably have been isolated from each other for several thousand years, possibly since the post-glacial warming trend forced them upstream. Such small, isolated populations are vulnerable to inbreeding and extinction.

The only species of the family Salmonidae native to the Appalachians and one of the most important sport fishes in eastern North America, brook trout inhabit a few headwater streams from Maine to Georgia. Anglers hit large populations so hard that natural age compositions are radically altered. Small populations are especially vulnerable to depletion. As a fisher friend says, "They're dumber than dirt and will bite to the last fish."

Today's brook trout, essentially a Pleistocene relict, occupies a challenging niche: streams that are cold, steep, scoured, well oxygenated, clear, and infertile—and therefore niggardly with food. Although they dwell in some hard-water streams in fertile valleys, brook trout are more abundant in the soft water of infertile mountain creeks. Perhaps the most temperature-sensitive native mountain fish, brookies need colder water than brown and rainbow trouts do. Optimal temperatures range from 50 to 61 degrees Fahrenheit, with brook trout seldom inhabiting water above 68 degrees. These trout are also intolerant of silty or turbid water.

Most brook trout streams are unproductive ecosystems whose energy comes from surrounding land. Erosion-resistant Devonian shales and sandstones yield coarse substrates, few nutrients or dissolved solids, and clear waters. In these forest-shaded, nutrient-poor streams, slow-growing attached algae provide negligible food. Here, trout likewise tend to grow extremely slowly.

Brookies do not prefer these streams, but are forced into them. In central and southern Appalachia, the species' original range extended from about 2,100 feet above sea level upward to the headwaters. By the turn of the century, brook trout had been excluded from low elevations by logging, railroad building, forest fires, overfishing, and transplanted exotic trouts. By 1910 logging companies were heavily stocking rainbow trout, a practice that in part allowed much of the brook trout's former range in the southern Appalachians to be monopolized by rainbow and brown trout. In more modern times, acid rain has been added to the list of pressures on the brook trout's habitat.

As warm water, unsuitable habitat, and exotic trouts press the brook trout from lower elevations, freezing water temperatures exclude them from higher country. Appalachian brookies spawn in the fall, during September and October, and their eggs incubate through the winter. At high altitudes in winter, anchor ice and dwindling flows imperil the trout's gravel nests, or redds, exposing them to air and allowing the eggs to freeze.

Brook trout in headwater streams build redds at the sides or tails of pools. After the female cuts the redd, the beautifully reddened male fertilizes the eggs as they settle into the gravel. Fecundity ranges from 20 eggs for a 4-inch female to 200 eggs for a 7.5-inch female. The eggs incubate unattended until spring. Embryonic mortality during prolonged subfreezing weather contributes to the low replenishment of populations in higher reaches.

Within the gravel, newly hatched brookies depend on their large yolk sac for nutrition. After emerging from the gravel in the spring, the fry feed on minute drifting prey, and by July they begin to capture insects at the water's surface. Shortly after emerging from the gravel, a young brook trout protects its food source by defending a territory ranging in size from 25 to 300 square inches. Young brook trout can afford to aggressively displace others because the contested area yields more food than it costs to defend. This behavior forces weaker individuals into suboptimal habitat.

Brook trout are generally visual, opportunistic predators that eat any animal their mouths can grasp, including insects, crustaceans, fish, even small mammals—but the brookie's visual hunting strategy loses effect when high, silt-laden spring runoff obscures prey. One study reported that creek chubs were absent from clear-water streams prowled by sight-oriented brookies, but were abundant in turbid tributaries. In this situation, turbidity promotes a stable coexistence between predator and prey.

In their mountain streams, brook trout grow slowly, mature at a small size, and maintain sparse populations. In these habitats, they typically reach only 6.5 inches long at 3 years of age. In contrast, those in fertile streams grow faster, mature at the same age but larger size, and maintain abundant populations. In Pennsylvania, an infertile stream produced only 20 percent of the brook trout pounds per year that a fertile stream yielded. Annual production of brook trout in a Minnesota stream was tied closely to the abundance of the fish's primary invertebrate food, the small, shrimplike amphipod *Gammarus*. When land development intensified around the Minnesota stream, the silt load increased, amphipod populations decreased, and the annual production of brook trout dropped by 44 percent—further illustrating the brook trout's sensitivity to stream quality.

In eastern Canada some brook trout hatch in freshwater, migrate to sea where they grow to maturity, and then return to breed in freshwater. Exclusively freshwater populations may exist in different rivers with-in the same region. In Canada, the brook trout is called the brook char, a char of the genus *Salvelinus*, not a trout of the genus *Salmo*. The seagoing, or anadromous, brook char remain near shore, close to their rivers of origin, and grow four to five times faster than fish remaining in freshwater. The fast growth at sea presumably reflects bountiful food.

Rainbow and brown trouts have displaced brookies in many stream reaches. Following severe winter floods in Minnesota, two year-classes of brook trout were lost at the egg and fry stages. Consequently, the mass of brook trout dropped by 92 percent, and adults matured more slowly. This gap in the fish community was filled by rainbow trout that moved in from downstream. In this case, winter floods killed brook trout eggs, whereas spring floods would have depressed rainbow trout, whose eggs incubate in the spring. Over the course of 15 years, this trout community changed from 100 percent brook trout to 70 percent brown trout and 15 percent each of brook and rainbow trouts. Brown trout's pugnaciousness and large body size give them an edge in monopolizing foraging and spawning areas. Further, brown trout populations seem to be more resistant to predation and angling pressures. These competitive advantages have enabled brown trout to gradually move upstream through many runs that originally hosted brook trout.

As if that were not enough, acid rain clobbers the reproductive success of brook trout. The number of viable eggs decreases sharply at a pH of 5.0, and to a lesser extent at higher (5.5 to 6.5) pH levels. The growth and survival of young fish also drop at lower pH levels.

The estimable brook trout appears caught in a desperate evolutionary squeeze. Pressed from low elevations by warm water, exotic trouts, and effective anglers, excluded from upper reaches by freezing temperatures, and stressed everywhere by increasingly acidic precipitation, native brookies have come to occupy dwindling, suboptimal habitats. Sandwiched and isolated, a few populations of native brook trout continue to persist without help from us—although we could give them a few breaks along the way.

The survival of the brook trout in Appalachia depends to some extent on what we do to help them. We can encourage our state fishery agencies to deploy liming devices. The released buffer will neutralize some of the acid entering streams. Stimulating utilities to burn low-sulphur coal will reduce the acid in rain. I have seen modest movements in these directions. We can also sensitize state fisheries units to avoid dumping rainbow and brown trouts near brook trout populations. Perhaps there is hope—if we continue working together.

15

A Lungless Salamander Trilogy

Primer

SALAMANDERS, those moist, smooth, lizardlike amphibians, are hardly material for a Madison Avenue style logo. Yet if asked which animal best symbolizes the Appalachian highlands, I would nominate a salamander. Of Appalachia's 34 species of "spring lizards," my candidate is one of the woodland species of lungless salamanders, members of the genus *Plethodon* and the family Plethodontidae. They, more than any other group of living things, reflect the quintessential features of evolution in the Appalachian Mountains. Their small size and limited powers of movement, placed in the context of Appalachia's fragmented topography, have led to a fascinating complex of species.

The Plethodontidae is the largest salamander family: of the 325 salamander species worldwide, more than 200 are plethodontids. In fact, new species of lungless salamanders are still evolving. In Appalachia, Jordan's salamander on one mountain is noticeably different from those a few summits away. All told, there are 21 high-elevation, geographically isolated populations of Jordan's salamander, each in the process of evolving its own unique body features.

Why have lungless salamanders undergone a major radiation in Appalachia? Lizards have been unable to build large populations in the cool, moist forest, possibly because they require direct sunshine to maintain their high metabolic rate. This apparently has left salamanders with little competition. Further, the plethodontid's independence from surface water has allowed it to move freely through the forest's ground cover. Together, freedom from competition and independence from water have allowed lungless salamanders to spread successfully across the landscape. Once they were widely distributed, lungless salamander populations became fragmented by geographic barriers and changing climate.

Not only are plethodons geographically widespread, they are also frequently numerous. For example, the red-backed salamander, which is the most abundant woodland salamander in North America, may live in densities of up to ten per square yard.

Plethodontid salamanders span a continuum from aquatic to fully terrestrial species. The completely terrestrial woodland salamanders of the genus *Plethodon* do not visit streams or seeps to lay eggs. They deposit their eggs in moist, protected sites on solid ground where the female broods them for up to eight months. Upon hatching, a fully functional little salamander emerges. I devote the remainder of this, and most of the next two chapters, to the biology of these completely terrestrial lungless salamanders.

Of the 21 species of *Plethodon* in eastern North America, only the red-backed salamander ranges extensively into northern Appalachia; the remainder are restricted to non-glaciated areas. Only the red-backed forages on the surface during cool weather, a trait that may have allowed it to colonize vast stretches of formerly glaciated terrain.

You have probably been wondering how in the world an animal without lungs could possibly breathe. Lungless salamanders absorb oxygen and release carbon dioxide through their moist skin by the slow, simple process of diffusion. Envision diffusion as the process by which perfume molecules move, by bouncing around slowly and randomly, through a room filled with perfectly still air. Diffusion suffices only if the animal has a lot of surface area in comparison to its body mass—if it is shaped like a hot dog rather than a ball. A long, thin shape maximizes the flux of matter or energy between an object's interior and its environment. In essence, the evolutionary jettisoning of lungs was permitted by a skinny body. A serious disadvantage of this breathing style, though, is that the skin must be kept moist, which restricts the salamanders to damp micro-environments. And this opens up a whole other can of salamanders.

Because above-ground activities such as foraging and courtship are restricted to wet nights, woodland salamanders spend long periods of their lives resting in the moist atmosphere under cover, punctuated by brief periods of above-ground activity. *Plethodons* do not engage in activities that require a great deal of energy, such as running, prolonged fighting, or producing huge quantities of eggs. Their low metabolic rate and large energy stores enable them to survive long stretches between meals.

After emerging from deep underground in early spring, red-backeds often congregate in groups of two to seven under rocks and wood. On rainy and foggy nights, red-backeds crawl up from the forest floor to forage for small insects on plants. During their arboreal forays in darkness, red-backeds rely on odors to locate their motionless prey. Individuals spread out uniformly through summer as competition for food intensifies. During summer droughts, terrestrial salamanders move little, foraging in areas under and bordering protective cover. The survival of a terrestrial salamander is in large part determined by its ability to defend its cover against competitors. By releasing and scenting airborne molecules and through aggressive behavior, plethodontids advertise and protect their crevices. This seasonal change in dispersion suggests that some individuals repel others from the shelters, an example of interference competition.

A salamander's abilities to communicate with other salamanders and to locate and assess stationary prey at night attest to a good sense of smell. An adult red-backed salamander can distinguish between its own home site and those of other individuals on the basis of olfactory cues in body secretions. Male red-backeds prefer substrates with their own excretory odors over those marked by unfamiliar members of their species. Chemical markings on the ground allow communication among red-backeds and between individual red-backeds and Shenandoah salamanders. Picture a male dog lifting his leg on a fire hydrant and you have the idea. The chemical enforcement of territorial boundaries confines the movements of woodland salamanders to small areas.

Adult male red-backeds employ "dear enemy" recognition—individuals are less aggressive toward familiar territorial neighbors than toward strangers. Individual recognition reduces the odds of escalated contests between established neighbors. Salamanders detect other individuals by tapping their fleshy whiskers to fecal pellets. They leave their scent by touching chin and cloacal areas to the substrate. This ability to recognize specific individuals via smell is an unappreciated talent of lower vertebrates.

In addition to chemical signals, red-backeds have a small repertoire of visual displays they use in territorial contests. Threat displays include raising all of the trunk and looking forward; submissive displays include lying flattened and looking away. Males are more aggressive to each other than to females, whereas females display no such intersexual differences.

Fertilization takes place within the female's body—but the males have no penis. They solve this sperm-transfer problem by passing a spermatophore, a packet filled with sperm. During courtship, the male deposits a spermatophore on the ground. If his movements and phero-mones stimulate the female to courtship, she picks up the spermatophore in her cloaca, the common opening for both the excretory and reproductive systems. She stores sperm in the cloaca until the eggs are ready to be fertilized and then lays the clutch in a protected site.

Although other groups of salamanders brood their eggs, this behav-ior is most elaborately developed in plethodontids. Brooding defends the eggs against predators, infection, and desiccation. The female also rotates the eggs to prevent yolk stratification, which causes birth defects and a low hatching rate. Brooding females rarely eat their own eggs unless the eggs are dead or infected. These the mother eats before the infection spreads to the rest of the clutch. A female Allegheny mountain salamander maintains throat contact with her eggs, her throat pulsa-tions somehow contributing to egg survival. Laboratory experiments have shown that clutches attended by female Allegheny mountain salamanders are less susceptible to predation by other salamanders and ground beetles than are unattended clutches. Further, clutches deprived of females but protected from predation usually succumb to a fungal parasite within 12 days. While brooding her eggs, a female Allegheny mountain salamander eats little and consequently loses body weight. Brooding, then, like all adaptations, has costs and benefits for individual reproductive success.

Amid Appalachia's diverse animal species live these common yet inconspicuous amphibians: lungless, skin-breathing salamanders that recognize neighbors by smell, practice internal fertilization without a penis, and brood their young. As you wander Appalachia's hills and hollows, turn over a rock or a log—you never know what strange and wonderful thing might be waiting for you.

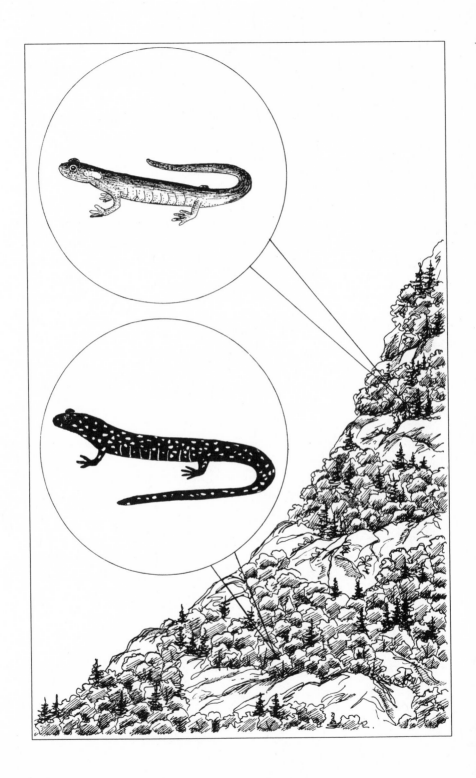

16

A Lungless Salamander Trilogy

Coexistence

SEVERAL SPECIES OF LUNGLESS SALAMANDERS live in the same habitat, forage at the same time on the same prey, and use the same sites for brooding their eggs. In my hollow, the red-backed and slimy salamanders commonly live side-by-side. Yet a great deal of ecological theory and empirical evidence indicates that two or more species cannot exploit forever the same set of limiting resources. Either their resource requirements diverge through evolutionary time to reduce competition or one of the species becomes extinct. So how do several plethodontid species manage to coexist?

Several field studies have demonstrated that competition between species of plethodontids sets the limits for their coexistence. In West Virginia, the Cheat Mountain salamander inhabits spruce forests, relics of the formerly widespread boreal forest. In some sites, the Cheat Mountain salamander appears to exclude the red-backed salamander, but in most localities the two coexist. It appears that the Cheat Mountain salamander, unable to compete with the red-backed in deciduous forests, has become extinct over most of Appalachia's boreal forest.

In the Great Smoky Mountains of North Carolina, the distributions of two other salamanders—the slimy, so called because of its slick, viscous coat, and Jordan's—reflect one of the great evolutionary acts of Appalachia. In southwestern North Carolina, Jordan's consists of twelve geographic isolates, local, genetically distinct populations of a species. On some mountains, the slimy and Jordan's cohabit throughout the entire isolate; on others the two species replace each other altitudinally with varying amounts of elevational overlap. It is as if in some isolates, the two species have evolved mechanisms that permit cohabitation over large areas, while in other areas competition seems to have been so strong that they can coexist only in narrow overlap zones.

In the Great Smoky Mountains, the altitudinal overlap between Jordan's and slimy amounts to only 230 to 400 feet of elevation, whereas in the nearby Balsam Mountains, the two overlap at least 3,900 feet. This comparative observation suggests that competition between the two species has been stronger in the former isolate than in the latter. This hypothesis has been tested: The experimental removal of Jordan's resulted in significant increases in the abundance of the slimy in both areas, but the increase appeared earlier in the Smokies. This experimental outcome demonstrates that competition between species is stronger in the zone of narrower overlap, the Smokies, than in the zone of wider overlap, the Balsams.

In this experiment, both the Jordan's and the slimy benefited from the removal of the other. Yet there were a total of seven salamander species in the study areas. The remaining five (other than Jordan's and slimy) did not increase in abundance after the removal of either of the two abundant species. Thus, we must not automatically assume that competition is a significant factor in all coexistence.

Another competition between species plays on the north-facing slope of Hawksbill Mountain in Virginia's Blue Ridge. Most populations of the Shenandoah salamander inhabit small, isolated pockets of shallow soil tucked within the rocky confines of talus. Both the Shenandoah and red-backed prefer moist spots, but the Shenandoah tolerates dry conditions better than the red-backed. Each species responds differently to drought. Red-backeds, which live in deep soil, simply descend deeper. When forced to dehydrate, red-backeds lose more water, are less tolerant of the water losses, and do not survive as long as Shenandoahs.

Red-backeds are excluded from the dry talus slopes because they cannot traverse the rocks or tolerate periodic dry conditions in the shallow soil. As successful competitors for food, red-backeds employ aggressive territorial behaviors to exclude Shenandoahs from the soil of surrounding forests. The geographic distribution of red-backeds, then, results from habitat selection, whereas the distribution of Shenandoah is best explained by competitive exclusion.

Experiments suggest that, if red-backed salamanders were to suddenly disappear, Shenandoah salamanders would occupy the forest's soil. Competition between the species at the talus-soil interface currently prevents such ecological release. All sizes of Shenandoahs emigrate from talus into soil, but only the largest, which are big enough to feed on prey that are too awkward for red-backeds, are able to invade more than a few yards into their competitor's territory. Even this incursion represents eventual failure, though, because the offspring of pioneering Shenandoahs, which eat the same foods as red-backeds, lose in competition. Shenandoahs, then, survive only in suboptimal habitat where red-backeds cannot penetrate.

Red-backeds appear to be expanding their range at the expense of Shenandoahs. In the Blue Ridge, Shenandoahs live on only three mountains, each completely surrounded by red-backeds. This distribution suggests that current populations of Shenandoah salamanders are relics of a formerly more widespread form that has been squeezed out of its original habitat, much like the Cheat Mountain salamander.

The talus habitat, left from the Pleistocene glaciation, is gradually disappearing. As soil washes into the talus slopes, red-backeds invade the fingers of soil and Shenandoah populations lose numbers. One comparison is particularly telling. Eight years after a severe drought, one population of Shenandoah salamanders finally recovered from a few individuals that persisted in soil patches. In another talus pile, without soil patches, Shenandoahs became extinct. Competition between species and climatic change can thus interact to cause the demise of a population or even an entire species. Shenandoah is experiencing an evolutionary bottleneck. Will it squeeze through and pop out the other side, or are these the details of a forthcoming extinction? I am not optimistic.

In addition to this Hawksbill Mountain isolate, there are two other distinct populations of Shenandoah salamanders. Populations at Stony

Man Mountain and The Pinnacle, in the Blue Ridge about five miles from Hawksbill Mountain, are also surrounded by deep soil and red-backs. Red-backed salamanders are playing out a similar scene of encroachment with yet another species, the Peaks of Otter salamander, on a single mountain of the Blue Ridge. Thus, three relict plethodons, the Cheat Mountain, Shenandoah, and Peaks of Otter, seem to be disappearing at the hands of imperialist red-backs.

The red-backed salamander ranges from Nova Scotia to North Carolina, west to Ontario and Missouri, and continues to incrementally usurp the habitat of other salamander species. Some of the less competitive species have found temporary relief in relict habitats not accessible to red-backs, such as talus for Shenandoah and spruce forest for Cheat Mountain. Others, such as Hoffman's and ravine salamanders, inhabit deciduous forests suitable to red-backs and have been able to accommodate various levels of interspecific competition. Theoretical models predict that species of lungless salamanders will not be able to coexist indefinitely. However, their recent arrival and extensive geographical overlap in Appalachia mean their long-term relationships are still evolving. Some plethodontids compete for limiting resources, others do not. Of the former, some species pairs have been competing intensely and are diverging evolutionarily; others have competed only weakly and have diverged little. Still other species are being competitively displaced, possibly to the point of extinction.

But the humbling fact is that, after all of our ecological and behavioral studies on everything from single-celled animals to salamanders and mice, we still cannot predict which species will win a particular competitive struggle. Are we witnessing something that is not knowable and therefore ultimately unpredictable? This possibility gives ecologists high anxiety.

17

A Lungless Salamander Trilogy

Mimicry

IN THE GREAT SMOKY MOUNTAINS, an amazing similarity exists between two salamander species, Jordan's and Allegheny Mountain. Both include some red-cheeked and some red-legged individuals. It's as if they are copying each other. The evolutionary cause of this improbable likeness lies in the tastes of salamander predators. Any meat-eating bird that feeds by scratching the forest floor will try to eat a salamander. The blue jay, brown thrasher, and wood thrush are all confirmed salamander predators. All species of woodland salamanders in the genus *Plethodon*, however, seem to be at least mildly distasteful to birds, and some salamanders are downright poisonous. Upon ingesting a "bad" salamander, the birds' reactions range from gagging to regurgitation. (The skin secretions of salamanders are said to numb human taste, although I haven't had the temerity to lick one.)

In the continuum of salamander palatability, birds find the Allegheny Mountain tastier than Jordan's. Although not poisonous, Jordan's exudes viscous, noxious skin secretions, and experienced birds avoid it. Jordan's salamander is tastier than the poisonous red eft, but is passed over by most birds because of its bright warning coloration and overt defensive behavior. (You may know the red eft as the familiar, bright red juvenile stage of the red-spotted newt that wanders about boldly in broad daylight.)

103

In the Great Smoky Mountains, some isolates of Jordan's display red cheek patches. Four other Jordan's isolates in Nantahala National Forest south of the Smokies have red legs. Some populations of the Allegheny Mountain possess, with varying frequencies, red legs, red cheeks, or both. Here are the crucial observations: The red-legged form of Allegheny Mountain occurs only within the range of red-legged Jordan's; within the range of red-cheeked Jordan's, the imitator sports red cheeks. There seems to be a lot of copying going on.

If they have had previous experience with Jordan's salamanders, birds avoid the tastier but incognito Allegheny Mountain. Some bird predators transfer their distaste for red-legged Jordan's to red-legged Allegheny Mountain, avoiding them both. Likewise, birds that have been conditioned by the unsavory red-cheeked Jordan's avoid red-cheeked Allegheny Mountain salamanders as well. The selective advantage of the false warning colors of red legs or red cheeks on the Allegheny Mountain has been demonstrated experimentally. Simply, birds learn to associate red patches with unpalatability.

The phenomenon in which a palatable species evolves an exterior appearance or behavior that is similar to that of a distasteful or poisonous species is known as Batesian mimicry. Members of the tasty species thereby gain protection from predators. Allegheny Mountain salamanders with red legs, instead of the usual black, are interpreted as Batesian mimics of the range-sharing red-legged Jordan's. Analogously, red-cheeked Allegheny Mountain are Batesian mimics of neighboring red-cheeked Jordan's. The model is the large, black Jordan's salamander, which exists as 21 geographical isolates, and the mimics belong to the highly variable Allegheny Mountain salamander complex.

The mimicry between Jordan's and Allegheny Mountain salamanders appears to be a weak Batesian mimetic system. The system is based on only one model—Jordan's—which is only mildly unpalatable to begin with. The success of a Batesian mimetic system with a weak model depends on the availability of alternate food sources for the predators. The greater the availability of other foods, the less predation on the model and the greater the protection for the mimic. Another aspect of this system is consistent with weak Batesian mimicry: natural selection favors variable forms in the mimic—that is, the mimic occurs in several color forms—when the model cannot support an extensive mimetic population.

The red-backed salamander and the red eft carry on another mimicry. In this system, the red eft serves as the model for an all-red phase of the red-backed. A classic example of warning coloration and behavior, red efts are extremely toxic to mammals and birds—their skin contains tetrodotoxin, a powerful neurotoxin and the strongest emetic known. This is why red efts can crawl around fearlessly during the day. As you would expect, where it coexists with red efts, the all-red color phase of the red-backed repels bird predators. The system is not quite this simple, though, because the red-backed itself is mildly distasteful, and therefore some predators might avoid it without the mimicry. However, it is fair to conclude that exposure to red efts reinforces the predators' avoidance.

With the red-backed mimic being distasteful, the red-backed-red eft mimetic system has another type of mimicry superimposed on its essentially Batesian foundation. Mullerian mimicry is the phenomenon in which unpalatable species mimic each other. Mullerian mimics share both warning colors and noxiousness. The selective advantage here is not in deceiving the predator but in training predators more quickly. In this case, the mildly distasteful red-backed is both a Batesian and Mullerian mimic of the highly toxic red eft.

From an original, ancient lungless salamander, a burst of adaptive radiation has rewarded us with diversity. Our fascination with these small animals rests in their habits of breathing air without lungs, chemical recognition of neighbors, laying eggs on land, and egg brooding by females. Among some of the resultant species, competition has produced coexistence; with others it is leading to extinction. Further, in some cases of coexistence, evolution has led to complex mimicry. These small, undemanding creatures, so instructive to those willing to look, embody evolution in Appalachia. Fine logo material too, I might add.

18

Love among the Frogs

THE FIRST COLT'S FOOT, eastern phoebe, garter snake—
all help us chart the arrival of spring. Although I pay
polite attention to these and other harbingers, a chorus of spring peepers is my personal watershed. In his
essay, "The Day of the Peepers," Joseph Wood Krutch
agreed: "I wonder if there is any phenomenon in the heavens above or
in the earth beneath which so simply and so definitely announces that
life is resurgent again."

Not just a single warm evening, which might be misleading, but an
accumulation of a minimum number of degree-days signals the chorus
to convene. As you might suspect, their serenade hides conflict. Behind
the music, a war is raging.

Appalachia is not prime frog country. A paucity of standing water
makes breeding habitat rare. Further, the ability of frogs to travel widely
precludes the formation of the small, reproductively isolated populations that speed the evolution of new species. For these reasons, only
14 species of frogs and toads inhabit southern Appalachia. These few
species, however, enrich us with song.

Wood frogs are first to emerge in the spring, after overwintering in
logs and stumps and under leaf litter. Often with snow still on the
ground, wood frogs migrate to their woodland breeding ponds. Because
they breed in ephemeral waters, the time they have is limited. By

breeding in temporary waters early in the season, wood frogs reap the benefits of no predation by fish, fairly decent odds of metamorphosis before the pond dries, and attainment of large adult body size by the time predators become active. These advantages must exceed the disadvantages of occasional freezing of adults and eggs.

Wood frogs arrive at their breeding pond with precise synchrony. One biologist witnessed the arrival of 500 frogs within 90 minutes. Calling males float at the surface, sometimes in pools that still contain ice. Although each male's horse-clacking call is weak, the chorus carries a long way. Choruses are often intense. Males search, struggle among themselves, and intercept females as they enter the pond. Females are passive. After coupling, which may occur anywhere on the pond, pairs swim toward the single communal egg-laying site. Here, in full sunlight, females deposit their eggs directly onto the growing egg mass. Late breeders lay their eggs on the outside of the clump. The presence of eggs stimulates a female to release eggs. More than 100 females may contribute to a single cluster, and most deposit their eggs on the night they arrive.

This explosive breeding is short-lived, lasting at most ten days, but often ending after a single night of mating. Essayist Annie Dillard's metaphysical exploration of fecundity well describes the wood frog's orgy:

"I don't know what it is about fecundity that so appalls. I suppose it is the teeming evidence that birth and growth, which we value, are ubiquitous and blind, that life itself is so astonishingly cheap, that nature is as careless as it is bountiful, and that with extravagance goes a crushing waste."

Within a clump, eggs insulated in the center are about six degrees Fahrenheit warmer than those around the periphery, and in turn, eggs on the edge of a cluster stay warmer than single eggs. Dark embryos absorb sunlight, and jelly envelopes around them retain the heat. In addition to passive solar heating, heat generated by normal metabolic processes increases the temperature of embryos. The temperature of the egg mass increases with the size of the clump. In the cluster's warm microenvironment, embryos develop rapidly and normally.

The thermal advantages of being one of the first females to breed quickly become obvious. Because of their higher temperatures, eggs in the center of the mass have a 90 percent chance of hatching compared with 45 percent for peripheral ones. Further, central clutches have more eggs (1,125) than peripheral ones (750). Large females, which breed earlier, hold an edge: they not only produce more eggs than smaller females, but their eggs have the thermal benefits of centrality. Selection pressure favoring early breeding is presumably limited by how quickly the frogs are able to emerge in the spring and when the ice melts at their breeding pond. The combination of a minimum temperature threshold and the ephemeral nature of its breeding habitat explain the wood frog's early, explosive, spawning behavior.

As swiftly as they arrive, wood frogs recede into the forest, where they spend the summer away from water. The next chorus issues from spring peepers in March and April, followed by cricket frogs, chorus frogs, and pickerel frogs. Bullfrogs drone on through summer. Spanning the late spring-early summer time slot is the gray tree frog, which breeds from April to late July. The gray tree frog is a small (1.2 to 2 inches from snout to anus) frog that typically calls from bushes and small trees near water. Suction cups on the undersides of its toes identify this creature as a tree frog.

Clinging to reeds, stems, and other suitable perches, male gray tree frogs use the mating call—a loud, resonant trill—to enforce spacing among themselves. They defend territories at least two feet across by using encounter calls, occasionally fighting off intruders. The encounter call sounds like an abbreviated rooster's call. Females are attracted by the males' chorus and trickle in singly during the long breeding season. In contrast to wood frogs, female gray tree frogs approach calling males and initiate the mating embrace with a nudge, after which the pair may remain coupled for over four hours.

Females move toward louder calls more frequently than weaker ones. In one field study, the sound level one yard away from good perches—ones that led to mating—averaged 89.5 decibels, whereas it was only 87.1 decibels at poor perches. Poor perches may be near acoustic obstructions or may lack sound amplifiers, such as the surface of still water. Males occupy good perches earlier in the season and for more nights than poor perches.

This priority on calling sites places male tree frogs in conflict with each other. Dominant large males relegate many smaller males to inferior perches. In fact, only one-fourth to one-third of the males that call mate successfully. This explains the observation that male tree frogs caught in the act of mating are larger than single males.

Noncalling males, frogs that have lost vocal or physical contests, often remain close to calling males. Termed noncalling satellites because they hang around dominant males, these opportunists intercept and mate with one-third to one-half of the approaching females. A satellite remains motionless near a calling male until a female moves into the vicinity, then he swiftly grabs her. Calling males try to repel noncalling males by pulsed encounter calls, butting, and wrestling. When a calling frog vacates his perch, a subordinate male quickly occupies the site and begins calling, often within four minutes. Because males leave their perches to couple with females for over four hours, good calling perches become available to satellite males for lengthy periods. In essence, small satellite males sexually parasitize large vocalizing males of the same species. About 80 percent of the males are callers; the rest are consistently satellites or switch back and forth.

Each mating tactic of the male gray tree frog—calling from a territory, noncalling in a peripheral satellite position, and opportunistic switching—leads to at least some degree of mating success. A male's best strategy depends on what others around him are doing. If a male is surrounded by calling territorial males, he might fertilize more eggs by forgoing the costs of fighting and behaving as a noncalling satellite.

What leads to such contrasting mating behaviors as those of the wood frog and of the gray tree frog? Wood frogs, explosive breeders in temporary ponds of early spring, form dense aggregations for highly synchronized chorusing and egg-laying. Females add their eggs quickly to the communal clump, ensuring that their eggs will be insulated by later clutches and develop quickly. Such explosive breeding systems place a premium on acquiring mates quickly, so female wood frogs do not exercise a great deal of discrimination in choosing mates. Males search widely, clasp every female frog, and do not defend a specific resource such as an egg-laying site. This combination of factors accounts for the explosive orgy.

Gray tree frogs, which breed in permanent warmer waters, call over a period of several months from established perches within defended territories. The territory offers undisturbed courtship and habitat crucial for egg survival. Because there is plenty of time for females to discriminate and choose large males, natural selection has favored a way in which small males salvage at least some matings: they linger as satellites around their dominant counterparts and pick up the reproductive scraps.

Frog song can signal either a mad sexual scramble or meticulous courtship. Among frogs, both get the love job done.

19

Box Turtle's Independence

FEW OF US PURPOSELY SEARCH for box turtles, so it's no wonder we have few first-hand impressions of them in their natural habitat. However, most of us have vivid memories filed away of desperate swerves to avoid squashing them on the road. Instead of allowing these images of a lethargic, indifferent creature to mislead you, envision these pedestrians as reptiles insulated from vagaries of their environment. In fact, land tortoises seem more divorced from environmental stresses than any other Appalachian vertebrate.

The turtle's home provides our first hint of its independence. Box turtles live in a variety of terrestrial habitats—though permanent water does not seem to be a requirement. High densities of these reptiles commonly reside in woodlots with large trees, canopy gaps, and a diversified ground cover. The turtles bask in openings in the canopy and munch on a variety of short plants. The close ground cover of woody shrubs and leaf litter provides shelter. To feed and bask, box turtles frequently also enter open areas adjacent to the woods.

Much of what we know of box turtle biology comes from the labors of Charles and Elizabeth Schwartz, biologists who tracked turtles for 20 years. By training Labrador retrievers to locate and retrieve turtles, they were able to study unprecedentedly large sample sizes. During 19 years of the Schwartzes' study, the average size of the area a turtle covered routinely, or the home range, increased from 5.2 to 12.8 acres. Home ranges were essentially equal for males and females. Another study at a different field site concluded that box turtles restrict their movements to home ranges that average only about 100 yards in diameter, which translates to about 2.5 acres. For comparison, the home ranges of snapping and wood turtles, two Appalachian relatives, average 8.4 and 3.2 acres, respectively.

When not traveling, box turtles rest in forms, depressions made in vegetation and the top inch of soil. During their active season, April to October, box turtles remain in their forms until the morning sun warms them, then travel slowly and feed for about an hour. If it is sunny but cool, they bask; if it is warm they may crawl under a few leaves or a clump of grass. A turtle may meander up to 70 yards per day, or he may move just a foot or two before making a new form for the night. On any given day, one turtle might be active while another is quiescent. Some individuals are simply more sedentary than others.

Intuitively, it seems that resting forms should contribute to a turtle's independence from environmental changes because the forms insulate the turtle's belly plate, or plastron, during hot days and cool nights. However, recent study suggests that there is no pattern in when or why turtles use their forms. Use is not related to an individual's sex or size, nor to a consistent difference in air or soil temperatures. Neither have we found an obvious reason for how long they stay in a form. In essence, each individual box turtle seems to have its own internal agenda, acting independently of the environment in determining when or where to settle into a resting form or how long to stay there.

One environmental condition turtles do respond to is a cold snap in autumn. Box turtles enter hibernation with the first killing frost. A wet fall without a sudden freeze provides good conditions for entering hibernation. Dry weather, which makes digging difficult, and a sudden freeze may trap some turtles above ground. Surprisingly, box turtles do not hibernate below the frost line, but remain dormant at depths down to five inches below the leaf litter. How they avoid freezing is unknown. In some areas, box turtles emerge from hibernation and move about on warm winter days. Final spring emergence occurs between the last week of March and the last week of April, an interval that roughly coincides with the last killing frost.

Most box turtles establish home ranges, but others are transients. Turtles found crossing roads, especially those we commonly see after warm spring rains, are likely to be transients. Only a few individuals wander, but those that do may fulfill the important function of transferring genes from one sedentary population to another, thereby reducing the deleterious consequences of inbreeding. Of highway-crossing turtles, half are youngsters, smaller individuals less than nine years old, with equal numbers of each sex, and the other half are mostly adult males. Transients move one way through the environment—no returning. Road kills, by the way, are particularly hard on this long-lived, low-fecundity species, and I seethe when a mountaineer cites his turtle-squashing score.

Box turtles mate from May through October. In copulo, the male's concave plastron complements the female's convex back shield, or carapace. His recurved hind first claws play a crucial role during mating: he wedges them between the female's upper and lower shells so that she can't clamp down on his penis. Newly hatched and juvenile box turtles are seldom found, so we know precious little about baby box turtles. When they're not paired, you can still tell the sexes apart by noting a combination of characteristics. Compared to females, males have a deeper depression in their belly plates; thicker, shorter, more recurved hind claws; and redder heads and eyes.

The age of a box turtle is evident in some characteristics of its carapace. Individuals with shells up to 4.6 inches long fall within age class I. They are actively growing, show obvious new growth rings on their plastron and carapace, and are up to nine years old. Class II includes young adults that are 4.6 inches or longer. They show wear on old growth rings and have no obvious new rings, particularly on the plastron. They are 10 through at least 32 years old. Sexual maturity appears to be related to size, not age. Individuals 4.7 inches long have well developed sex-specific characters, whereas the 4.3- to 4.7-inch size class includes both immature and mature adults. Old adults, in age class III, are also longer than 4.6 inches but carry worn, even smooth, uniformly colored carapaces. These old "bowling balls" are 33 to over 51 years old.

Some young individuals shift their residence before establishing a permanent home range. As a turtle grows, its home range enlarges, at least through the first two age classes. Specifically, the home ranges for Class I through Class III turtles average 4.2, 9.2, and 8.9 acres, respectively.

During the Schwartzes' long-term study, the turtle population fluctuated between 400 and 600 individuals, which in the context of a wide variety of animal population studies is a fairly stable enrollment. Stable population numbers score as yet another indicator of independence.

Published reports suggest the box turtle's sex ratio favors males, but males are more active than females, so these estimates may reflect a sampling bias. Interestingly, where the Schwartzes used dogs to find turtles, sex ratio was equal. Maybe to a dog's nose turtle essence is not sex-specific.

A box turtle's daily behavior seems to be divorced from the caprice of its immediate environment. The condition of a turtle at any particular time appears more an integration of its past experiences than a reflection of its present stresses. At least three adaptations create this apparent time lag. Most obviously, a box turtle's shell takes the edge off temperature extremes by insulating its body from environmental stresses such as heat and drought. During severe drought, the tortoises do not concentrate around creeks—they merely seek moist sites within their home ranges, make a form under a pile of leaves, and rest peacefully. Second, their forms conceal them from what few predators they do have, such as raccoons. Third, box turtles have a low metabolism. Coupling that with omnivorous food habits, box turtles enjoy a high supply-low demand economy and do not need to hustle. They eat insects, earthworms, strawberries, fruits, mushrooms, and many other foods, yet they burn these calories slowly. In these ways, box turtles enjoy a tremendous hedge against environmental stresses.

In essence, the box turtle's uniqueness results from the scale of time it adopts as relevant. What you see lumbering across your Appalachian road is not an organism reflecting its present and immediate history, like the rest of us, but rather an easy-going, independent time lag living in the past.

20

Copperhead's Year

ALONG PINE CABIN RUN—and probably throughout Hampshire County, West Virginia—I am one of those rare humans who is pleasantly surprised to encounter a copperhead. After summer rains, these vipers slither down the hill past our cabin on their way to local frog-hunting grounds. So, I come across them fairly often.

Before our daughter Leah arrived, Nancy and I would coax the serpents into a grain sack and covertly release them on a nearby hill. (I hope our neighbors do not ostracize us now that we have gone public.) Then two events converged: Leah learned to toddle, and I researched this essay. We were then confronted by a brutal trade-off: accept the risk that Leah might be bitten, or kill the copperheads because, if released as before, they would return to their home range—our yard. We settled on the procedure of catching, bagging, and depositing the vipers in the freezer—admittedly not much of a compromise from the snake's point of view, but at least they seemed to die painlessly and yielded perfect study specimens. Now that Leah is a competent walker, we once again enjoy our copperhead friends basking out by the mailbox, where our daughter exhibits only naïve curiosity toward them.

Our risk of death by copperhead bite is far less than that by auto accident, yet of the two, the snake elicits involuntary shudders. This is perplexing. Although serpents are ingrained evils of our folklore, I will go out on a limb and propose that our reaction to them is learned, not genetically predetermined. After seeing this common Appalachian reptile in a less evil light, you may even learn to appreciate the copperheads you encounter in your Appalachian wanderings.

Copperheads spend about half of the year, from late October to mid-April, in hibernation. Dens where several snakes hibernate, called hibernacula, most frequently occupy rocky hilltops with a southern exposure, probably because such sites are warmer and drier than surrounding habitats. The snakes gather peaceably in the autumn, and within the hibernaculum, each individual benefits from the heat and moisture generated by the group. Copperheads coil together when hibernating, and infrequently, timber rattlesnakes join them. In this torpid state, their body temperatures may dip to 39 degrees Fahrenheit.

Copperheads arouse in the spring when the temperature reaches 45 to 50 degrees. After exiting the den, they lie under nearby rocks that hold the warmth of the sun and provide insulation during cool spells. Some individuals remain near their den through the summer; others travel varying distances. Copperheads migrate seasonally between rocky hilltops and lower summering areas. One study found the average distance traveled between the den and summer sites was 0.4 mile for males and 0.25 mile for females. As summer approaches, copperheads either stay within a clearly delineated zone, or home range, near their overwintering site, or abandon the original home range for another. Most individuals are "home-rangers," but of those that move on, males shift more often and farther than females. Home ranges average 1.7 acres for males and 8.9 acres for females, but the actual sizes vary with habitat. Within its home range, a snake seems to wander about in an irregular, circuitous course.

Copperheads mate between spring emergence and late May, when females ovulate. The snakes mate at night, the odor of skin apparently stimulating courtship. As with other reptiles, male copperheads have paired copulatory organs, each called a hemipenis, lodged at the base of the tail and covered with spines. The spines lock the male into the female and irritate the female's reproductive tract. By locking and irritating, the male precludes mating by other males, reducing competition from other males' sperm.

Like most members of the pit viper family, which includes rattle-snakes, fer-de-lance, and bushmasters, copperheads are viviparous—they produce living young whose embryonic development is fostered by nutrients conveyed from the female's body. When they emerge in spring, females carry small whitish eggs in their ovaries. During May, eggs grow, turn yellow, then are ovulated. The mature elliptical eggs average 1.4 inches long and 0.7 inch wide. To delay fertilization, female copperheads store clumps of sperm in stretches of the convoluted oviduct. Females carry young internally through the summer, the embryos growing slowly during the 102- to 110-day gestation period. Compared to other copperheads, gravid females are docile, secretive, and more likely to bask, which speeds embryonic development. Some pregnant females gather in small groups, but most remain alone. The typical female does not produce a litter every year, probably just in alternate years. After several weeks of development, the fetuses assume an elongate serpentine form coiled within the egg. Birth dates of the young vary from August 3 to November 6, but at any one place, births are concentrated within a two-week interval.

The number of young in a litter depends on the size of the female. Females less than 23 inches long from snout to anus produce 3 to 6 young; those longer than 25 inches bear 6 to 14 snakelets. Females in the east produce an average of slightly more than six young, several fewer than their midwestern counterparts. Newborns, called neonates, are about 8.5 inches long.

A neonate uses its egg tooth, a thorny, chisel-like projection on the tip of its snout, to puncture the flexible fetal membrane around itself soon after birth. Once punctured, the membrane collapses about the head. The egg tooth drops off soon after hatching. With nostrils exposed, the neonate remains coiled for several hours. If all goes well, a newborn copperhead can strike immediately after rupturing its fetal membranes.

Mothers extend no significant care to snakelets. After birthing, the mother becomes irritable and menacing, and advertises her unpleasant disposition by vibrating her tail, arching her neck, and darting her tongue.

A copperhead spends most of its time in a flat resting coil—its tail outside, its head and forebody in an S-shaped loop near the center, and the remainder of its length wound compactly in one or two cycles. Coiled and well concealed from potential prey, it waits in ambush for a meal, for several days if necessary.

Sight, scent, ground vibrations, or infrared radiation alerts the snake to the presence of prey. The facial pit, between the eye and nostril, is highly sensitive to infrared wavelengths, such as thermal radiation emitted by warm-blooded animals. This allows copperheads and other snakes to locate prey in the dark. Preparing for a strike, the snake brings more body length into the coil nearest its head, extending its reach. These slight movements—cocking the head, shifting the coils—are not readily noticed by the victim. A short jab, often at a distance of less than six inches, delivers the bite. The copperhead aims, opens its mouth, erects its fangs, and injects venom. Typically, the bite penetrates the prey's chest. Strikes may be wildly inaccurate—to which I gratefully attest! After striking, a copperhead immediately releases its prey and snaps back into a coil. This ensures that the prey, perhaps a sharp-toothed mouse, will not bite the snake.

The primary function of the copperhead's venom is to rapidly kill small prey; poisoning enemies is a lesser, secondary function. A slightly viscous, watery liquid, often cloudy yellow in color, copperhead venom kills prey by inducing blood clotting, circulatory arrest, and respiratory paralysis.

The poison fang holds a fascination. The copperhead's axillary bone, to which the upper teeth are attached, can rotate almost 90 degrees. This rotation permits the poison fang, which is just a greatly enlarged tooth, to be either erected or folded against the roof of the mouth. The poison fang has evolved from a solid cone to a highly effective hypodermic needle, with a hollow channel leading to an opening near the tip of the tooth. The fang's tip is solid. Compared to other related snake species, copperheads have short fangs. In individuals of equal size, the copperhead's fang is about half the length of a rattlesnake's. Fangs have short functional lives, and the snakes shed them almost monthly, swallowing them with food and passing them unaltered through the digestive tract. Several replacement fangs in various stages of development wait behind each functional fang.

Copperheads produce a relatively weak venom; most rattlesnakes have venoms two to six times more potent. Young copperheads inject two drops of venom, adults three drops, and exceptional individuals four drops. Among different individuals, venom varies greatly and unpredictably in quantity and potency. One study found the strongest venom was three times as toxic as the weakest.

Although copperheads bite people more often than any other snake species does, their venom is rarely fatal to humans. In uncomplicated cases, recovery is virtually assured without the aid of antivenin. Copperhead venom acts on the blood, the walls of the blood vessels, and the central nervous system, causing, in succession, muscle twitching, swelling and discoloration, severe throbbing, numbness, respiratory congestion, intense pain, and vomiting. The bite causes no extensive hemorrhaging, and all body functions return to normal within a month.

Adult copperheads typically consume only eight meals per growing season. Well adapted for fasting, they prey on large animals and store fat in their abdominal cavities. As sedentary animals whose body heat comes from the environment, their food requirements are modest. Copperheads digesting large food items spend most of their time coiled beneath shelter.

Few animals prey on copperheads. Moles and opossums eat first-year young, and king snakes and red-tailed hawks take a few adults. Against such predators, a copperhead's most effective defense is to lie still and depend on its camouflage. If vulnerable and threatened, a snake rotates its head suddenly, faces the danger, then cocks its head back 45 degrees and prepares to strike. When severely alarmed and ready to strike, the snake vibrates its tail against the surrounding leaves and twigs producing a rattling or whirring sound. If caught in the predator's grasp, the snake's last resort is to spray musk from anal glands and defecate its cloacal contents.

The serpent must periodically replace its inelastic skin as the animal grows. During an active season, copperheads shed two to four times, living an average of 85 days within each coat of skin. Young that do not shed promptly stiffen inside their dry outer layer and cannot assume the compact resting coil. Shedding also beautifies: snakes are dull and dark before shedding, bright and vivid afterwards.

In *A Country Year*, Sue Hubbell observed that there is no record of a human death caused by a copperhead bite in Missouri, and I have heard similar nonstatistics cited for West Virginia. Hubbell wrote calmly and with respect about sharing the Ozarks with copperheads, just another species with its own set of strengths, weaknesses, and desirabilities. I appreciate her point of view. You may not embrace the first copperhead you come across, but I hope this annual account eases the anxiety a bit. In the process, both snake and human will gain.

21

Oaks and Squirrels

DURING LATE SUMMER AND EARLY FALL, in years when acorns are plentiful along Pine Cabin Run, two or more squirrels work the big white oak brooding over my lab. The lab's metal roof reports the rhythm of their labors. Last summer, after some listening practice, I learned to discriminate between the pings made by the cuttings of acorn husks and the plonks of acorn bodies, which in turn allowed me to estimate the number of bites it took a squirrel to exploit an acorn— about five. Over the years, I have also noticed that my roof gets pelted only in certain summers, an important insight into the relationship between oaks and squirrels. As with most relationships, there are two points of view here: the oak's and the squirrel's.

Oaks fruit irregularly. In some years a white oak 24 inches in diameter might produce 2,000 acorns, then several years may pass without any crop at all. Similarly, chestnut and scarlet oaks may produce a good acorn crop only once every four or five years. Year-to-year variation in the quantity of nuts produced, known as mast-yearing, has been documented for a variety of oak species and other nut-bearing trees.

Nut production also varies among neighboring trees during any given year. Within a single stand, some trees produce large crops while others produce none at all. In one study covering 14 years, only one tree in 12 had good-to-heavy yields, and only during 5 of the years. Many of the remaining 11 trees produced only a few acorns.

What causes such variation in acorn production within a stand? Trees shaded by neighboring trees produce fewer good crops than those with crowns exposed to direct sunshine. The extent of crown suppression is only a partial answer, though, because thinning enhances fruiting in only some of the surviving trees. Other influences remain a mystery.

From year to year, spring temperatures strongly affect acorn yields. White oaks produce good crops of acorns in years when a warm 10-day period occurs in late April, with mean night temperatures of 55 to 61 degrees Fahrenheit, followed by cooler temperatures of 45 to 50 degrees for 13 to 20 days in early May. Conversely, a year featuring a cool April and warm May will yield a small acorn crop. Freezing temperatures when chestnut oaks flower in early April to early May greatly reduce acorn production. April and May seem to be important for oaks because female flowers emerge in late April or early May, five to ten days after male flowers. The early warm period increases the development of viable pollen, while the subsequent cool period enhances ovary development and fertilization.

Springtime weather does not affect the mast crops of all oaks in the same way. Although white oak acorns ripen in one year, acorns of black oak species require two years to mature. Mast failure of trees in the black oak group is due to six consecutive nights of frost in May of the previous year. A frost that causes failure in white oaks one year will ruin the black oak's crop a year later. Oaks offset the consequences of irregular reproductive success, at least in part, by their extreme longevity. A 600-year-old white oak, with a trunk a yard in diameter and 50 yards tall, has experienced many seasons favorable for acorn production.

The trick from the oak's point of view is to have at least some of its acorns germinate. Many forces mitigate against it, though. White-tailed deer, wild turkey, squirrels, and an army of insects and fungi leave few acorns embryologically intact. Further, acorns seem to have better odds of reaching adulthood if they take root outside the influence of their parent's canopy. Not only will the parent shade the seedlings, but experienced seed predators and adapted pathogens are likely to concentrate there.

Squirrels enter the scene as the acorns' transportation. In gathering and caching nuts for their winter food supply, they inadvertently improve the oak tree's reproductive success. A tree that produces only an occasional large crop may disperse its seeds farther than a tree that consistently produces a small crop. For a moment, make the simplifying assumption that squirrels bury nuts at a constant density in a rough circle around the base of a tree. Accordingly, a tree that produces twice as many fruits as its neighbor would benefit from having the nuts spread over twice as large an area. Since the radius of a circle with double the area is 1.4 times as long as the radius of a circle with half its area, a tree that annually alternates between large and no crops would theoretically have its nuts dispersed 1.4 times farther than a tree that consistently produced half as big a crop every year. Perhaps, then, oaks do not "fail" as such to produce mast in some years—natural selection may have favored individual trees that produced few or no acorns in some years because this increased the dispersal of acorns in years of high production.

Natural selection could favor mast-yearing for another reason. Poor years may depress the populations of seed predators, allowing trees to overwhelm the seed-eating abilities of predators during peak years. In this sense, trees may be "setting up" squirrels in a bad year to be swamped by a large volume of acorns in the following good year. This could improve the odds that some seeds will escape being eaten and will germinate. The word "failure" may have crept into our interpretation because the "success" of "our" game species depends on mast.

Squirrels, however, do not care about the germination rate of acorns. They obsessively pursue their own survival and reproductive priorities. Squirrels seem to rank nuts by how efficient they are to gather. In general, a squirrel will choose to forage in a patch with abundant, low-quality food that yields a high rate of energy intake over a patch with sparse, high-quality food.

Gray squirrels exhibit definite acorn preferences. In one area, they prefer in decreasing order red oak, chestnut oak, and white oak acorns. They choose all acorns over black walnuts and shagbark hickory nuts. Squirrels simply take less time to shell acorns than to hull walnuts or hickory nuts, netting more food value in less time—a true fast food. Gray squirrels not only prefer particular foods, they also discriminate among trees within a species and even among seeds on a single tree. As it turns out, acorns from lightly harvested trees contain more tannin, a poisonous acid, than nuts from heavily harvested trees. The desirability of a nut increases as its concentration of tannin decreases. Tannin acts as a natural insecticide, so the variation of tannin content in acorns among and within trees may stem, at least in part, from the tree's battle with herbivorous insects.

After a squirrel decides where to forage, it proceeds to store nuts for winter. Squirrels bury nuts to reduce competition from birds, mice, deer, and, of course, other squirrels. Squirrels consume or bury acorns of favorite species as they ripen in late summer and autumn and use them heavily thereafter while stocks last. Nuts of oaks, hickories, and walnuts make up at least 83 percent of their autumn and winter diet.

Through most of winter, gray and fox squirrels usually have plenty of stored nuts to eat. The survival bottleneck comes in late winter and early spring when their caches begin to run low but fresh foods are not yet available. Squirrels often lose weight during this time. To get through this critical period, the animals employ a specific strategy of food hoarding.

Fox squirrels bury individual nuts in widely scattered locations. This is called scatterhoarding. Animals that eat seeds will likely store food in numerous, widely scattered, small caches if they are unable to defend the food against competitors. The optimal spacing of scattered caches reflects the tradeoff between two constraints. The more scattered the caches, the fewer will be lost to competitors, but the more time and energy will be spent storing the nuts. Scatterhoarding balances these costs and benefits.

In contrast, the red squirrel larderhoards conifer cones, storing all of its food in one large cache. For the red squirrel, spreading the food over a large area would not reduce losses to other animals that can open cones, such as mice, chipmunks, and other red squirrels.

Once they have buried the nuts, how do squirrels find them again? Some animals, such as Clark's nutcracker, a jay of western North America, have the extraordinary ability to remember the exact locations of thousands of seed caches. Squirrels do not remember specific sites. However, resident squirrels remember a cache's general location, giving them an advantage over naïve newcomers. Squirrels locate individual buried nuts using their keen sense of smell. Experiments have shown that squirrels can smell the nuts that other squirrels buried and even recover nuts through a foot of snow. Remarkably, fox squirrels can smell the differences in densities of buried nuts, then concentrate their search in those high-density areas. This ability, plus their powerlessness to defend caches from larger species such as deer and turkey, may have led to the evolution of the scatterhoarding strategy of nut storage. Despite the squirrels' keen nose, many acorns escape becoming a meal and sprout later.

With their dependence on acorns, squirrel populations fluctuate with the mast crop, but with a time lag of one year. A good food supply in the fall and a mild winter result in earlier and larger litters the following spring. A poor mast crop leads to delayed, or even cancelled, spring breeding. When black oaks, beech, walnut, butternut, and hickory produce small crops, the harvest of squirrels by humans also drops the following year. Since 1930, squirrel populations in West Virginia have fluctuated radically, primarily as a function of mast availability, which incorporates both mast production and winter harshness.

Oaks and squirrels are tight partners in a mutually exploitative relationship. The reproductive success of oaks depends on squirrels to disperse their acorns and plant them in favorable sites. Oaks accomplish this by producing good acorn crops only occasionally. In turn, squirrels depend on oaks for winter food, but pay the time and energy costs of scatterhoarding. Scatterhoarding and the squirrel's imperfect sense of smell ensure that at least some acorns escape to germinate. Thus, a causal chain connects springtime weather, pollination success of oaks, annual variations of acorn crops, with the squirrel's overwintering success, reproductive rate, and population density. The pings and plonks on my tin roof remind me of one of the great coevolved acts of the Appalachian play.

22

Highlanders

I DO NOT KNOW WHEN humans first set foot in Appalachia. Most anthropologists agree that we have been here since the last ice age, about 12,000 years ago; a few argue for a far more ancient colonization, possibly 100,000 years ago. I cannot settle the question, but I can suggest a historical sequence of human habitation in the Appalachian Mountains: indigenous Americans, European settlers, and finally mountain lovers.

Native Americans named the mountains Appalachia, or "endless mountains." In pre-Columbian times, eastern North America was covered by a seemingly endless forest. Closer examination may have revealed a mosaic of different forest communities interspersed with occasional openings. North American Indians used broadcast fire to clear the woods of underbrush and preclude the clandestine approach of raiding tribes. Because new grass attracted grazers such as deer, Indians used fire to maintain the wild game habitat along the forest-grass edge, even using fires to drive deer to waiting hunters.

In the late seventeenth century, several tribes inhabited the Blue Ridge. The Cherokee, for example, were numerous in southern Appalachia, especially from the present site of Asheville, North Carolina, to the Great Smoky Mountains of eastern Tennessee. One census estimated 25,000 Cherokee thinly dispersed through the region.

Humans have also occupied West Virginia for at least 12,000 years. This time of first colonization, which is fairly typical of many North American sites, coincides with the existence of Beringia, a land bridge that connected Russia and Alaska during the last ice age. Most anthropologists think that Asians colonized North America 10,000 to 15,000 years ago. Based on gross anatomy, the closest relatives of Native Americans are Siberians. After crossing the north Pacific, the first people dispersed southward to inhabit the entire Western Hemisphere.

At first, American aborigines lived as nomads and hunted large mammals, but by 4,000 B.C. they adopted a semisedentary life-style. The hunting-gathering economy of pre-1,000 B.C. was gradually supplemented by small-scale horticulture. Around 800 to 900 A.D., the Mississippian Mound Builders grew corn, beans, and squash. By 1,000 A.D., dense populations of the Late Prehistoric Village Farmers lived in permanently stockaded villages and practiced intensive agriculture.

Paleontological evidence suggests that prehistoric Appalachian humans consumed a complete and varied diet. During the Pleistocene, from about 2 million to 10,000 years ago, North America supported a community of large-bodied mammals as diverse as that roaming Africa. The southern Appalachians sustained 90 species of mammals, more than any other area of eastern North America. North American plants, such as Kentucky coffee tree, Osage orange, and paw paw, that produce large seeds seem out of ecological context as no animals currently eat and pass their seeds. This incongruity suggests that recently extinct, large-bodied herbivores dispersed their seeds. Further, the extreme spininess of some trees, such as honey locust, does not make sense without invoking the existence of large mammals. It is not unreasonable to surmise that humans, the most opportunistic animal, dined on this diversity.

The preceding paragraphs may report the conventional chronology of Native Americans in eastern North America. But as an interesting aside, how do we explain the purported Christian messages in Old Irish script carved in sandstone throughout West Virginia? Some anthropologists claim that the Wyoming County and Horse Creek petroglyphs were written in Celtic Ogam, an alphabet that appears in rock-cut inscriptions from the sixth through eighth centuries throughout the

Old World. Who wrote them? What impact did the author have on aborigines? Did they leave descendants? Here is a genuine mystery.

Europeans began to move into Appalachia in the early 1700s. The first settlement in eastern West Virginia was built near Shepherdstown in 1719. Settlers invading the hunting grounds of the Kanawha, Mingo, Delaware, and Shawnee peoples in West Virginia found the forests little disturbed. The lush wildlife that provided sustenance to early European settlers apparently depended on habitat that the Native Americans sustained with fires. Fires also helped maintain grassland corridors, such as the Shenandoah Valley, that provided a major thoroughfare for the dispersal of settlers.

As seen through the eyes of this zoologist, European immigrants, like other dispersing animals, may have been escaping environments that limited their reproductive success. Specifically, people were eager to escape intolerance, taxes, and other forms of oppression. Playing a major role in the peopling of Appalachia were the Scotch-Irish, or Ulstermen. Persecuted by the crown, they arrived en masse in Pennsylvania around 1682, where they settled outside German settlements, which in turn were already located west of the Quakers. This was only a temporary home for the Ulstermen, though. As game, land, and other resources became scarce in Pennsylvania, and the French and Indian War of 1763 secured the countryside for settlement, a surge of Scotch-Irish homesteaders penetrated central and southern Appalachia. A few brave souls struggled westward over the Blue Ridge escarpment, but most followed the easier Great Valley route southward and settled land from West Virginia through North Carolina.

The first homesteaders raised their log cabins where they found water, gentle slopes, and fertile soil—generally on sites with bedrock of granite or basalt. Areas underlain by sandstone or shale offered thin, rocky soil, steep slopes, and intermittent springs. The earliest arrivals cleared the broadest valleys and erected cabins. When the generous lowlands filled, the homesteaders' children and other late arrivals moved into the coves and hollows of higher elevations. Temperatures in the Blue Ridge averaged 5 to 13 degrees lower than in adjacent lowlands, but precipitation and winds were greater in the mountains. Accordingly, many homesteaders chose sites strategically located with

135

protection against westerly winds but exposed to maximum sunlight. In these marginal sites, people scrabbled for a living. Later homesteaders were left with only hillsides to clear, which quickly became infertile when their off-contour plowing allowed the already thin soil to erode. Again, humans conformed to a pattern seen in other animals: dispersing individuals were forced to colonize increasingly marginal habitats.

The log cabin—a single large room and stone fireplace and chimney—could be erected in one day by four men. Logs were notched to fit together at the house's corners, and the wide spaces between logs were filled with wood, rocks, mud, or anything that happened to be handy. Using German or Scandinavian building methods (our cabin's corners are of German design), these early settlers constructed sturdy log cabins, many of which continue to house families in comfort today.

European immigrants found one of the richest natural environments on earth. Flocks of passenger pigeons darkened the sky. Woodland bison, elk, and timber wolves roamed the mountains. Where *Homo sapiens* and the Kentucky long rifle moved in, though, these large-bodied animals disappeared. Woodland buffalo were wiped out by about 1800; elk and mountain lion disappeared by 1855; and wolves vanished by 1900. By the early 1900s, suffering from the combined blows of overhunting, lumbering, and farming, white-tailed deer became virtually unknown throughout the southern Appalachians.

In little more than a century, the settlers thoroughly logged the vast, virgin eastern deciduous forest. Colonists cut trees to clear fields for agriculture and to feed a hungry lumber market. Shipbuilding, with its demand for tall, straight wooden masts, became a major colonial industry. By the end of the eighteenth century, the British shipbuilding industry imported a large proportion of its lumber from the American colonies. The greatest decline in forest area occurred between 1750 and 1850; by 1880 less than 35 percent of southern Appalachia's virgin forest remained. Around 1880 railroads opened the mountain summits to systematic logging, and with help from the rails, almost all remaining tracts of virgin timber were converted to lumber, turpentine, and ship masts.

Today's "mountain whites" descended from migrants who settled in mountains such as the Alleghenies, Blue Ridge, and Unakas. With the prime land already taken, many latecomers moved westward, to Kentucky and beyond. The Cumberland Gap, found in 1750 by British surveyor Thomas Walker, funneled the westward dispersal. This natural breach, only 1,600 feet above sea level, and other mountain gaps played a major role in the settlement of the United States.

The dispersal behavior of humans points to the possibility of different genetic predispositions for sedentary versus dispersing behaviors. Conjecturing, there may be a "wanderlust gene" in the human population. Daniel Boone, who in 1769 pioneered the Cumberland Gap by following a Cherokee and Shawnee hunting trail, may have had such a gene—two of Boone's preceding generations and one succeeding generation also sought the frontier. Boone's contribution was to hack out the 208-mile Wilderness Road, which allowed Carolina and Virginia families to pour into the lush lands of Kentucky.

The story of Appalachian highlanders is one of hard knocks. They girdled trees to clear new ground, producing quick canopy gaps. Plowing the soil with a bull-tongue, a wide blade attached to a plow, the highlanders grew staples of corn, cabbage, and beans. They raised tobacco and ginseng for the market, harvested wild bloodroot and ginger for medicinal purposes, and grazed livestock on balds. Not long after they cleared their acreage, however, rains washed the topsoil away, and the land reverted to poor pasture or second growth forest. Forest nutrients that had been accumulating for eons left as muddy water.

For generations, highlanders scratched a living from steep hillsides and narrow valleys. From 1700 to 1900, the fractured topography limited human intercourse much as it has isolated salamander populations since the last ice age. Each enclave of highlanders superimposed its own vocabulary on the Queen's English. The dialect of mountaineers still includes words and phrases common to Elizabethan England, including the old Anglo-Saxonisms "hit" which means "it," "hisn" for "his," and "aims to settle down." Verbs are prefixed with "a," as in "I'm a-goin'." Some linguists consider mountain talk to be the closest surviving relative of the Elizabethan language of Shakespeare.

A constellation of interesting behavioral traits also arose. With the custom of settling close to kin and intermarrying, many valleys became the domain of a single family. Even though mountaineers knew well the consequences of inbreeding, first cousins still married, sometimes to the extent that entire districts were interrelated. To this day, double first cousins, the children of brothers marrying sisters, are not unusual.

By the early 1900s, many mountain folk were still cut off from greater society. Five or six generations did without improved tools, medical advances, and long-distance communication. Some mountaineers had never seen a town. The world as they knew it extended a few miles from their cabin. In Greene County, Tennessee, I have talked to people who were born, grew up, married, had their families, and no doubt will die in a single hollow. No other ethnic group in America remains so unmixed.

The music of the southern mountaineer is uniquely American. Because a large proportion of mountain folk descended from Scotch highlanders, their music evolved from the ballads of England and Scotland. Tunes brought to the mountains by eighteenth century colonial settlers took root and flourished, hidden from the outside world. Though some of these tunes were already dead in Britain, they thrived in the southern hills. Appalachian people still have a native fondness for music and dancing, and they hold the fiddler and banjo player in high regard.

Antic, bawdy, or mournful, many mountain songs were homemade and passed along by word of mouth. Appalachian songs packed a punch, a primordial intensity, that the mellow, sweet British versions often lacked. Mountain tunes were also freer, more spacious. The best Appalachian ballads came from the most backward areas, with certain valleys in western North Carolina, southwestern Virginia, and eastern Kentucky being especially rich musically.

In the old country, moonshining had been perfected by the poorer classes of Irish as a weapon against the government. Immigrants brought this craft to North America, typically hiding the still in a rhododendron thicket along a run. Making moonshine, "blockadin'," was a family activity. Mountaineers still get excited over good, cold water, in large part because of its crucial contribution to good moonshine. Dependable springs are guarded like a favorite fishing hole or reliable ginseng patch. I have heard men damned to hell for "ruinin' a good spring."

Clans were patriarchal. Intense individualism and clan loyalty led to a general disregard for the law. It is logical, therefore, that Appalachian frontiersmen were the first to establish governments of their own, in defiance of the king.

Most women married young, then proceeded to have seven to ten children. High infant mortality ensured that hillside family cemeteries contained several children.

Because their small reference group was of overwhelming importance, extended communities did not develop. Human relationships were personal, based on kinship. Mountain folk were passionately attached to their homes. Emotional dependence, not shared activities, bound one to another—a relationship that leads to insecurity in the face of broader challenges. Suspicion reigned, filling mountain societies with intense anxieties. This behavior contributed to wars between families.

Life on a small mountain farm was hard, and the occupants languished in isolation. As the nation as a whole progressed, the gap between townfolk and highlander widened. However destitute, they were seldom abject and never resorted to begging. Haughtily independent, they could not stand to be bossed. They were existence-oriented, not future- or improvement-oriented. They did not strive for objects, but for being liked and accepted within their reference group. This made them supersensitive to slights and criticisms.

Passive resignation was normal. Sharp limits in the amount and quality of land led to fatalism. In the mountains, nature did not yield, and the harshness of the land overcame the man. Mountaineers had little confidence in their own abilities because they had little experience meeting and overcoming problems. A residue surfaces even now when I see local people offered an opportunity: they promptly cite an inability to handle the responsibility and decline.

The highlanders' behaviors seemed inconsistent. On the one hand, the average mountaineer was lean, inquisitive, and shrewd. Yet the individual felt little control over his or her own destiny and consequently planned little for the future. The mountain folk regarded hospitality as a sacred duty towards "furriners"; nevertheless, the average mountaineer was schooled to dissimulate.

The highlanders' fierce independence and individualism, so adaptive in the habitat of an isolated mountain hollow, became a stumbling block in the modern world where cooperation was essential in work, education, and progress. Possibly because it seemed irrelevant, mountaineers derided education. Folks signed contracts they could not read, leading to outside control of the coal and timber resources, and thereby of the land. Many landowners sold the mining rights when deep mining depended on the relative harmlessness of picks and shovels. Surface mining, however, brought disaster to their descendants. Miners diverted water, poisoned wells and streams, piled refuse, withdrew support timbers in mine tunnels, and cut roads. Courts upheld the coal companies in all of this. Absentee parties bought coal rights at 50 cents to a few dollars per acre and were free to do with the land as they saw fit. For many mountaineers, strip mining destroyed the economic base of their existence. To this day, mountain people have no national organization to represent their needs.

With poor diets and joint problems, mountaineers were not notably healthy. Many with physical defects and little education remained in the home hollow and reproduced. The high rate of illegitimate births apparently stemmed from the girls' desire for purpose and self-worth. In the mountains, birth control is still poorly understood; poverty, self-perpetuating.

By the 1930s, one was considered poor if he or she lived in a log cabin, so most log homes were covered with milled wood to resemble the then-fashionable board-and-batten homes. Our log cabin bears the scars of this swinging pendulum. Built in the 1820s, the logs were left exposed for many years. Then, studs were retrofitted to hold weatherboard. Coming full cycle in the 1960s, the weatherboard was removed, reexposing the logs.

Through the years, the mountains have been a physical, social, cultural, economic, educational, and religious barrier. The late 1950s were bust years, part of a three-decade-long depression when people deserted the mountains for factories in Chicago, Cleveland, and Detroit. A modest reversal began in the 1970s.

Peopling the mountains today, in addition to the mountaineers' descendants, are educated drop-outs, weekenders, summer vacationers, retirees, and outdoor enthusiasts. What I call "mountain love" has motivated this third wave of Appalachian habitation. We mountain lovers are attracted to mountains because they help us find who we are—in the hills, our minds drift towards fundamental questions. The convoluted topography invites exploration—eyes, ears, and nose become alert as we walk through the hills and hollows. Together, the sensuousness of the mountains and the curiosity they excite give strength and clear-eyed vision.

Annie Dillard expressed mountain love well when, finding inspiration in a valley of Virginia's Blue Ridge, she opened her senses to nature's excitement, transcended her daily blinders, felt the pulse of the seasons, and shrank before the overwhelming fecundity of life around her. Humans have changed Appalachia—the mountains have touched us, too.

Seasonal Acts

23

Autumn Leaves

IT HAPPENS EVERY FALL. I'm hell-bent on splitting a pile of wood, winterizing the old truck, or jogging from the house to the lab when I feel the tug. Resist as I might, my concentration wanes. I give in and indulge by inspecting the colorful leaves. The meander takes me farther and farther from my task. During these rambles I am reminded of a favorite yet deceptively complex question, "Why do leaves change color and drop?"

When biologists confront "why" questions, two camps usually emerge and commence battle. One group argues that each feature of every living thing has a purpose, that in some way every trait is an adaptation that contributes to the survival or reproduction of the individual. The other school counters that some life processes have no reason for being, are adaptively neutral, just happen. (As you know by now, I generally subscribe to the former paradigm.) The recent history of evolutionary biology is punctuated with the ebb and flow of this debate. With these conflicting possibilities in mind, let us try to interpret the meaning of autumn leaves.

Leaves change color, then fall. Let us consider these events in their natural sequence. We all know that leaves are green in the summer; what may be news is that summer leaves also harbor other pigments. July's dogwoods certainly contain chlorophyll, a molecule that reflects green light and plays a crucial role in photosynthesis, but they also contain carotene and xanthophyll, molecules that reflect orange and yellow light, respectively. Together, the three pigments allow a plant to absorb light of a wide range of wavelengths and thereby enable the plant to capture more energy from sunshine than if it had only one pigment. Because summer leaves contain all three pigments and yet are green, the green of chlorophyll must overpower the other colors.

The process of photosynthesis continually breaks down chlorophyll, but as long as the weather is warm, plants continue to produce it. Through the summer, plants maintain a fairly constant chlorophyll concentration and thereby go on reflecting green wavelengths. As the temperature drops, leaves absorb less water and minerals, and chlorophyll synthesis decreases. By late summer, chlorophyll breaks down faster than it is replaced. What little photosynthesis still occurs in the fall completely exhausts the remaining chlorophyll molecules. Suddenly, the other pigments are unmasked. Though the yellow of October's hickories seems to appear spontaneously, it was there all along. From this perspective, the yellow and orange shades of autumn leaves, leftovers of previously functioning biological mechanisms, have no adaptive significance themselves.

Red autumn leaves, on the other hand, develop in a different way. During the cool nights and sunny days of fall, leaf cells begin to synthesize a new kind of molecule, anthocyanin, which reflects red wavelengths. Anthocyanin accumulates in the sap of leaf cells. Anthocyanin's formation depends on the breakdown of sugars in the presence of bright light and a decrease in phosphate concentration caused by the diminishing water supply. The brighter the light during this period, the greater the production of anthocyanin and the more brilliant the colors. The most flaming reds develop when autumn days are bright and cool and the nights chilly but not freezing. As was the case for orange and yellow leaves, we know of no purpose for the trait "red leaves." Thus, the colors of tree leaves in the autumn appear to be adaptively neutral—they convey neither advantages nor disadvantages to the reproductive success of the individual tree.

The second feature of a tree's seasonal change is its loss of leaves. For the past several years, I have watched a sugar maple sprinkle its leaves through still air. (I use the languid plume from my wood stove to verify total calm.) Leaves falling through quiet air betray an active process of self-amputation.

During summer, long days stimulate leaves to synthesize a hormone called auxin. This molecule helps maintain cells throughout the leaf's stem that are firmly glued to each other and to the stem. Shorter days cause auxin production to drop, which allows the development of cells that only weakly attach the leaf stem to its branch. This resulting abscission layer consists of a band of cells that separate easily from each other. Imagine how easy it would be to topple a brick wall in which the bottom two rows were set without mortar. Similarly, with its abscission zone in place, a leaf will drop at the slightest breeze, or even, as was the case with my maple, just from the weight of the leaf itself. After separation, a thin layer of cork cells quickly seals the wound.

I am again led to ask "why?" Why do trees shed their leaves? Leaves are thin, full of water, and thereby exquisitely vulnerable to freezing. In autumn, trees drain their leaves, but a tree covered with dry leaves would never do. Should fall gusts snap off drained leaves, a tree would face winter with thousands of open, hollow wounds. If water could enter these openings, a single winter of alternating freezes and thaws would yield a tree that looked like a frazzled lightning target. At least in part then, today's trees shed their leaves and seal the scars because this saved their ancestors from being ripped apart by wedges of ice.

When you find yourself contemplating a blazing autumn hillside, consider two notions. Although the colors may inspire you to daydream, wax poetic, or paint a landscape, the hues are probably irrelevant to the trees' reproductive success. Further, when those gay leaves flutter groundward, the tree is actively amputating its own members to prevent a shattering trauma. At least that's how the teleological metaphor would go. I offer these musings not to cancel mystery, which we all crave, but to foster a deeper understanding of some of the biological reasons for the events of autumn in which we rejoice.

24

Window on Bird Politics

Busy BIRDS COME AND GO, helter-skelter, about the pile of sunflower seeds. One comes to expect this when birds have been conditioned by easy calories. When I watch casually, this is all I see. But when I really examine the scene, I discover that my bird feeder serves as a window into a subtle world of dictators, parasites, and liars. Read this chapter on a cold winter day, feet propped up and hot chocolate within reach, overlooking a stocked bird feeder. You may find that your backyard birds reveal some intriguing politics.

In the winter, my feeder attracts single-species flocks of northern juncos, American goldfinches, evening grosbeaks, and purple finches, and mixed-species flocks featuring black-capped chickadees, tufted titmice, white-breasted nuthatches, and occasionally downy woodpeckers and brown creepers. A mixed-species flock includes individuals of two or more species. Although pairs of cardinals and of rufous-sided towhees occasionally feed here, flocks bring most of my customers. The two reasons birds flock—for greater protection against predators and higher feeding efficiency—provide insight into the scene at our feeders. Let us take a look at each.

Many of us have seen on television a film in which a lioness fixates on and then attacks an isolated zebra, the one that strayed from the herd or behaved differently. The pruning of marginal individuals favors the evolution of centripetal instincts, the tendency to move inward. For this reason, flocks of small birds tighten in the presence of a raptor. This point was driven home not long ago when I saw a flock of starlings flying in a highly synchronized formation. Based on their tightness, I thought a predator might be nearby. Sure enough, a few seconds later, a sharp-shinned hawk glided into view. Under my breath, I hoped a stray would trigger a stoop, but on that day the squadron was disciplined.

In many bird species, when one member of a flock sees an aerial predator, it gives a special alarm. Chickadees and titmice respond to the alarm by diving into bushes and remaining quiet for several minutes; downy woodpeckers simply freeze on the tree trunk. Regardless of the type of response, alarm calls present us with a difficult evolutionary problem. Some flocks include both genetically related and unrelated members of the same species. In such flocks, alarm calls ring out not only to kin, which would make them explainable by kin selection, but also to unrelated members of the same species. Thus, the warning caller could increase the fitness of unrelated flock mates. This would represent genetic altruism, reproductive selflessness, a phenomenon unexplainable by natural selection. How do we account for alarm calls?

Perhaps the individual that sees the hawk and gives the warning is manipulating its flock mates into heading for cover even though the responders do not know the predator's position. Then the caller heads for the far side of the flock. Thus, straightforward natural selection may have favored a gene for calling because the caller increases its own chance of survival to the detriment of its flock mates.

On the other hand, we know that some flocks reflect the action of kin selection. During winter, black-capped chickadees and tufted titmice, the nucleus of natural mixed-species flocks, forage with their mates and offspring. The high pitched alarm calls of chickadees and titmice are ventriloquistic, making their source hard to locate. These observations suggest that chickadees and titmice may experience the benefits of helping genetic kin.

Flocking also improves the odds of finding food. Look at the northern junco, which normally feeds on the ground below a feeder. Snowbirds, as they are also called, feed in large winter flocks. They peck and scratch, and deplete a spot before searching elsewhere. Chase-offs by other juncos are common: a bird might deplete its own feeding spot, observe a neighbor feeding, make a quick approach to chase it off, and then feed at the conquered spot. If the site proves empty, the bird will make another approach-attack. Dominant displacers tend to be large, dark males.

The individual members of a junco flock conform to a stable peck order. Within this society, subordinate individuals are at a disadvantage. They carry less body fat and thereby have less fuel for winter than dominant birds, they possess larger adrenal glands (an indication of a high level of stress), they feed at the periphery of the flock where they are more vulnerable to predators, and they burn more energy avoiding other birds. The dominant birds' great fat stores and favorable surface-to-volume ratio give them an edge in surviving the winter.

Apparently, juncos find it more profitable to chase off subordinates and conquer feeding spots than to search for food independently. Most of the encounters below a feeder are of this parasitic type. Dominant juncos serve as parasitic shepherds and subordinates as food-finding sheep. From the low-ranking bird's point of view, the food-finding ability of the flock reduces the probability of outright starvation—seeds are clustered, and groups seem to find them more efficiently than individual birds do. Regardless of a bird's standing, then, the advantages of flocking seem to outweigh the disadvantages.

Flock size also improves an individual's feeding efficiency. As flock size of the yellow-eyed junco, a western relative of our northern junco, increases, individuals spend less time scanning for predators, which in turn allows more food pecks. Even though individuals spend more time in aggressive interactions as flock size grows, the mean rate of food pecks still increases with flock size.

The behavior of the white-throated sparrow, which breeds in Canada and overwinters in Appalachia, reflects this trade-off between feeding efficiency and predation risk. Like juncos, white-throated sparrows form loose winter foraging flocks with dominance hierarchies. In one experiment, when birds of known rank were provided food at varying distances from dense shrubbery, individuals preferred to feed near the cover rather than in open areas. They would nearly exhaust the food in secure areas before moving farther into the open. Dominant birds fed nearer to shelter than subordinates since their high rank allowed them access to preferred sites. Subordinate white-throated sparrows enjoyed high foraging efficiency but were relegated to more exposed sites where they faced high odds of falling prey.

The make-up of winter foraging flocks varies among species. The black-capped chickadee and tufted titmouse make an interesting contrast. During spring and summer, black-capped chickadees live as monogamous pairs and defend breeding territories that provide a rotten stump for a nest and enough caterpillars and other foods for both the adults and chicks. In September, the molting adults and their fledged young gather into flocks and repel other chickadee flocks from their communal territory, an area two to three times larger than the breeding territory. In winter, each individual chickadee takes on one of two possible behavioral modes. It either becomes a flock regular and spends its entire winter in a single flock, or it behaves as a floater that moves among three or four flocks. About 80 percent of the members of a flock are regulars, with an average of ten regulars per flock. Future mates pair when the flock forms in the fall, so it is a safe bet that a flock with ten regulars contains five mated pairs. Floaters, though reproductively mature, are prevented from breeding by dominant individuals.

Within a chickadee flock of regulars and floaters exists a clear-cut linear peck order, meaning that each member of the flock is consistently either dominant or subordinate to each flock mate. Chickadee pecking orders, like those of the northern junco, are the same at or away from feeders. Within a flock, floaters rank below regulars of their sex. However, should the male at the top of the pecking order disappear, the highest ranking floating male takes over as the dominant male of the flock. Likewise, should a high ranking female vanish, the dominant female floater assumes the regular spot. Surprisingly, each replacement acquires the mate of the bird it replaced. Vacancies are not filled by the next highest regular, apparently because regulars are locked into their status by the rank of their mate.

Floaters do not fill every vacancy, however. If the mate of a newly inserted floater dies, a second floater will not pair with the first. Instead, the first reverts to floating. It seems that floaters only insert when a high-ranking bird of the same sex dies. Thus, regular, low-ranking widows and widowers remain mateless for the rest of the winter. Because only the top two or three pairs in a flock will gain a territory and breed, and because the fastest route to high-rank is via insertion as a floater, floating is actually more desirable than a low-ranking, regular position.

To reproduce successfully a chickadee should emerge from winter as a high-ranked regular. The positions offering the best chances of gaining a breeding territory, from highest to lowest, are high-ranked regular, high-ranked floater, low-ranked regular, and low-ranked floater. It makes sense, then, that this happens to be the order in which the slots of the flock fill as young birds arrive in the fall.

Contrast chickadee society with that of the tufted titmouse. Tufted titmice also form winter flocks in the fall, but their flock size ranges from only two to five individuals. Almost half of all titmouse flocks consist of only one adult male and one adult female. Further, since titmice do not float, the membership of a titmouse flock remains stable throughout the winter. The average territory of a titmouse flock covers 13 acres and, like the chickadee's, its boundaries are stable and delineated early in the flocking season. On or near their territorial boundaries, the birds engage in interflock aggression—jeering loudly, displaying erect crests, and flitting about with quick, spastic movements. Like juncos and chickadees, titmice exhibit linear dominance hierarchies within their flocks. Males dominate females, and seniority on the flock territory determines dominance within a sex. Again, titmouse ranks assigned away from feeders hold at the feeders as well.

When a winter titmouse flock disbands in March, the dominant male and female, which are mates, establish a breeding territory within the winter flock range. This pair will most likely be the only titmouse couple to breed within the flock range.

Chickadees and titmice sometimes forage together in mixed-species flocks during winter. Flocks composed of black-capped chickadees, tufted titmice, and several follower species, such as downy woodpeckers, hairy woodpeckers, and white-breasted nuthatches, are common in Appalachia. Birds form mixed-species flocks for the same reasons that members of the same species flock together. Feeding in mixed-species flocks proves profitable for sponging individuals. For example, white-throated sparrows chase off juncos, providing an interspecific example of the shepherd-sheep relationship. Reducing the risk of being caught by a predator works the same for birds that look similar, regardless of whether they are members of the same species. Chickadees, titmice, and nuthatches are gray above, white below, and about the same size. Presumably, individuals of these three species look enough alike that birds hiding behind each other do not betray an odd size or color.

All five species—chickadees, titmice, the two woodpeckers, and nuthatches—fall prey to raptors and respond to each others' alarm calls. Within these flocks, chickadees and titmice give most of the alarm calls. When downy woodpeckers forage with chickadee-titmouse flocks, the woodpeckers spend less time being vigilant and thereby eat more. The core species seem to get nothing in return from the woodpeckers.

I invite you to view new intrigue by critically exploring the action at your bird feeder. You may notice that winter-flocking birds are slow to visit a newly stocked station, but then descend in droves after that first visit. Even this simple observation allows two inferences. First, winter-flocking birds often overlook good food in new places, possibly because their natural food is patchily distributed among known locations. Second, that first visit by a single bird assures a visit by the entire flock, thereby demonstrating one of the big advantages of group living, namely that birds learn from each other where the food is. Do not underestimate the power of simple, local scenes to illuminate the Appalachian play.

25

Thwarting Swords of Ice

LIVING THINGS ARE MADE OF CELLS. With an electron microscope, we can see that these tiny chambers hold criss-crossing tubules, packages of high-powered fuel, and bins of enzymes that could digest the cell itself— all suspended in jelly and wrapped in an ultrathin membrane. These fragile, interacting parts import and process food, consume and disperse oxygen, generate and export waste products, and by cooperating, build exact copies of themselves. Life is possible only if each component occupies its proper place in the subcellular neighborhood. The medium for this machinery is an exquisitely versatile fluid, water. Exquisitely versatile, though, only so long as it remains liquid.

Freezing weather challenges living things to keep the water in their cells from freezing. Vincent Dethier, an insect physiologist who made his mark by discovering how a fly is able to taste, skillfully identified the problem. In his book, *The World of the Tent-Makers*, he declared that the sword of winter is the ice crystal. If you want to get a feeling for the unyielding character of an ice crystal, deflect your breath, inch your nose up to a frosted window, and study the rapiers stretching across the pane. If these lances could gain a toehold inside a cell, they would displace specialized structures, shred tubules, and perforate the cell's membrane. Yet even on bitterly cold mornings, when dry snow squeaks under my boots and my mustache freezes solid, a variety of hardy animals keep the spark of life. How do Appalachian animals thwart these swords of ice?

Organisms employ two broad strategies to avoid frozen tissues. They either meet winter's full force head on or move to sites that do not freeze. Let's first focus on species that, like ourselves, face winter's Arctic blasts. Within this broad category, animals exhibit two entirely different ways of avoiding cellular ice: by being winter-active or by supercooling. Those that continue to forage and avoid predators through the coldest months must be able to find food, generate body heat, and retain that heat.

If a bird or mammal has any hope of living through a West Virginia winter, it must consume seeds, dormant plants, or other winter-active animals. It is no coincidence that January's birds are primarily seed eaters—purple martins and ruby-throated hummingbirds have followed the bugs and blossoms south. Birds and mammals produce heat primarily in the abdomen. Metaphorically, food fuels an abdominal stove. As long as the animal can find suitable and sufficient food, it can maintain its torso above freezing.

Shivering, the rapid contraction and relaxation of skeletal muscles, also contributes to heat production. Because shivering requires no external work, energy is released in the form of heat. In severe cold, shivering can elevate an animal's metabolic rate up to five times its basal level. We now think that many small birds, including titmice and chickadees, shiver continuously all through winter. Their pectoralis muscles, the major breast muscles that stroke the wings, produce most of the heat they generate by shivering.

Heat generation alone, however, cannot sustain life. Winter-active animals must also be able to retain their hard-won warmth. Good insulators, such as fur or feathers, impede radiation and convection, thereby trapping a layer of warm air around the skin. In some animals, a layer of fat under the skin serves as both insulation and stored energy.

Beyond the minimum requirements of feeding, and generating and capturing heat, winter-active species exhibit more subtle adaptations. The first of these involves the animal's body shape. Heat is produced in the body's mass but escapes through the surface. In general, heat escapes more slowly from an animal shaped like a sphere (with a small surface area and a large volume) than from one shaped like a hot dog (with a high surface area and relatively low volume). As a set, arctic animals are plumper than tropical ones: polar bears and Aleuts are rounder than orangutans and Masai. It is also no accident that igloos are hemispheres. The few long, skinny mammals in cold areas, such as weasels, pay a tremendous price in heat loss and therefore compensate by voracious predation. It is not quite that simple though, because although very few winter-active animals are hot-dog-shaped, tropical species come both skinny and round.

The principle that an animal's surface-to-volume ratio determines its rate of heat loss is illustrated within single species as well. The subspecies of the white-tailed deer living in Maine weighs up to 300 pounds. In New York, white-tails weigh 150 to 200 pounds. On the Florida mainland, this species weighs up to 150 pounds, and on the Keys, only 80 to 110 pounds. Small animals in general, including deer, have a higher surface-to-volume ratio and therefore lose heat faster than large deer.

Because of their large surface areas and poor suitability for heavy insulation, limbs might appear to be thermal liabilities. In fact, legs and wings lose little heat. To minimize the loss of heat from extremities, animals come equipped with a fascinating set of blood vessels called a counter-current heat exchanger, in which arteries feeding the limbs pass intimately alongside veins returning blood to the torso. Heat passes by conduction and radiation directly from the warmer artery to the cooler vein. In this way, arterial blood with its oxygen and nutrients continues its surge to fingers and toes, but most of its heat short-circuits the extremities. Some duck legs have such efficient heat exchangers that blood arriving at the foot is just half a degree above the ambient temperature. This permits smooth function with little heat loss, even in icy water. Counter-current heat exchangers exist in beaver tails, human arms, and the legs of deer and wading birds.

Insects, in contrast to the heat-producing animals discussed so far, do not generate body heat. Even so, many insects, including larval tent caterpillars and adult paper wasps, live through winter without being compromised by ice crystals. Millions of years ago, insects evolved the second strategy of coping with winter's bitterness, supercooling. The molecules of a liquid constantly ricochet off each other in random fashion. Normally, as a liquid cools, its molecules slow and eventually

159

reach a point where they move so sluggishly that their mutual repulsion is exceeded by their mutual attraction. At this point, the molecules of the liquid line up in a definite, geometrical pattern and form a crystal. Once that initial crystal forms, it serves as a seed for the alignment of other molecules. The crystal grows rapidly, and the liquid turns solid. Apparently, mixing increases the chances that the molecules will randomly conform to the critical angles required to form that first crystal.

If, however, a liquid cools slowly and without agitation, its molecules may not strike each other at just those specific angles. If cooled slowly and with care, a liquid's temperature can drop far below its freezing point without starting the crystallization process—the liquid supercools.

Insects evolved the knack of supercooling the water in their cells and blood. The key was subduing the odds of forming that first seed ice crystal. They accomplish this by remaining absolutely motionless. Nudge a supercooled insect, though, and it instantly freezes solid. Plants can also supercool. Liquid in the cells of the shagbark hickory does not freeze until its temperature drops to -42 degrees Fahrenheit. Other trees and shrubs may persist unharmed down to -53 degrees.

Insects employ yet another mechanism to avoid frozen cells. As winter approaches, the cells of some insect species synthesize and concentrate an antifreeze called glycerol. Like the antifreeze in your car's radiator, glycerol lowers the freezing point of water. In *The Days of the Year*, Hal Borland reported mourning cloak butterflies flying in New England during the warm days of winter. You can witness a similar sight through the open winters of central Appalachia. One of the few butterfly species that overwinter as adults, mourning cloaks probably combine the tactics of supercooling and antifreeze synthesis to persist through winter in a state of suspended animation.

Some insects are actually more like birds and mammals with abdominal stoves. Clustered in a tight sphere, a honeybee colony functions as a heat-generating superorganism. Bees in the core produce heat and rotate with peripheral individuals that temporarily serve as insulation.

A few insects seem to defy the laws of physics. In Maine and Vermont, two types of winter moths can fly through freezing air. Adults in the subfamily Cuculinae emerge in the fall and fly during winter when ambient temperatures approach 32 degrees. Some species warm by shivering at temperatures as low as 26 degrees and continue to shiver until their thoracic muscles reach 86 degrees, the minimum for sustained flight. For these species, prolonged shivering, a one-twenty-fifth-inch-thick layer of insulating pile on the thorax, and reduced heat flow from thorax to abdomen allow them to fly in subfreezing conditions.

Another group of winter moths, in the family Geometridae, is even more amazing. Also emerging in the fall, they fly from late November until the first heavy snowfall. These small-bodied moths cannot generate their own heat, yet they fly in temperatures at or above 26 degrees—without employing shivering, basking, insulation, or high thoracic temperatures. In fact, they fly when their muscle temperatures are below freezing! Further, they do not have specialized enzymes that operate at subzero temperatures. We just don't know how they do it. The moth befriended by Robert Frost in his poem "To a Moth Seen in Winter" was probably one of these winter-active species. Alas, it was perfectly normal and probably did not go loveless as he lamented.

The second broad strategy for precluding the formation of ice crystals in cells is to overwinter in a place that does not freeze—either migrate or hibernate. A discussion of migration could easily fill an entire chapter, so I will treat only the latter topic here. Hibernation is one of those biological concepts that is attractive and intuitively understandable, but as we shall see, difficult to generalize.

Let us consider the groundhog, a true hibernator. A hibernating whistle pig remains rolled in a ball, with head between hind limbs, unresponsive to disturbance for six months. While normally at 99 degrees, the hibernating woodchuck's body temperature drops to between 43 and 57 degrees. Its breathing slows to a point that cannot be detected by sight alone. In July, adult groundhogs start accumulating a fat layer that grows to one inch thick by autumn. They hibernate when they have amassed the requisite amount of fat—in New York, about mid-September. They store no food in the burrow; fat is their only fuel. During winter, a groundhog burns 33 to 40 percent of its body weight. In one study, adults that weighed 9.2 pounds in September averaged 5.5 pounds when they awoke in March.

The only other Appalachian mammals that clearly hibernate are several species of jumping mice, chipmunks, and some bats. All other mammals display varying levels of metabolic depression—they may sleep for long periods, but they do not depress their metabolism as severely as true hibernators. Raccoons, for example, often den in hollow trees, do not cache food, and usually remain near their dens during the coldest three or four months. Because the raccoon's abdominal stove burns enough fat to remain above 95 degrees, a raccoon may lose up to half its body weight in a severe winter. Although commonly thought to hibernate, black bears in North Carolina and West Virginia are not true hibernators because they rove about to feed during winter's warm spells.

Small birds such as chickadees have such high surface-to-volume ratios that they cannot generate enough heat to compensate for the heat lost through their skin. Instead, they save fuel by allowing their body temperatures to drop at night. In one experiment, the body temperatures of chickadees exposed to freezing dropped by 23 degrees during the night. Nocturnal hypothermia seems to be a normal part of the bird's winter life. This adaptation saves birds up to one-fourth of the energy required to maintain normal body temperature.

In contrast to heat-producing birds and mammals, some vertebrates, including fishes, amphibians, and reptiles, do not produce significant amounts of internal body heat, and consequently, their body temperatures reflect ambient conditions. Formerly and inaccurately called cold-blooded, these vertebrates exhibit two strategies for avoiding frozen cells: moving to a site that does not freeze or depressing the freezing point of cellular water.

The gray tree frog overwinters beneath leaf litter and survives freezing. The leopard frog, which overwinters in aquatic sites, lacks such a cold-tolerance. How does the gray tree frog survive freezing conditions? The key is that tree frogs accumulate the antifreeze glycerol in their body fluids, whereas leopard frogs do not. Leopard frogs, in contrast, hibernate in small pits at the bottom of ice-covered ponds, lightly covering themselves with silt and remaining capable of some movement. The leopard frog's pit is larger than the occupant, presumably allowing free movement of water and gas exchange through the animal's skin.

If an animal can generate heat in its belly and find fuel for its abdominal stove, and aided by body roundness, insulation, and heat exchangers, can hold on to enough heat to move its muscles smoothly, it is a candidate for an active life through the Appalachian winter. Lacking any of these adaptations relegates a species to inactivity via supercooling or antifreeze, or to overwintering in a site that does not freeze. Those plump chickadees cleaving sunflower seeds at your feeder, that "poor, cold" duck paddling through an icy pond, and those insects that mysteriously take to wing in the first few hours of a mild winter day bear witness to the amazing adaptations that sustain life through an Appalachian winter.

26

Spring Tensions

THAT FIRST WAFT OF WARM SPRING AIR, the pale green brush to a hillside, the first warbler singing in a treetop—all excite our senses and push aside the day's problems. It is fitting that the opening movement of Aaron Copland's "Appalachian Spring" captures the timid, cautious mood of the first few days of resurrection. Then comes the onrush. From a biological point of view, things change faster in spring than at any other time. Along Pine Cabin Run, phoebes flick their tails, hickory leaves unsheathe, and creek chubs vie for headwater pools. With a big shudder, everything shakes off winter and begins anew. With the spring emergence comes tension. Timing is everything.

The first warm sunshine of February rekindles the flow of sap on the south side of trees, and leaves soon begin to unfurl. In a locally predictable sequence, the leaves of various tree species emerge over the span of a couple of months. The timing of leaf-out appears to vary from year to year—late April one year, early May the next. But our calendar months lend little relevance because the immediate cue for leaf emergence is the cumulative thermal sum, or the amount of ambient heat available in the spring after a requisite cold period. When we relate the timing of leaf-out to thermal sums rather than to days on a calendar, we find it consistent over the years. When I speculate with my neighbors up the hollow about whether spring has come early or late, I know I'm applying the wrong yardstick, but I enjoy the rite just the same.

Most plants of the forest floor respond acutely to lessened sunshine as trees leaf out. The seasonal light hitting the forest floor runs out of synchrony with the temperature cycle. Ground cover plants receive strong sunshine or warm weather, but not at the same time. The woodland herbs of early spring produce flowers during the brief window of time between the first prolonged period warm enough for pollinators and the closing of the canopy. The heydays of herbaceous wildflowers end as the canopy closes in above.

Early-blooming, ephemeral herbs of the Appalachian forest include spring beauty, round-lobed hepatica, cut-leaf toothwort, squirrel corn, Dutchman's breeches, rue anemone, and bloodroot. Many of these early spring bloomers have white, bowl-shaped, sun-following flowers with reflective petals, and fuzzy pollen-producing and seed-bearing organs. These flowers stay warmer than the surrounding air because they reflect visible light and other forms of radiation onto the flower's sexual organs. Such tiny parabolic solar ovens speed the development of pollen, seeds, and fruits and aid the survival and reproduction of visiting insects by providing them with a warm microenvironment. Because these wild-flowers need the full energy of bright sunshine to grow and bloom, they retreat as the canopy thickens.

Some of the extremely early bloomers actually produce their own heat. With short bursts of intense metabolism, the eastern skunk cabbage heats its flowers to as much as 31 degrees Fahrenheit above the ambient temperature, allowing them to melt their way through ice and snow. Because the skunk cabbage plants produce heat, they get a jump on flowering and seed production. The spike of flowers inside the skunk cabbage's hood is warm to the touch, and the hood, which resembles Styrofoam, insulates the flower spike. The warmth inside the flower and the plant's characteristic smell of feces and decaying flesh lure insect pollinators. The heat may help to volatilize the odorous molecules. After pollination, the plant maintains a tropical climate for embryonic development.

The temperature of a skunk cabbage's flower spike varies little because a built-in thermostat helps regulate the plant's metabolic rate, and thereby its core temperature. In fact, the metabolic rates of skunk cabbage's flower spike and warm-blooded animals of similar weight are about equal, suggesting that both plants and vertebrates evolved the ability to generate heat via the common route of elevating their metabolic rates.

The sequence of wildflower bloom in West Virginia from late winter through mid-spring, goes something like this: skunk cabbage, bloodroot, spring beauty, hepatica, Dutchman's breeches, squirrel corn, violets, star chickweed, trilliums, crested dwarf iris, columbine, and fire pinks. Our trees also bloom in a definite order: downy serviceberry, flowering dogwood, black cherry, eastern redbud, and tulip poplar.

I find it curious that all the individuals of a given plant species do not emerge at the same time. For example, at a specific site, jack-in-the-pulpit individuals may emerge within a two-week period. Why don't all members of one species emerge simultaneously? Herein lies a conflict—or rather a *possible* conflict, as you will see in the following tentative musings.

When in the spring an organism mobilizes its biochemical resources and begins nudging, probing, and stretching strikes me as a period fraught with tension. The timing of emergence reflects a tug-of-war between competing priorities. Each plant must accelerate its metabolism, which is probably a non-reversible physiological change, and emerge from below ground without knowing what the weather will be in the near future. Presumably, each species of plant has evolved to leaf out within a certain time frame, determined by some combination of day length and thermal sums. From an evolutionary point of view, the timing of leaf emergence seems to reflect a trade-off between the potential photosynthetic gains from early leaf-out and the probability of leaf damage by late frosts. Leaves should open when the benefits gained from photosynthesis equal the costs of replacing frozen leaves. However, individual plants that bloom during their species' flowering peak often suffer low rates of fertilization and seed production, possibly because the pollinators are swamped. The currency in this cost-benefit transaction is, as always, the number of successful offspring the individual organism produces.

Consider bloodroot, an herbaceous flower of the forest floor. Individual plants that emerge early might risk being frozen before pollinating insects are active. Late individuals risk unfurling their leaves after the canopy has opened, thereby missing opportunities for photosynthesis. Late plants also may fail pollination because other flowers have already bribed, and thereby trained, the bees to visit them. Theoretically, within a specific area, bloodroot should emerge collectively within a short period of time, and these temporally clustered plants should have greatest survival and reproductive success in the long run.

Most of the time, that is. The catch comes with the nonsynchronous individuals during unusual years. These nonconformists occasionally gain huge reproductive advantages over normal individuals. Early individuals benefit if spring comes early. Likewise, late-emerging plants have high reproductive success in a late spring because all of their competitors have been frozen out, leaving all the pollinators to the latecomers.

Even though emergence within a brief window of time normally yields reasonable odds of pollination, fertilization, and production of viable seeds, a plant may occasionally gain even greater fitness by operating outside the norm. The question arises of whether a plant should conform, play with normal odds, and gain a modest payoff, or be a nonconformist gambling against low odds for a huge payoff. Natural selection may have led to a diversity of individual emergence times because every once in a while nonconformity paid off handsomely for the ancestors of some of today's flowers. This tension is the irony of spring.

27

Dawn Chorus

AT LEAST ONCE EACH SPRING, as dawn breaks, I hike up to our pine thicket and practice the brand of stump-sitting espoused by Charles Fergis, naturalist and cur-mudgeon of Pennsylvanian Appalachia. In his book, *The Wingless Crow*, Fergis suggested that stump-sitting would release me, allow me to open my senses to nature's bounty, permit me to see and feel new things. But try as I may, I am a lousy stump-sitter. Invariably, any sensory free association I manage to generate gets cut short by a sound or movement. More often than not, the distracter is a little bird high in the canopy that calls, then answers itself, a male red-eyed vireo competing for its slice of the dawn chorus. This common Appalachian bird illustrates the wonder of bird song. As I listen, I wonder why he sings, what is he saying, to whom, how, and why? Rational inquiry takes over; I step down from metaphysical stump-sitting and reenter science.

In monogamous species it is almost always the male that sings, to attract a mate or to proclaim his nesting territory off-limits to other males of that species. He thereby monopolizes an area with enough food for himself, his mate, and their offspring. In general, males aggressively guard only areas with tangible resources that are defensible at reasonable cost.

Natural selection seems to favor individuals that defend areas large enough to include just enough resources for their family's survival.

However, a few ornithologists argue that some birds defend super-territories, areas that provide more than enough resources, as a way to reduce the reproductive success of less aggressive individuals. The idea is that by monopolizing more food than needed, a male bird limits the food available to other potential competitors. There may also be non-resource reasons for superterritories: to reduce the odds of being distracted by neighbors and thereby surprised by a predator. Like international boundaries, the borders between bird territories often remain stable even though their occupants change. If a bird disappears, a single individual replaces it and inherits the territory and the established neighbors.

Although male birds usually direct territorial aggression at other males of the same species, some repel members of other species. Territoriality between species can evolve if two species, such as red-eyed and Philadelphia vireos, compete for the same resources. Both of these species have highest breeding success in areas they occupy jointly, so a male vireo must repel members of both species from his territory. Some animal behaviorists have suggested that *inter*specific territoriality is just misdirected *intra*specific territoriality, and therefore not adaptive. However, I believe that the frequency and regularity of aggression between the two species of vireo are signs that natural selection maintains this behavior.

Definite benefits accrue with larger and better territories. Male field sparrows with larger territories weigh more and mate more frequently than males on smaller territories. On average, such benefits go to older males because they occupy their territories for longer portions of the year than first year males. In many species, clutch size varies as a function of territory quality, such as the amount of food or availability of refuge sites. Presumably, a female lays the optimal number of eggs for her territory—the number of offspring the pair can feed. Thus, the kind and amount of resources within the defended area become crucial determinants of the reproductive success of both partners.

The songs of dozens of males simultaneously advertising their territories comprise the dawn chorus. During the height of the breeding season, the dawn chorus can be deafening, seemingly chaotic. Though, like the crescendo in Rimsky-Korsakov's "Scheherazade," sophisticated structure underlies the cacophony.

Most birds sing in the morning when there is little wind or con-vection. Calls voiced then broadcast up to 20 times farther than songs of equal amplitude broadcast at midday. Many birds sing from treetops, again to take acoustical advantage of a favorable microclimate. Like light, sound can be blocked, deflected, or absorbed to create a sound shadow. Near the ground, steep temperature and wind velocity gradi-ents cause such sound shadows. Since greater elevation reduces the effects of these near-surface refractions, singing high above the ground increases the broadcast coverage.

Two dominant variables influence identification and localization of sound in a forest: changes in volume and reverberations. Fluctuations of volume, caused by the scattering effects of turbulent air, vary in strength with weather conditions. The degree of volume fluctuations determines how intelligible the call will be. Reverberations, caused by surfaces that scatter sound, also interfere with the receiver's ability to recognize a call. However, one benefit of reverberation is the camouflage it provides the singer through ventriloquism. Ventriloquists produce sound whose source is hard to locate, presumably to make it harder for a predator to locate them.

Communicating animals employ special tactics to reduce sound degradation. First, they call when and where degradation is least, such as from treetops in morning. Second, birds may signal in patterns that differ from patterns created by scattering. Finally, the singers incorpo-rate redundancy into their signal. Repetition allows the receiver to predict the entire signal from part of it or to average the sound. However, broad leaves and other surfaces that reflect sound cause severe rever-berations in deciduous forests, so long-range callers there usually avoid signals that sound like reverberations. In general, forest-breeding song-birds also avoid rapid repetition in their long distance communications. For example, when communicating with others up to ten yards away, chickadees use the "gargle" call, which sounds like a small bird gargling with mouthwash. Over greater distances, though, the birds employ the long, plaintive "fee bee."

Even though they could use a huge range of potential frequencies, birds sing only at certain pitches. The sound window (1,585 to 2,500 Hz) forest birds use is limited at the low end by the frequencies of wind-generated noise and at the high end by the pitch of insect song. Birds exploit this range even though lower frequencies actually carry farther.

Within this frequency range, many male birds sing at the same time. To avoid the worst interference, species drop in and out of the chorus at different times of the day. Some warble in feeble predawn light, others sing when the sun is well overhead.

To further preclude audio interference, male birds avoid singing at the same moment others call. The males of the least flycatcher and red-eyed vireo communicate with short advertising songs of similar pitch repeated through the day. When they breed in the same place, the flycatcher and vireo avoid superimposing songs. Forbearance is more marked in the flycatcher: the male avoids beginning its song while an adjacent vireo is singing. Specifically, the flycatcher inserts its short (12 seconds) song in between the longer (46 seconds) songs of the vireo. Other Appalachian birds have solved this problem in a similar way. The wood thrush, eastern wood peewee, tufted titmouse, white-throated sparrow, and great crested flycatcher tend to avoid singing during the songs of other species, usually by beginning their song immediately after the neighbor has stopped. Singers must also solve this interference problem within their own species. In one experiment, male ovenbirds overlapped an artificial ovenbird stimulus song in only 10 of 251 trials. Further, most of the ovenbirds sang during the first tenth of the silent interval in order to avoid interference.

Male birds master a repertoire of stereotyped songs—one endlessly repeated song will not do. The sizes of repertoires vary greatly both between and within species. Two hypotheses, which unfortunately are not mutually exclusive, attempt to explain the evolution of large repertoires. A large repertoire may indicate to a female a male's superior age, experience, and territory. Such a male may be more successful in copulating with their own mate and neighboring females than are males with a small repertoire. In experiments, female canaries that listen to playbacks of large song repertoires build their nests faster and lay more eggs than females exposed to smaller repertoires.

The second hypothesis states that large repertoires contribute to territorial defense. Labeled the Beau Geste hypothesis, it claims that a territorial male can inflate the apparent density of singing males in his region by singing several distinct song types. Prospecting males then avoid such an acoustically dense area. So far, however, the Beau Geste hypothesis has been only partially supported by experimental data.

Some species of birds exhibit local dialect. Neighboring birds may sing similar or identical songs, while just a mile or two away the songs of the same species may sound noticeably different. Like human language, bird dialects do not blend at boundaries to form intermediates, and their basic pitch and rhythm are stable over many years. Although local subdialects may involve as few as two to five birds, a specific dialect usually characterizes several hundred individuals.

Some evidence indicates that dialects are population-specific. The "gargle" of the black-capped chickadee is a sputtery, explosive, complex threat emitted when males from neighboring flocks meet along their mutual territorial boundary. Syllables at the end of the vocalization are shared among several small interbreeding groups, but introductory syllables usually differ, even at sites less than four miles apart. Flock members also share a great similarity in the "dee" elements of "chick-a-dee" calls. These findings, in view of the flocking and mating adaptations of chickadees, suggest that each interbreeding group develops its own unique dialect.

Why do birds have dialect? Perhaps because young males copy the songs of established neighbors to gain an advantage in territorial defense or mate attraction. Male white-throated sparrows, ovenbirds, and indigo buntings respond more aggressively to the recorded songs of strangers than to those of established neighbors. In other words, males habituate to familiar songs. Such "dear enemy" recognition saves neighbors the time and energy of expensive contests. Copying the local dialect may allow a young, new male to establish a territory relatively painlessly, as other males would mistake him for an older resident male. Thus, song dialects may reflect mimicry within a species that leads to social elevation. This hypothesis holds merit. In southern Michigan, first-year male indigo buntings that matched the songs of adult territorial neighbors had greater success in mating, nesting, and fledging young than first year males that did not match those songs. No disadvantage fell to the males being mimicked.

It makes sense that song learning depends on socialization fairly late in life, not simply on hearing a song at the birthplace. For example, young rufous-sided towhees and indigo buntings disperse from their birth site, then settle and begin singing like their new neighbors.

Birds have developed foolproof ways to recognize each others' song. In experiments, the white-throated sparrow identified its neighbor after hearing only the first three notes of a five-note song. Ovenbirds also discriminate between the songs of neighbors and those of noncontiguous males, but by using the singer's location as the main cue. When a neighbor's song was played from the territorial border farthest from the neighbor's usual location, the ovenbird responded as if it were defending against a stranger. Unfamiliar songs would presumably be sung by a transient, unsettled male looking for a territory. "Dear-enemy" recognition saves the costs of territorial contests with established neighbors that present little threat.

The last time I settled onto my favorite stump, I felt overwhelmed by the skill of the red-eyed vireo. His pitch and simple expressions carry through broad leaves; he sings most assertively at dawn when broadcast conditions are best; he recognizes his neighbors and listens to them to avoid acoustic interference; his lovely repertoire may stimulate his mate to reproductive readiness; and his dialect marks him from a specific area. When I apply these adaptations to another species in the dawn chorus the complexity compounds; consider the entire chorus and it becomes overwhelming. The counterpoints in Bach's Brandenburg Concertos pale by comparison.

28

Trees and Caterpillars

Mᴜᴄʜ ᴏꜰ ᴛʜᴇ ᴇɴᴇʀɢʏ passing through an Appalachian ecosystem follows a single path. Arriving as sunshine, energy then flows through deciduous leaves, moth caterpillars, and fecal rain. This is why, by late summer, it is nearly impossible to find an intact leaf. A forest of holey leaves proves that caterpillars are exerting tremendous feeding pressure on broadleaved trees. Yet the struggle between trees and caterpillars would not have become a dominant act in the play had trees served merely as passive targets. In their own subtle way, trees fight back.

Let us first consider the larva's role in the relationship, focusing on the eastern tent caterpillar. Residing in the eastern half of North America from Nova Scotia to Florida, this well-known insect overwinters communally in egg masses on its principal host trees, cherry and apple. Deposited near branch tips the previous summer, eggs hatch as leaf buds unfurl. Because a female lays all her eggs, which contain fully formed caterpillars, in a single cluster, the "cats" that develop from one egg mass are siblings.

A few days after hatching, the caterpillars construct a tent near their tree's center, a site offering branches for support and a central position from which to forage. This permanent tent is enlarged several times a day to accommodate the growing larvae. Cats enlarge the tent one layer at a time and the spaces between partitions provide room for up to 300 individuals during the morning and afternoon rest periods. Small circular openings in the tent allow entry and exit.

During feeding excursions to nearby leaves, the caterpillars secrete strands of silk. Collectively, the strands form a conspicuous silk trail that provides purchase on smooth bark. When a hungry caterpillar leaves the tent in search of food, it lays an exploratory trail chemical signal, or pheromone. Returning from a successful foraging trip, it lays a recruitment trail pheromone by brushing the tip of its abdomen on newly deposited silk trails. Using an old trail, the caterpillar elevates its abdomen, leaving no chemical. Because they are able to discern the age of a pheromone on a silk trail, caterpillars can distinguish between trails to fresh food and paths to exhausted sites. Recruitment via pheromones leads to the efficient forwarding of caterpillars to the most productive foods, as well as the prompt abandonment of areas without young, tasty leaves. As cherry leaves age, they get tougher and drier, and provide less nutrition. As we shall see, from the tree's point of view these changes may represent an adaptive strategy to protect itself from herbivory.

Tent caterpillars create a microenvironment that allows them to be active on cool spring days. Like little greenhouses, tents admit solar radiation and retain some of the converted heat within the silk layers, maintaining temperatures up to 40 degrees Fahrenheit warmer than the surrounding air! By adding more silk to the bright side of the tent, cats enlarge their greenhouse in the direction of the sun. Eventually, these sophisticated larvae turn into short-lived, plain brown moths.

Albeit social and thereby efficient, the tent caterpillar is just one of thousands of species of Appalachian moths whose larvae eat tree leaves. Damage by insect herbivores decreases tree growth, seed production, and seed viability. Trees seem so vulnerable—they are a large target, rooted to one spot, without a fly-swatting tail. Yet by hook or by crook trees persist, in part through alliances with birds.

Birds lend trees a little help. At Hubbard Brook, New Hampshire, ecologists used netting to exclude birds from patches of striped maple, an understory tree. After several days of protection, the densities of moth larvae were significantly greater inside the cages than outside.

The researchers estimated that birds, such as warblers, thrushes, and vireos, removed an average of 37 percent of the caterpillars from the understory. This effect was most intense from late June to mid-July when adult birds were feeding their demanding nestlings.

Bird predation most effectively controls insect numbers when the densities of caterpillars lie within a normal range. At such endemic population levels, birds reduce and thereby regulate the densities of larval moths on forest vegetation. During epidemic outbreaks, though, birds may take only 0.1 to 1.0 percent of the caterpillar biomass. The situation of caterpillars going amuck describes our current gypsy moth invasion.

Trees also get some help from larval parasites, which, like birds, probably make their most significant impact at normal levels of pests.

Trees have a defense problem, though. Compared to their insect pests, trees are long-lived and therefore evolve slowly. In the tree-caterpillar arms race, insects would appear to have the edge. How do trees persist in the face of rapidly evolving pests? We have recently discovered that trees deploy sophisticated chemical and genetic defensive weapons. For example, oaks produce tannin, an organic compound used in the process of tanning leather. When ingested as part of mature oak leaves, tannins bind proteins into indigestible complexes that inhibit the growth of moth larvae. In Vermont, leaves of red oaks that had been defoliated by gypsy moth larvae two years in a row were drier, tougher, and had a higher concentration of tannins and phenolics, another natural insecticide, than leaves of undamaged trees. Gypsy moth larvae grow more slowly, produce smaller pupae and fewer eggs, and decline in vigor when they eat leaves of such defoliated trees.

These observations suggest that trees engage their antiherbivore defenses fairly quickly. A wide variety of plants rapidly mobilize defenses in surrounding leaves and tissues after an herbivore bites. Some plants are induced to synthesize toxins that poison herbivores; others produce complex compounds that interfere with the attacker's growth cycle or digestive ability. Thus, a leaf's suitability as food is not so much a function of its primary metabolites, which contribute to the growth and maintenance of the plant's cells, but of secondary metabolites, compounds synthesized specifically for defending against herbivores. There is tremendous variation of secondary compounds among species.

181

Such toxic chemicals can render an otherwise suitable plant repulsive to an insect. One type of inducible defense works as follows. After a plant is attacked, it releases yet unknown substances from the wound. These chemicals disperse throughout the plant and stimulate the production of molecules that impede the breakdown of protein molecules in the insect's gut. This makes poor food of the plant's leaves.

In Finland, researchers performed a series of interesting experiments on white birch, which is defoliated by the autumnal moth. Larvae that were fed undamaged leaves of shoots from which one leaf had been torn two days earlier grew more slowly and attained lower final weights than individuals that ate leaves from intact shoots. The biologists noticed that birch leaves in an area of heavy herbivory maintained an elevated concentration of phenolics for three years, while trees outside the zone maintained a normal level of phenolics. The level of resistance seemed to depend on the amount of damage.

In these studies it appeared that white birch induced two types of responses to insect predation: a resistance that was rapidly enhanced and rapidly lost in leaves of the current year, and a high resistance that lasted several years thereafter. The former tended to stabilize defoliator populations, whereas the time lag inherent in the latter may have contributed to population crashes and explosions.

Then the Finns made an astounding discovery. The growth, survival, and egg production of moths correlated positively with the distance between their food tree and the closest birch defoliated the previous year—the farther their food source was from the previously defoliated birch, the more successful the moths were. Incredibly, this suggested the presence of aerial chemical communication among nearby trees. A similar phenomenon has been reported in some trees of northern Appalachia. Perhaps this is a response to airborne chemicals released by the attacked trees. As I write, the possibility of a molecular early warning system among trees is being hotly debated among forest ecologists.

In Vermont, trees similarly inhibit gypsy moths. Gypsy moths reared on previously defoliated black oaks grew slower, produced lighter pupae, and had higher mortality than gypsy moths that ate leaves from unaffected oaks. These changes are great enough that they could influence the course of outbreaks.

Currently, inducible defenses are thought to spread to undamaged leaves on the same tree, to leaves on the same tree in successive years, and even to nearby trees. Not all biologists accept these ideas, though. Some assert that these defenses may be present, but that they have negligible effects on herbivore populations. They further counter that the studies, based in laboratories, are statistically flawed. I accept the ideas that defenses spread to other leaves within a tree and exert an influence in succeeding years in the same tree, but I question the evolutionary basis of intertree communication. Kin selection may maintain aerial communication within a group of related individuals or clones, such as aspen and beech, but kin selection is less likely to work in a randomly interbreeding population, such as oaks and hickories.

In addition to inducing defenses, trees fight back in a totally different way—by being many individuals. To understand this idea, picture each tree as a population of buds. If a genetic mutation arises in a cell of a growing bud, the descendant cells will also carry the deviation. Mutations in buds give rise to different kinds of leaves, seeds, and defense compounds within a single plant. In essence, a tree becomes a mosaic of defense types as its buds evolve new variations.

Long life, large size, and annual regeneration of buds make it likely that variation will arise among different parts of an individual plant. Take the wildflower, spring beauty, for example: Different parts of single plants have different chromosome numbers. In one population, 68 percent of the individuals exhibited variation within themselves. Many biologists believe that this situation exists—and will be found—in trees, as well.

With two forms of within-plant variation—inducible defenses and genetic mosaics—trees present attacking insects with a complexity that normally prevents pests from overwhelming the host's defenses. Such plant complexity has several effects on herbivores. If a pest makes a poor decision as to where to settle and feed, it will grow slowly and suffer poor reproductive success. Further, chemical and genetic variation allow parts of individual plants to escape being eaten. If the tree concentrates pests in patches of tasty foliage, it may increase competition among and predation of the pests.

Ultimately, plant defenses may catalyze the evolution of counteradaptations in the pests. For example, some insects are able to convert normally harmful substances into sources of nutrition or even use the nasty substances to defend against animals that may in turn eat them. Caterpillars of the monarch butterfly feed on milkweed leaves, which are rich in cardiac glycosides, powerful toxins that interfere with basic cellular processes. The poison the adult butterflies retain provides some protection against bird predators.

Although I have reported some controversial observations, some of which originate outside Appalachia, this essay conveys what I consider to be a likely scenario in Appalachian forests. Chemical weapons and genetic variation within individual trees provide potent defenses against voracious caterpillars that would otherwise hold an overwhelming edge. Appalachian trees are not merely large, passive, targets under attack by an efficient herbivorous army—they probably have adaptations at least as sophisticated as those portrayed here.

Epilogue

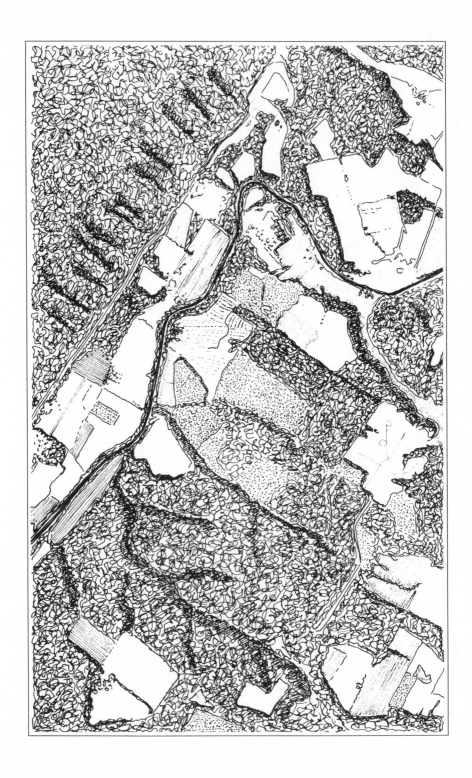

29

The Remnant Archipelago

As I HIKE THE RIDGES AND HOLLOWS of Appalachia, I am dogged by some disturbing questions. Like cockleburs, these doubts cling to me, tainting my Appalachian experience. I can't end this book without at least trying to deal with my baggage of anxiety. What is the fate of Appalachia? What will happen to our cove forests, lungless salamanders, dawn choruses, and, yes, even our copperheads? Despite a feeling of urgency, I freely admit that I do not have the corner on truth. Simply, I have observed some things that concern me and have some ideas on what we might do about them.

Before Europeans arrived, an almost unbroken forest blanketed Appalachia. European colonists exploited this resource so efficiently that by 1910 all the trees accessible by rail or river had been logged. Except in a very few areas, forests were cut to yield the largest possible immediate return—without the slightest thought for the future. After three centuries of farming, logging, and development, less than 1 percent of the virgin forest remains.

Most of today's Appalachian forest is an archipelago of second-growth woodlots in an ocean of pasture. Logging, farming, road cutting, and other human activities have fragmented the forest. This habitat fragmentation lowers the odds that native populations will survive and therefore decreases the diversity of indigenous species. Throughout the

189

world, habitat fragmentation is one of the most serious causes of the present extinction crisis.

So what? Why should we care about biological diversity? Biological diversity, defined as the number of different kinds of living things and their genetic variability, counts for several reasons. First, the number of species in a particular place indicates that ecosystem's health. Polluted streams have bullhead catfish, carp, and a few other hardy species; an untainted Appalachian run will support dozens of fishes. Second, we feel greater delight in a landscape hosting many kinds of organisms than in one that is species-poor. How do you feel at dusk surrounded by fireflies, listening to the whippoorwill, and smelling trailing arbutus? Third, we don't have the slightest idea which species will serve our future needs. Scientists have explored the drug potential of only about 2 percent of the world's plant species. Who would have ever predicted that the horseshoe crab would become crucial to hematology? Would the passenger pigeon's liver have been the ideal system for studying human liver cancer? Finally, human-caused extinctions betray the attitude that other species were put here on earth for our benefit, to exploit as we see fit. We will not transcend this selfish heritage—and therefore will not be able to take credit for the next act in the evolutionary play—until we vow to maintain biological diversity.

As a forest becomes fragmented, the average size of the stands, total habitat area, and habitat diversity decrease, while the insularity and the ratio of forest edge to forest interior increase. The first two effects require no explanation. When habitat diversity decreases, shrinking ecological islands offer fewer kinds of habitats than larger fragments. Compare the variety of temperatures, sunshine, and moisture in ridges, hollows, and streams with the relatively uniform conditions on a single mountainside. Insularity, or the effects of isolation, increases as the distances between islands increases. Geometry dictates that as an island shrinks in area, its edge overwhelms its interior area. The smaller a circle, the greater the circumference per unit of interior area—and many species need the cover, shade, humidity, echoes, and other features of interior habitat.

These five environmental effects contribute to the loss of biotic diversity in three ways. Populations may be outright destroyed, severely reduced, or subdivided. Further, sources of immigrants may be lost, lowering the odds that a species will reestablish itself where it has become extinct. And the environmental changes may impede immigration that normally takes place among habitat patches.

The size of the habitat is important because area alone strongly influences the number of species present. In cities, for example, more weed species live on large vacant lots than small ones. This pattern, known as the species-area relationship, has been documented for many kinds of habitats. Assuming similar habitat, large areas contain more species than small areas, in part because, compared to small areas, large areas support larger populations, which are less likely to become extinct than small populations.

The degree of isolation from other habitat patches also affects the number of resident species. When animals cannot efficiently move among islands, each patch comes to support an isolated population rather than part of a large population. Inbreeding is more likely to occur in small populations than in large ones. Further, small populations may experience genetic drift, random genetic changes that deplete genetic variance. Both inbreeding and drift contribute to genetic *homo*zygosity, the condition in which an organism has identical genes for a given characteristic—a person with two genes for blue eyes, each acquired from one parent. Compared to *homo*zygous individuals, *hetero*zygotes not only avoid the deleterious effects of inbreeding, such as slow growth, depressed survival, and poor reproduction, but their development yields fewer congenital defects. Homozygous individuals are more likely than heterozygotes to develop nonidentical left and right halves.

We can examine the problems of inbreeding by studying the cheetah. When skin grafts are exchanged between unrelated individuals, they are fully accepted, suggesting that all cheetahs are genetically very similar. How do we account for this completely unexpected characteristic in a wild population? It is possible that a climatic catastrophe or hunting spree reduced the cheetah to a few individuals, wiping out a population's worth of genetic variation, and then the population rebounded from these few founders. Whatever the historical cause, its present genetic uniformity has the cheetah on the verge of extinction—they are susceptible to epidemics and experience high juvenile mortality.

191

So, how many individuals must a population have to preclude extinction? Several geneticists have estimated that the minimum number of reproductive adults needed for self-perpetuation is in the range of 50 to 100. Conservation biologists use 1,000 individuals as a general minimum for viable populations. Theoretical evidence suggests that even populations as large as 500 may lose genetic variation faster than they gain it via mutation.

Forest fragmentation reduces effective population size by limiting each organism's ability to move among subpopulations. One remedy is to connect habitat islands, as currently advocated by the greenways movement. Effective population size may be increased by maintaining dispersal corridors among physically isolated patches of habitat. Species subdivided into small, interconnected populations will persist when the rate of population extinction is less than or equal to the rate of population founding.

All this points to one simple idea: Rarity seems to be the best indicator of how vulnerable a species is to extinction. Before you dismiss this as self-evident, consider the power it gives us to predict the most likely candidates for extinction: top predators (golden eagle), large-bodied species (black bear), habitat specialists (Cheat Mountain salamander), and species at the outer fringe of their geographic distribution (wood turtle in the eastern panhandle of West Virginia).

In general, mammals are particularly vulnerable to extinction by insulation. Not only do they have low powers of dispersal, they also have high metabolic needs. Compared to wood thrushes, which can fly between woodlots, a population of waddling opossums depends more on the food and shelter of a single patch of habitat. In fact, of all vertebrate classes, mammals exhibit the fastest rates of species loss. Extreme insularity, with absolute dispersal barriers, could thoroughly extirpate mammals and other nonflying vertebrates.

Species that disperse among patches are a bit better off. Because they can fly from patch to patch, birds maintain higher numbers of species at equilibrium than do other vertebrates. But even here fragmentation is taking its toll—breeding populations of songbirds have been dropping in small forest tracts. For bird communities in forest islands, the smaller the habitat area, the fewer the number of bird species; the greater the degree of isolation of forest islands, the fewer the number of species; and the greater the extent of forest fragmentation, the fewer the number of species typical of the forest interior.

Ironically, with the possible exceptions of the ivory-billed woodpecker and Carolina parakeet, North American birds have not yet been pushed to extinction because of deforestation. However, the mix of species, particularly the representation of migrant songbirds, has dropped. In general, neotropical migrants, those birds that breed in North America and overwinter in Latin America, comprise up to 90 percent of the breeding pairs in Appalachia. In many places the diversity of our migrants has plummeted. For example, the worm-eating warbler, ovenbird, and American redstart, often found in large forests, are rarely seen in small woodlots. Even populations of the red-eyed vireo, possibly the most common bird in Appalachia, have declined dramatically in many forest fragments.

At least two possible reasons arise for the disappearance of neotropical migrants. Because migration imposes high energy costs and short breeding seasons, neotropical migrants lay few eggs per clutch and produce only one brood per year. Compared to resident birds,they are less buffered against reproductive failure. Further, neotropical migrants lay their eggs in open, cuplike nests that are vulnerable to predation and parasitism. Compared to a large expanse of unbroken forest, small woodlots have proportionately more edge, which supports high numbers of predators (crows, raccoons, cats), competitors (sparrows), and parasites (cowbirds). Several studies bear this out. Predation rates soar from 2 percent in the 510,000 acres of Great Smoky Mountains National Park to 75 to 100 percent in woodlots of 25 acres.

The second reason for the decrease in migratory songbirds lies in the tropics—the slash-and-burn destruction of winter habitat. Tropical rain forest, where many of our birds overwinter, are being cleared at the rate of three acres per minute. Sadly, the life histories of many neotropical migrant birds may be incompatible with our fragmented forests.

On a more general scale, fragmentation may be having subtle, insidious effects on Appalachian forest communities. For example, the spores of mycorrhizal fungi may disperse among habitat islands by hitchhiking on small mammals, which, as I have already said, are severely affected by insularity. Thus, the health of trees in small, isolated woodlots may depend on the minimum area and insularity requirements of small mammal populations. Here's a totally unexpected connection with huge implications.

So what can we do to slow or reverse the heavy toll of fragmentation? Given limited amounts of money and land, how should nature preserves be designed to minimize isolation, inbreeding, predation, and ultimately extinction?

Some ecologists approach this problem by applying the equilibrium theory of island biogeography. According to this theory, immigration of new species into a patch should decrease with greater isolation, and extinction should increase with smaller island size. The theory predicts that smaller and more isolated islands will have a lower equilibrium number of species than islands that are larger and less isolated. The problem is that this theory, despite its intuitive appeal, is insufficiently validated to support its application to conservation. Some ecologists argue that one large refuge will save more species than an archipelago of smaller refuges of equal total size; others press the contrary. Until this scientific question is settled, community ecologists will be unable to offer straightforward, practical advice to county commissioners, land developers, and other people who make decisions on land use.

I offer this: the answer to each particular situation lies with the specific conservation goals. If the priority is to protect black bears, hawks, or other widely ranging animals, many small habitat islands, preferably with connecting corridors, might work. In contrast, migrant songbirds such as the Acadian flycatcher, ovenbird, and veery would benefit from large blocks of unbroken forest. Organisms—the summer tanager and cardinal, for instance—that live along habitat boundaries such as the forest edge would do better with long, skinny reserves.

Ideally, we would provide a system of habitat islands that would allow the development of local, genetically differentiated subpopulations but would not block the flow of genes among habitat islands. Many small stepping-stone islands would link a few large and distant preserves; riparian strips would allow travel between isolated islands.

Because conflicts among ecologists surface whether considering reserve area, reserve spacing, or reserve shape, people who attempt to preserve land and its living community are left with ambiguous scientific guidance. As irrevocable changes impact the Appalachian forest, we don't even know enough to plan the salvage operation. Even so, we must not let ignorance justify inaction. One solution to the problem is the international system of biosphere reserves.

UNESCO launched the biosphere reserve project in 1971 to conserve genetic and ecological diversity and to provide opportunities for research and education. The ideal biosphere reserve is large enough to include a complete ecosystem, including its full range of physical and biological processes. The core zone, the heart of the reserve, is strictly protected and administered as a global benchmark for studying how ecosystems function. In the United States, some wilderness areas, national parks and monuments, and wildlife sanctuaries could serve as suitable core zones. A buffer zone designed to absorb the most severe impacts of the surrounding countryside insulates the core.

The Southern Appalachian Biosphere Reserve cluster, with the Great Smoky Mountains National Park (Tennessee and North Carolina) as the core and Oak Ridge National Laboratory (Tennessee) and Coweeta Hydrological Laboratory (North Carolina) as buffers, has served as a model for cooperative research. In northern Appalachia, Hubbard Brook Experimental Forest (New Hampshire) represents a buffer for a yet-to-be determined reserve. There is talk of establishing a biosphere reserve in central Appalachia that would include Shenandoah National Park (Virginia).

Philosophically, I view biosphere reserves as another step in our ethical evolution—they affirm our commitment to the future of living things. From a more practical point of view, biospheres represent one of the last bastions of natural Appalachian diversity, the last pockets from which broader areas will draw powers to convalesce.

Biosphere reserves are just part of the solution. The ultimate strategy must also include a form of land-use planning that incorporates the preservation of biological diversity. When we begin to plan how to use a given piece of Appalachia, we must set out from the start to save the full complement of native species. Nothing less will do.

30

Abuse, Resurrection, Hope

THE DEPTH OF MAN'S ABUSE of the Appalachian landscape came about 1920. Uncontrolled hunting had extirpated game, the railroad had spurred clear-cutting of the forest, and an introduced blight was decimating the elegant American chestnut. A modest reversal came with the emergence of the conservation ethic, which Aldo Leopold so forcefully expressed in A Sand County Almanac: "In short, a land ethic changes the role of Homo sapiens from conqueror of the land-community to plain member and citizen of it. It implies respect for his fellow-members, and also respect for the community as such."

Since then the environmental health of Appalachia has been gradually recovering. White-tailed deer now abound in some areas to the point of becoming serious farm pests; pine, oak, and hickory reforest old eroded homesteads; and government agencies have begun to at least partially reclaim abandoned strip mines. I savor this progress, yet see a plethora of remaining obstacles. Three big environmental problems interfere with the successional recovery of Appalachian ecosystems: haphazard land use, acid rain, and exotic species. Even though landfills crop up next to farms and surface mines appear next to schools, local governments eschew land-use planning—not to mention the "z word." Acid rain sterilizes our streams. Ironically, emissions from high-sulphur coal that is torn from Appalachia's landscape and then burned in the

Midwest blow back to Appalachia as a second affront. Finally, exotic species endanger native plants and animals. In the forest around my cabin, feral cats and cowbirds wreak havoc on the native warblers.

The most harmful problem, lack of land-use planning, is a crime of omission. Land-use planning allows local communities to develop a regional strategy that defines the types of changes that we may visit upon the land. A zoning ordinance codifies those desires. Most Appalachian counties have neither planner nor ordinance.

When land development proceeds without a broad plan, environmental impacts are usually worse than if an ordinance had been on the books. Common consequences of this omission are the building of homes and sewage treatment plants in flood plains, and the digging of septic drain fields in soils that cannot assimilate the volume of sewage generated by modern households. In my area, why were people allowed to replace their trailers along the South Branch's riverbank after a huge flood had washed them away?

Lack of land-use planning also leads to erosion and muddy streams. Road builders expose bare soil without shielding it from erosion, developers clear subdivisions of plants that would have stabilized the topsoil, loggers clear-cut without regard to slope, and farmers plow off contour. All of these practices lead to soil erosion and concentration of silt in streams, where it settles on living things. Silt is particularly deadly to attached and slow-moving organisms, such as aquatic plants, snails, insect larvae, and fish eggs, because it interferes with their ability to exchange gas.

A further consequence of the lack of land-use planning is the loss of biotic diversity due to haphazard forest fragmentation. We ignore the contributions of reserve size, shape, and spacing to maintaining a full set of plant and animal species.

Why do governments in Appalachia lack, even resist, efforts to regulate land use? Both resident and absentee landowners seem to play roles. Highlanders are independent and skeptical of authority. A bureaucrat from the county seat telling a mountaineer what to do with his land has never "set" well. Absentee landowners also have a vested interest in resisting land-use planning. Absentee landowners own 72 percent of West Virginia, and they thwart planning through political routes. In order to institute land-use planning, both types of landowners must realize the greater potential income from planned economic development versus totally unregulated land uses. Communities that passively allow aimless land-use changes attract fly-by-night developers and toxic waste dumps.

The Appalachian Mountains, steep and covered by thin soil, cry for controls of land development based on sound ecological principles. Without a comprehensive land-use policy, visitors will reject Appalachia; its people will continue to wither on the vine.

Highlanders have been slow to adopt Leopold's land ethic. The idea that God created these hills for us to use as we see fit is deeply ingrained. In my opinion, education is part of the answer. Highlanders will be more willing to change their ways when they learn that their hills are the basis of a sustainable paycheck. Scattered throughout the hills lies the blueprint: a landowner charges hunters and anglers to recreate on his land; a couple hosts tourists in a restored bed-and-breakfast; a mechanic nurtures ten acres of Christmas trees. All depend on a healthy environment. Preservation through appreciation will not be quick or cheap, though. In many regions, it will take nothing less than a fundamental revolution of priorities.

Acid deposition, a pervasive, insidious poison produced elsewhere and imported by rain, snow, fog, sleet, and hail, is another major environmental problem. Acid deposition is a contemporary example of the principle Garrett Hardin articulated in his classical essay, "Tragedy of the Commons." Hardin revealed how resources that support all of our lives, such as air, space, and water, are endangered by a few selfish individuals. Now, a little background.

A liquid's acidity depends on its concentration of hydrogen atoms with a positive electrical charge. Acidity, measured on the pH scale, ranges from 0, the most acidic, to 14, the most alkaline; a liquid with a pH of 7 is neutral. Your stomach juices have a pH of 2, tomato juice is 4, milk is 7, ammonia is 11, and lye is 13. As a logarithmic scale, one unit of change in pH represents a ten-fold difference in the amount of acid. A liquid with pH of 5 is one hundred times more acidic than a neutral solution.

Unpolluted rain has a pH of 5.6. The modest acidity of natural rain has three sources. First, carbonic acid forms when carbon dioxide in the atmosphere dissolves in water vapor. Second, volcanoes, geysers, and decomposing organic matter release sulphur oxides, which change to sulphuric acid in rain water. And third, electrical storms spark the formation of nitric acid in rain.

Highly acidic rain, though, is human-caused. Westerlies import sulphur-rich emissions from the major industries of the Midwest. The winds strike Appalachia, then force air upward, where it cools. The condensate falls to the ground, cleaning the air of sulphur—but becoming sulphuric acid in the process.

The concentrations of charged hydrogen atoms, sulphate, and nitrate in the precipitation of eastern North America have increased with our rising consumption of fossil fuels. Tall smoke stacks eject their effluent high into the air, enabling the long range transport of acidic gases. In general, sulphur and nitrogen compounds are responsible for two-thirds and one-third, respectively, of the acid deposition. The area suffering from the greatest acid deposition (pH less than 4.2) is a broad oval reaching southwest from New York and New Jersey to Tennessee and Ohio. Somewhat less affected (pH less than 5.0) are the other eastern states and southeast Canada.

In Greenland, ice caps contain thousands of years worth of frozen precipitation. When the pH of this standard is compared to that of contemporary rain in the eastern United States, ours is at least 30 times more acidic. The extensive impacts of acid rain and snow, however, did not exist prior to World War II.

Two natural elements—the forest canopy and the buffering capacity of rocks and soil—partially neutralize the human-caused acid in precipitation. In New Hampshire, where the average pH of precipitation is 4.1, the rain falling through the northern hardwood canopies, liquid known as throughfall, is less acidic than the direct precipitation. Neutralization of throughfall seems to be caused by the removal of hydrogen ions by deciduous foliage and the leaching of neutralizing bases from the canopy. Limestone buffers surface waters, imparting resistance to pH change because it dissolves easily and neutralizes acid. Hard, resistant bedrocks such as basalt and granite provide little buffering potential.

Softwater lakes, which formed in areas with hard rocks such as sandstone, contain few buffers, so their pH changes rapidly when subjected to acidic precipitation. The young glacial soils of New England are naturally acidic and lack lime. Consequently, they only slightly neutralize acid deposition and allow nutrients to leach from these already poor soils. The Adirondacks are characterized by soils with little neutralizing capacity and acidified lakes. In contrast, even though they also receive acid precipitation, the Great Lakes are not acidifying because the surrounding soils buffer them well. Thus, in many areas acid deposition overwhelms the soil's neutralizing powers.

Acid rain leaches potassium, sugars, proteins, and amino acids from tree leaves. Severely acidic rains damage the waxy coverings of leaves, which then desiccate and become susceptible to attack by fungi and bacteria. Conifers are more susceptible to damage from acid deposition than are deciduous trees because their needles remain exposed year-round, and because fogs that sweep through their high-elevation habitats are often more acidic than rain at lower elevations. In conifers initial symptoms include the loss of needles in the crown, and then over the course of several years the disease progresses downward through lower branches. Twenty years ago, dense healthy evergreen forests grew on Camels Hump in the Green Mountains of Vermont. Today, 50 percent of the red spruces are dead and firs look sick. Skeletons loom everywhere. Commercially important sugar maples are dying, too. Dead and crown-damaged trees commonly mar the White Mountains of New Hampshire, the central Appalachians of West Virginia, and the Great Smoky Mountains of Tennessee and North Carolina.

Compared to a pH-neutral solution, acidic precipitation dissolves higher quantities of aluminum, nickel, cadmium, manganese, zinc, lead, and copper from soils. Most of these metals are toxic at relatively low concentrations. The synergism between acid and heavy metals is lethal to a wide variety of living things. After acid deposition intensified, roughly about 1950, the concentration of aluminum increased dramatically in the annual rings of trees. Inorganic aluminum, present in the soil, is insoluble at a pH of 5.6 but quite soluble at 4.6. Plant roots absorb soluble aluminum, which hinders water uptake. Eventually, leaves turn brown and drop off, and the tree dies.

Acid also harms aquatic organisms. Below a pH of 6, fish experience various forms of reproductive failure, forcing the population to dwindle to a few, old, large individuals. Below a pH of 5, the fish community shifts to a few resistant species, for example, from a fishery offering brook trout and small mouth bass to one dominated by rock bass and yellow perch.

Most amphibians breed in the spring, when streams and puddles receive the largest input of acid from snowmelt—a winter's worth of stored pollutants. Such acid shock can wipe out an entire generation of an amphibian species. Because the winters of central and southern Appalachia characteristically alternate between freezing and thawing, the most severe springtime acid shock hits northern Appalachia. The spotted salamander, which breeds in temporary pools formed by snow-melt, illustrates the effects of acid shock: egg mortality is less than 1 percent if the pH is neutral, but greater than 60 percent in springtime pools with a pH of up to 6.0.

Slowly, inexorably, Appalachia is being sterilized by this insidious cancer. What can we do about it? It might be possible to develop a strain of acid-tolerant fish. Also, adding limestone to lakes and streams works temporarily. But these measures treat only symptoms. Because the effects of acid rain are subtle and partially hidden, it has been difficult to assess their environmental significance. Focusing research solely on acid deposition has been unrealistic because synergistic effects are involved. Thus, some scientists have been unwilling to make a firm statement about the cause and effects of acid deposition.

Recent studies that combine analytical chemistry and meteorology have located the major polluters in the north-central states between the Allegheny Mountains and the Mississippi River. Within this region, municipal power plants are the major source of sulphur dioxide. From source to deposition, pollutants travel an average distance of 300 to 700 miles. We can even recognize the chemical signatures of regional polluters by the proportions of elements such as arsenic, antimony, selenium, and zinc in their effluent. For example, eastern utilities that burn heavy residual oil (what is left after the removal of other distillates) produce an aerosol that is distinct from that of inland coal burners. When air flows eastward, a midwestern aerosol becomes superimposed on eastern pollution.

In essence, acid precipitation is a subtle ecological change visited by humans on our Appalachian ecosystems. In the environment, it is difficult to perform controlled experiments to test acid rain's effects because of confounding variables. Because it is an interstate and international problem involving large industries, huge financial issues are at stake. The combination of scientific ambiguity and money interests account for the incomplete action by government officials. In Europe, even though Scandinavian scientists concluded that acid rain from industrial Britain and western Europe was killing lakes, British government officials did not accept it. The Europeans' stance of denial is analogous to current foot-dragging by American officials. Our government's position that we need more scientific information before we can make correct decisions is simply an excuse for doing nothing.

Exotic species, those recent arrivals from other areas, make up Appalachia's third major environmental problem. Exotic species destroy native organisms via herbivory, predation, competition, parasitism, or by being pathogens. A native species can be wiped out by a newcomer in a few years. Human-assisted immigrants include several honeysuckle species, kudzu, tree of heaven, English sparrow, pigs, and cats.

The American chestnut originally thrived throughout the Appalachian Mountains from southern Vermont and New Hampshire southward into northern Georgia. Attaining a height of 130 feet, and occupying up to 60 percent of the canopy, American chestnut reached its largest size and greatest concentration in the Great Smoky Mountains. By 1925, an introduced blight had reached all parts of Appalachia. Chestnut blight did not eliminate the American chestnut from the forest, but it removed it from the canopy. Chestnuts continue to sprout today because the fungus did not kill the roots, but the blight kills the saplings before long.

The gypsy moth, an exotic species, is currently wreaking huge damage on Appalachian forests. In 1868, Professor Leopold Trouvelot of Medford, Massachusetts, imported several gypsy moth egg masses from southern France. He wanted to produce a better silkworm by cross-breeding gypsy and silk-worm moths. When a specimen jar fell from his window, a few moths escaped. Since then, this exotic has expanded its range an average of nine miles per year, in large part because North America does not have the natural enemies that keep the moth in check throughout Europe. It arrived in West Virginia in 1972. By an unsettling quirk of fate, as I was researching this essay, I found the first gypsy moth egg mass along Pine Cabin Run, on the trunk of a black walnut tree. The moth's current range includes all of the New England states, west to Michigan, and the pest continues to spread southward through West Virginia and west to Ohio. This picture will be out of date by the time you read this—most authorities see nothing to stop the moth's spread across the continent.

Gypsy moth caterpillars have strong food preferences. They readily eat oak leaves; white oaks suffer more than red oak species. They also like to eat apple, basswood, willow, and birch. The moths will attack, though not favor, American beech, black cherry, black gum, eastern hemlock, hickories, hornbeam, maples, pines, sassafras, and spruces. Larvae must be starving before they will defoliate the following tree species: eastern red cedar, flowering dogwood, mountain laurel, black locust, persimmon, sycamore, tulip poplar, and black walnut.

When half or more of its leaves are eaten, a hardwood tree will produce a whole new set of leaves by midsummer. This extra outlay decreases the tree's food reserves, weakens it, and leaves it more susceptible to drought, fungi, insects, and the stresses of winter. For one or two years following defoliation, the tree refoliates with small, off-color leaves, and twigs and branches die back. One heavy defoliation can cause subtle reductions in a tree's health that are detectable for a decade. Weakened trees are attacked and killed by shoestring fungus and the two-lined chestnut borer. A single defoliation kills some softwoods, while hardwoods die after two or more defoliations. In general, the effects of gypsy moth defoliation depend on the amount of foliage removed and the number of consecutive defoliations.

The gypsy moth's life cycle is supremely suited for converting broad leaves into caterpillar tissue. Mercifully, there is only one gypsy moth generation per year. The moths overwinter in eggs amassed on stones, walls, and logs. Eggs hatch in late April and early May. Larvae leave their egg mass and climb the tree, trailing silk threads. Reaching the top, they arch their body, drop on silken threads, and then are tugged loose by slight gusts of wind. The silk strand and the caterpillar's long hairs contribute to buoyancy. After several ballooning episodes, they start feeding. Although most settle near the tree on which they hatched, some catch updrafts and float high above the canopy for tens or even hundreds of miles. Young caterpillars feed and rest during the day. Older individuals climb the tree at dusk, feed only at night, and descend at dawn to rest in protected sites. Larvae use silken threads to return to resting sites, such as wounds and gaps under bark.

Caterpillars mature when they are 1.5 to 2.5 inches long. They enter the cocoon stage in June or early July. Adult moths emerge in 10 to 14 days and lay eggs from July through September. Adult gypsy moths do not eat.

Gypsy moth invasions proceed through a predictable sequence. After the initial defoliation, the severity and duration of each suc-ceeding outbreak decline. Stable or growing moth populations produce few and large egg masses—1.5 inches long with 700 to 1,000 eggs. In contrast, many small egg masses—0.5 inch long, 75 to 100 eggs— indicate a declining infestation.

Stretching for the positive, there are two possible consolations balanc-ing the acute disgust of living through a gypsy moth invasion. First, where oaks cover 60 percent of the commercial forest, as in some parts of West Virginia, repeated outbreaks may reduce the proportion of oak. This would yield tree stands of greater species diversity and resistance. Reducing the proportion of oaks, the moth's preferred food, to 15 to 25 percent of the dominant trees would give the pest less start-up momentum towards an outbreak. After the original oak-chestnut forest recovered from chestnut blight, it became the more diverse oak-hickory forest. Post-gypsy moth, we may live in an even more diverse ash-tulip poplar forest. The second potential benefit of defoliation is that it speeds nutrient cycling through larval feces and thereby increases ecosystem production.

Scientists are studying several strategies, including parasites, sex attractants, and genetic defenses of trees, to control gypsy moth popu-lations during non-outbreak periods. Further, some native ground beetles, 38 species of birds (including the black-capped chickadee and yellow-billed cuckoo), and several mammals, such as shrews and squir-rels, are significant predators. So there is plenty of hope for peace after the initial invasion has waned.

In "Field Days," essayist Roger Swain expressed his desire to get along with gypsy moths, and that sooner or later biological controls will rein them in. This is fine if you are managing a forest for perpetuity, but if you are suffering through the few years of peak populations, or if your livelihood in recreation or forestry depends on healthy trees, you would be justified in cursing the things.

I have chosen to illustrate the effects of exotic species by focusing on the gypsy moth, probably because it just recently began imposing itself along Pine Cabin Run. Other imports are also changing Appalachian ecosystems. Multiflora rose, locust leaf miner, pine sawfly, rainbow trout, and European starling are recasting the Appalachian play right before our very eyes. And there's precious little we can do about it.

In this epilogue, I have considered four environmental problems facing contemporary Appalachia: forest fragmentation, lack of land-use planning, acid deposition, and exotic species—all forces that are changing our highlands forever. For the sake of Appalachia's children, including my daughter Leah, I counsel a balanced commitment to managing them all.

We have witnessed together this vast Appalachian play. From the opening act of tectonic collisions hundreds of millions of years ago, through the broad scenes of forest origins and narrow vignettes of small bugs' sex lives, we have been delivered into today's environmental issues. I cannot rest knowing the joys of Appalachia may not last. The biggest things must start with a first small step. If this book helps in some small way to preserve Appalachia, possibly by fostering a deeper appreciation, then I'll be satisfied when I'm old in my rocking chair.

You are entitled to ask me what I have done, other than write a book, to help the Appalachian cause. I have committed the profit from the sales of this book to protecting local Appalachian ecosystems, especially several rivers in eastern West Virginia. My turn: What are you doing to assure continuity of the evolutionary play in Appalachia? "If I had only . . ." is one of life's great tragedies. I challenge you to take that first constructive step. To the extent that we rise above good intentions and do the work, the evolutionary play in Appalachia will continue.

Common and Scientific
Names of Plants and Animals

Plants

alder - *Alnus* (birch family, Betulaceae)
alpine azalea - *Loiseleuria procumbens* (heath family, Ericaceae)
alpine bearberry - *Arctostaphylos alpina* (Ericaceae)
American basswood - *Tilia americana* (basswood family, Tiliaceae)
American beech - *Fagus grandifolia* (beech family, Fagaceae)
American chestnut - *Castanea dentata* (Fagaceae)
American hornbeam - *Carpinus caroliniana* (Betulaceae)
apple - *Malus* (rose family, Rosaceae)
balsam fir - *Abies balsamea* (pine family, Pinaceae)
balsam poplar - *Populus balsamifera* (willow family, Salicaceae)
bigtooth aspen - *Populus grandidentata* (Salicaceae)
black cherry - *Prunus serotina* (Rosaceae)
black locust - *Robinia pseudoacacia* (legume family, Leguminosae)
black oak - *Quercus velutina* (Fagaceae)
black walnut - *Juglans nigra* (walnut family, Juglandaceae)
black willow - *Salix nigra* (Salicaceae)
black tupelo - *Nyssa sylvatica* (dogwood family, Cornaceae)
bloodroot - *Sanguinaria canadensis* (poppy family, Papaveraceae)
blueberry - *Vaccinium* (Ericaceae)
boxelder - *Acer negundo* (maple family, Aceraceae)
bracken fern - *Pteridium aquilinum* (true fern family, Polypodiaceae)
bunchberry - *Cornus canadensis* (Cornaceae)
Carolina hemlock - *Tsuga caroliniana* (Pinaceae)
Carolina silverbell - *Halesia carolina* (snowbell family, Styracaceae)
chestnut blight - *Endothia parasitica* (fungi: class Ascomycetes)
chestnut oak - *Quercus prinus* (Fagaceae)
coltsfoot - *Tussilago farfara* (sunflower family, Asteraceae)
common persimmon - *Diospyros virginiana* (ebony family, Ebanaceae)
crested dwarf iris - *Iris cristata* (iris family, Iridaceae)
devil's walkingstick - *Aralia spinosa* (ginseng family, Araliaceae)
downy rattlesnake plaintain - *Goodyera pubescens* (orchid family, Orchidaceae)
downy serviceberry - *Amelanchier arborea* (Rosaceae)
dutchman's breeches - *Dicentra cucullaria* (Papaveraceae)
eastern hemlock - *Tsuga canadensis* (Pinaceae)
eastern redbud - *Cercis canadensis* (Leguminosae)

European white birch - *Betula pendula* (Betulaceae)
eastern red cedar - *Juniperus virginiana* (juniper family, Cupressaceae)
Fraser fir - *Abies fraseri* (Pinaceae)
fringetree - *Chionanthus virginicus* (olive family, Oleaceae)
flowering dogwood - *Cornus florida* (Cornaceae)
fire pink - *Silene virginica* (pink family, Caryophyllaceae)
ginseng - *Panax quinquefolium* (Araliaceae)
huckleberry - *Gaylussacia* (Ericaceae)
hickory - *Carya* (walnut family, Juglandaceae)
holly - *Ilex* (holly family, Aquifoliaceae)
hepatica - *Hepatica* (buttercup family, Ranunculaceae)
jack-in-the-pulpit - *Arisaema triphyllum* (arum family, Araceae)
Japanese honeysuckle - *Lonicera japonica* (honeysuckle family, Caprifoliaceae)
Japanese jack-in-the-pulpit - *Arisaema japonica* (Araceae)
Japanese lady's slipper - *Cypripedium japonicum* (Orchidaceae)
jack pine - *Pinus banksiana* (Pinaceae)
kudzu - *Pueraria lobata* (pea family, Fabaceae)
Kentucky coffee-tree - *Gymnocladus dioicus* (Leguminosae)
lady's slipper - *Cypripedium* (Orchidaceae)
maple - *Acer* (Aceraceae)
milkweed - *Asclepias* (milkweed family, Asclepiadaceae)
mountain azalea - *Rhododendron canescens* (Ericaceae)
mountain heath - *Phyllodoce caerulea* (Ericaceae)
mountain laurel - *Kalmia latifolia* (Ericaceae)
mountain oat grass - *Danthonia compressa* (grass family, Gramineae)
nodding ladies tresses - *Spiranthes cernua* (Orchidaceae)
paper birch - *Betula papyrifera* (Betulaceae)
paw paw - *Asimina triloba* (annona family, Annonaceae)
persimmon - *Diospyros* (Ebenaceae)
pignut hickory - *Carya glabra* (Juglandaceae)
pink lady's slipper - *Cypripedium acaule* (Orchidaceae)
quaking aspen - *Populus tremuloides* (Salicaceae)
red oak - *Quercus rubra* (Fagaceae)
red pine - *Pinus resinosa* (Pinaceae)
red spruce - *Picea rubens* (Pinaceae)
red top - *Solidago* (composite family, Compositae)
rhododendron - *Rhododendron* (Ericaceae)
sassafras - *Sassafras albidum* (laurel family, Lauraceae)
scarlet oak - *Quercus coccinea* (Fagaceae)
shagbark hickory - *Carya ovata* (Juglandaceae)
showy lady's slipper - *Cypripedium reginae* (Orchidaceae)

showy orchis - *Orchis spectabile* (Orchidaceae)
silverbell - *Halesia* (Styracaceae)
skunk cabbage - *Symplocarpus foetidus* (Araceae)
snowbells - *Styrax* (Styracaceae)
spring beauty - *Claytonia virginica* (purslane family, Portulacaceae)
squirrel corn - *Dicentra canadensis* (fumitory family, Fumariaceae)
star chickweed - *Stellaria pubera* (Caryophyllaceae)
stewartia - *Stewartia* (tea family, Theaceae)
striped maple - *Acer pensylvanicum* (Aceraceae)
sugar maple - *Acer saccharum* (Aceraceae)
sumac - *Rhus* (cashew family, Anacardiaceae)
sweet gum - *Liquidambar styraciflua* (witch-hazel family, Hamamelidaceae)
sweetleaf - *Symplocos* (sweetleaf family, Symplocaceae)
Table Mountain pine - *Pinus pungens* (Pinaceae)
tree-of-heaven - *Ailanthus altissima* (quassia family, Simaroubaceae)
trillium - *Trillium* (lily family, Liliaceae)
tulip poplar - *Liriodendron tulipifera* (magnolia family, Magnoliaceae)
violets - *Viola* (violet family, Violaceae)
white ash - *Fraxinus americana* (Oleaceae)
white oak - *Quercus alba* (Fagaceae)
white pine - *Pinus strobus* (Pinaceae)
witch-hazel - *Hamamelis virginiana* (Hamamelidaceae)
wild columbine - *Aquilegia canadensis* (Ranunculaceae)
yellow birch - *Betula alleghaniensis* (Betulaceae)
yellow lady's slipper - *Cypripedium calceolus* (Orchidaceae)
yellowwood - *Cladrastis kentukea* (Leguminosae)

Animals
Allegheny mountain salamander - *Desmognathus ochrophaeus* (lungless
    salamander family, Plethodontidae)
American goldfinch - *Carduelis tristis* (finch family, Fringillidae)
American redstart - *Setophaga ruticilla* (wood warbler family, Parulidae)
autumnal moth - *Epirrita autumnata* (measuring worm family, Geometridae)
belted kingfisher - *Megaceryle alcyon* (kingfisher family, Alcedinidae)
black bear - *Ursus americanus* (bear family, Ursidae)
blackbanded darter - *Percina nigrofasciata* (perch family, Percidae)
black-capped chickadee - *Parus atricapillus* (titmouse family, Paridae)
blacknose dace - *Rhinichthys atratulus* (minnow family, Cyprinidae)
black-tipped hangingfly - *Hylobittacus apicalis* (bittacid scorpionfly
    family, Bittacidae)
blue jay - *Cyanocitta cristata* (crow family, Corvidae)

211

box turtle - *Terrapene carolina* (turtle family, Testudinidae)
brook trout - *Salvelinus fontinalis* (trout family, Salmonidae)
brown creeper - *Certhia familiaris* (creeper family, Certhiidae)
brown trout - *Salmo trutta* (Salmonidae)
canary - *Serinus canarius*
cardinal - *Cardinalis cardinalis* (Fringillidae)
Carolina parakeet - *Conuropsis carolinensis* (parrot family, Psittacidae)
Cheat Mountain salamander - *Plethodon nettingi* (Plethodontidae)
cheetah - *Acinonyx jubatus* (cat family, Felidae)
Clark's nutcracker - *Nucifraga columbiana* (Corvidae)
copperhead - *Agkistrodon contortrix* (pit viper family, Viperidae)
cottonmouth - *Agkistrodon piscivorus* (Viperidae)
creek chub - *Semotilus atromaculatus* (Cyprinidae)
crow - *Corvus brachyrhynchos* (Corvidae)
downy woodpecker - *Picoides pubescens* (woodpecker family, Picidae)
dusky salamander - *Desmognathus fuscus* (Plethodontidae)
eastern phoebe - *Sayornis phoebe* (tyrant flycatcher family, Tyrannidae)
eastern tent caterpillar - *Malacosoma americanum* (tent caterpillar
    family, Lasiocampidae)
eastern timber rattlesnake - *Crotalus horridus* (Viperidae)
eastern wood peewee - *Contopus virens* (Tyrannidae)
elk - *Cervus elaphus* (deer family, Cervidae), extinct in Appalachia
English sparrow - *Passer domesticus* (weaver finch family, Ploceidae)
European starling - *Sturnus vulgaris* (starling family, Sturnidae)
evening grosbeak - *Hesperiphona vespertina* (Fringillidae)
fantail darter - *Etheostoma flabellare* (Percidae)
field sparrow - *Spizella pusilla* (Fringillidae)
fox squirrel - *Sciurus niger* (squirrel family, Sciuridae)
golden eagle - *Aquila chrysaetos* (hawk family, Accipitridae)
grackle - *Quiscalus* (blackbird family, Icteridae)
gray squirrel - *Sciurus carolinensis* (Sciuridae)
gray treefrog - *Hyla versicolor* (treefrog family, Hylidae)
great tit - *Parus major* (Paridae)
great crested flycatcher - *Myiarchus crinitus* (Tyrannidae)
green heron - *Butorides striatus* (heron family, Ardeidae)
groundhog - *Marmota marmox* (Sciuridae)
gulf darter - *Etheostoma swaini* (Percidae)
gypsy moth - *Lymantria dispar* (tussock moth family, Liparidae)
hairy woodpecker - *Picoides villosus* (Picidae)
Hoffman's salamander - *Plethodon hoffmani* (Plethodontidae)
horseshoe crab - *Limulus polyphemus* (subphylum Chelicerata: Class Merostomata)

imitator salamander - *Desmognathus imitator* (Plethodontidae)
indigo bunting - *Passerina cyanea* (Fringillidae)
Iowa darter - *Etheostoma exile* (Percidae)
ivory-billed woodpecker - *Campephilus principalis* (Picidae)
johnny darter - *Etheostoma nigrum* (Percidae)
Jordan's salamander - *Plethodon jordani* (Plethodontidae)
least flycatcher - *Empidonax minimus* (Tyrannidae)
leopard frog - *Rana pipiens* (true frog family, Ranidae)
mink frog - *Rana septentrionalis* (Ranidae)
monarch butterfly - *Danaus plexippus* (milkweed butterfly family, Danaidae)
mottled sculpin - *Cottus bairdi* (sculpin family, Cottidae)
mountain lion - *Felis concolor* (cat family, Felidae)
mourning cloak butterfly - *Nymphalis antiopa* (brush-footed butterfly family, Nymphalidae)
mud salamander - *Pseudotriton montanus* (Plethodontidae)
naked sand darter - *Ammocrypta beani* (Percidae)
northern junco - *Junco hyemalis* (Fringillidae)
orangebelly darter - *Etheostoma radiosum* (Percidae)
orangethroat darter - *Etheostoma spectabile* (Percidae)
ovenbird - *Seiurus aurocapillus* (Parulidae)
Peaks of Otter salamander - *Plethodon hubrichti* (Plethodontidae)
Philadelphia vireo - *Vireo philadelphicus* (vireo family, Vireonidae)
purple finch - *Carpodacus purpureus* (Fringillidae)
raccoon - *Procyon lotor* (raccoon family, Procyonidae)
rainbow trout - *Salmo gairdneri* (Salmonidae)
ravine salamander - *Plethodon richmondi* (Plethodontidae)
red-backed salamander - *Plethodon cinereus* (Plethodontidae)
red-bellied woodpecker - *Melanerpes carolinus* (Picidae)
red-eyed vireo - *Vireo olivaceus* (Vireonidae)
red-headed woodpecker - *Melanerpes erythrocephalus* (Picidae)
red salamander - *Pseudotriton ruber* (Plethodontidae)
red-spotted newt - *Notophthalmus viridescens* (newt family, Salamandridae)
red squirrel - *Tamiasciurus* (Sciuridae)
rufous-sided towhee - *Pipilo erythrophthalmus* (Fringillidae)
sharp-shinned hawk - *Accipiter striatus* (Accipitridae)
Shenandoah salamander - *Plethodon shenandoah* (Plethodontidae)
slimy salamander - *Plethodon glutinosus* (Plethodontidae)
spotted darter - *Etheostoma maculatum* (Percidae)
spring peeper - *Hyla crucifer* (Hylidae)
spring salamander - *Gyrinophilus porphoryticus* (Plethodontidae)
stripetail darter - *Etheostoma kennicotti* (Percidae)

summer tanager - *Piranga rubra* (tanager family, Thraupidae)
tessellated darter - *Etheostoma olmstedi* (Percidae)
tufted titmouse - *Parus bicolor* (Paridae)
two-lined salamander - *Eurycea bislineata* (Plethodontidae)
walleye - *Stizostedion vitreum* (Percidae)
white-breasted nuthatch - *Sitta carolinensis* (nuthatch family, Sittidae)
white-tailed deer - *Odocoileus virginianus* (Cervidae)
white-throated sparrow - *Zonotrichia albicollis* (Fringillidae)
wild turkey - *Meleagris gallopavo* (turkey family, Meleagrididae)
wolf - *Canis lupus* (dog family, Canidae)
wood frog - *Rana sylvatica* (Ranidae)
wood thrush - *Hylocichla mustelina* (thrush family, Turdidae)
woodland buffalo - *Bison bison* (cow family, Bovidae), extinct in Appalachia
worm-eating warbler - *Helmitheros vermirorus* (Parulidae)
yellow-eyed junco - *Junco phaeonotus* (Fringillidae)
zigzag salamander - *Plethodon dorsalis* (Plethodontidae)

Glossary

abdominal stove. Informal phrase for the central mass of an animal's torso that generates and retains heat.

abrasive breeding. Spawning in which a female fish is stimulated to release eggs by a male rubbing against her.

abscission layer. Zone of cells at the base of a leaf's petiole that are only weakly attached to one another and whose function is to jettison the leaf.

acid deposition. The falling of human-produced acid from the atmosphere via all forms of precipitation.

adaptation. A trait that contributes to the reproductive success of an individual organism.

adaptive radiation. The evolutionary process by which a variety of species arise from an ancestral one.

adhesion. Attraction between molecules in contact.

adipose tissue. Connective tissue in which cells store fat droplets.

aggregate. Rock composed of fragments of several kinds of rock.

aggressive mimicry. Imitating a different animal, such as another's prey or mate, to lure prey within reach.

alarm call. Sound produced by one animal that causes others to behave defensively.

alarm signal system. The warning and defensive reaction among fish, consisting of skin alarm cells, alarm substance, and alarm reaction.

allele. Alternate form of a gene; for example, alleles for brown versus blue eyes.

allopatric speciation. Evolutionary formation of new species from geographically separated populations.

altruism. Behavior that benefits the reproductive success of others; selfless behavior.

amino acid. Nitrogen-containing organic molecules from which protein molecules are built.

amphipod. A form of crustacean commonly called sand flea.

amplexus. The grasping of a female amphibian by a male with his forelimbs during mating.

anadromous. Fish that ascend rivers from the sea for breeding.

anchor ice. Ice formed on the bottom of a stream.

anther. Part of a flower that contains pollen and is usually borne on a stalk.

anthocyanin. Blue, purple, or red pigment in plants.

anticline. An arch of stratified rock in which layers bend downward in opposite directions from the crest.

antifreeze. A dissolved substance that lowers the freezing point of a liquid.

Appalachian Plateau. Westernmost physiographic province of the Appalachian Mountains, located west of the Allegheny Front, characterized by mild deformation.

Araceae. Family of perennial herbs with tuberous roots and a pungent cell sap.

arum. Common name for plants in the family Araceae.

asexual reproduction. Producing young without the union of sperm and egg.

assemblage. The collection of species in a given area.

asthenosphere. Part of the mantle below the lithosphere.

auxin. Plant hormone that causes cell elongation, among other effects.

bald. A naturally treeless area surrounded by forest.

Baltica. A continent that may have collided with Laurentia during the Paleozoic to produce the Acadian orogeny.

Batesian mimicry. Resemblance of an edible species (mimic) to a distasteful one (model) to deceive predators.

Beau Geste hypothesis. An idea that male birds display large repertoires to appear to be many singing males.

Beringia. The strait of land connecting Siberia and Alaska during the last glacial stage.

biogeography. The study of geographic distributions of living things.

biological diversity. The number of different kinds of living things and their genetic variations.

bioluminescence. Production of light by a living thing.

biomass. The amount of living matter, measured by weight or volume.

biosphere reserve. An area that preserves all the functions of a natural ecosystem.

bole. The large central trunk of a tree.

boreal forest. The spruce-fir zone stretching across Canada.

Brevard Zone. The suture formed by the collison of the European and North American plates. The Brevard zone is a long fault trending northeast-southwest through Brevard, North Carolina, and connecting Atlanta, Asheville, and Roanoke.

buffer. A dissolved substance that neutralizes acid and thereby contributes to maintaining the original pH of a solution.

Cambrian Period. Part of the Paleozoic Era, 590 to 505 million years ago.

canopy. The nearly continuous layer of leaves along the top of a forest.

canopy gap. A break in the canopy, commonly due to one or more trees falling.

carapace. Dorsal part of a turtle's shell.

Carboniferous Period. Part of the Paleozoic Era, 360 to 286 million years ago.

carrying capacity. The number of individuals than can be supported by a given area.

catastrophe. Sudden overwhelming stress to living things due to physical forces such as freezing, wind, fire.

Cenozoic Era. Part of earth's history between 65 to 1.8 million years ago.

chance pollination. Fertilization in plants where pollen is delivered by inefficient, or risky, means.

character displacement. Divergence in the traits of two similar species where their ranges overlap, presumably caused by natural selection to avoid competition.

chlorophyll. Green pigment in plants that captures the energy of sunlight.

chromosome. Long thin structure in the cell nucleus that contains DNA and bears genes.

climax. The end of succession; an ecological community that has reached a steady state.

cloaca. The opening in some vertebrates to the outside environment of the digestive, excretory, and reproductive systems.

clone. Identical, asexually produced offspring.

closed winter. A cold season in which the ground remains frozen .

club cell. Specialized cell in the skin of some fishes that stores and releases alarm substance.

Coastal Plain. A low, flat, sediment-rich physiographic province between the Atlantic Ocean and Piedmont.

codominant species. Two or more species that equally influence what other species live in the community.

coevolution. The evolution of adaptations in two or more species by mutual interactions of these traits.

cohesion. Attraction among elemental particles.

collembola. Type of insect commonly called springtail.

community. A set of species identified by the place they live or the nature of their association.

competitive exclusion. A hypothesis that two or more species cannot coexist indefinitely on a scarce resource.

congenital defect. Bodily imperfection acquired during development.

conglomerate. Rock composed of round fragments held together within a cementlike matrix.

conservation ethic. Philosophy that humans should live with nature, not try to conquer it.

convection. Transfer of heat by movement of a fluid with nonuniform temperatures; for example, rising hot air.

convergent evolution. Evolutionary change leading to increasing similarity.

core. Central mass of an endothermic animal's body.

corm. Thick underground stem of a plant.

cortex. Outer layer.

cost-benefit analysis. Evaluating alternative actions by comparing their ratios of costs and benefits.

Cottidae. Fish family that includes sculpins.

counteradaptation. Traits of two or more species selected because of their mutual antagonism, especially in the context of competition or predation between species.

countershading. An animal's coloring in which the belly side is lighter than the upward side, presumably for camouflage.

cove. Bowl-shaped valley of central and southern Appalachia that typically supports many plant species.

Cretaceous Period. Part of the Mesozoic Era between 144 and 65 million years ago.

Crotalidae. Family of snakes that includes pit vipers.

crown shyness gap. Small break in the canopy caused by abrasion between neighboring limbs.

crust. Outermost layer of the earth's lithosphere, less dense than underlying mantle.

crustal plate tectonics. The study of the movements of lithospheric plates.

Cuculinae. Subfamily of birds that includes cuckoos.

cruising behavior. Movement by male darters searching for females among a series of nest rocks.

crystallization. Process by which a liquid changes into a solid.

Cumberland Valley. Name of northern part of Great Valley.

Cyprinidae. The fish family that includes minnows.

cytoplasm. The jelly-like substance inside a cell.

darter. Common name for some bottom-dwelling species of the fish family Percidae.

dawn chorus. The collective singing by male birds in early morning.

decibel. Unit for measuring the loudness of sound.

deciduous. Having leaves that are shed in autumn.

degree-day. Unit for measuring cumulative heat.

dendritic drainage. Pattern of watercourses characterized by randomly branching tributaries.

detritivore. Animal that eats detritus.

detritus. Loose organic material resulting from breakdown of plant or animal bodies.

Devonian Period. Part of the Paleozoic Era, 408 to 360 million years ago.

diffusion. The random movement of particles from an area of greater concentration to an area of lesser concentration.

disjunct distribution. Geographic pattern in which related species are separated by zones lacking those organisms.

dispersal. One-way movement of organisms, typically from an area of high density.

divergence. Evolution of different traits by related organisms in unlike environments.

dominant species. Organism that influences what other species can coexist in that ecological community.

eastern deciduous forest. The vast hardwood, broad-leaved forest in eastern North America.

ecology. Study of interactions between organisms and their environment.

ecosystem. The set of living and nonliving things that interact in a given place.

ecotone. A zone of transition between distinctly different habitats.

ecotype. A genetically differentiated subpopulation restricted to a specific habitat.

effective population size. Size of a population, incorporating biased sex ratio, that would undergo the same amount of genetic drift as the actual population.

egg tooth. Short, horny point at the tip of the upper jaw of a hatchling used to puncture the egg shell.

emetic. A substance that induces vomiting.

endemic. Confined to a certain area.

endosperm. Nourishing tissue that surrounds the developing plant embryo in a seed.

energy flow. The pattern by which energy moves through an ecosystem.

environmental gradient. Regular change in the value of an environmental variable, such as temperature or humidity up a mountainside.

Eocene Epoch. Part of the Paleogene Period, 58 to 37 million years ago.

ephemeral. Lasting a short time.

epidemic. Sudden rapid spread of an organism.

epiphyte. Plant that grows on another plant.

equilibrium. State of balance between opposing forces.

Etheostoma. Largest and most diverse genus of darters.

Eurycea. A genus of lungless salamander.

evolution. Genetic change in organisms from generation to generation.

exotic block. Rock formation of distant origin.

exotic species. Organism not native to an area.

fat body. Long, slender structures in reptiles and amphibians used to store fat.

fault. Fracture in the earth's crust in which one side is displaced relative to the other.

fecundity. Rate at which an individual produces offspring.

fitness. Relative genetic contribution by an individual to the next generation.

floating male. Male animal that moves continually through his habitat because he is unable to defend a breeding territory.

flux. Rate of movement of matter or energy across a surface.

forest edge-forest interior ratio. The amount of surrounding forest edge compared to the area within a forest.

form. Depression made by a box turtle for resting.

fragmentation of habitat. Human-caused breaks in a formerly continuous ecological community.

frass. Rain of caterpillar feces.

fright reaction. Defensive behavior displayed by fish in response to alarm substance.

Gaspé Peninsula. A finger of land north of Maine in southeast Quebec.

gene. Section of a chromosome that determines a specific trait, or section of a DNA strand that codes a specific protein molecule.

gene frequency. The proportion of a particular allele in the gene pool of a population.

genetic drift. Random change in gene frequencies unrelated to natural selection.

genetic variability. Differences in hereditary makeup among individuals of a population.

genetics. Scientific study of heredity.

genotype. Genetic characteristics that determine the structure and function of an organism.

genus. Taxonomic category that includes closely related species; ranks between family and species.

Geometridae. Family of moths commonly called inchworms or measuringworms because their caterpillars move by looping forward.

glycerol. A sweet, syrupy alcohol that serves as an antifreeze.

glycogen. Polymer of glucose that serves as the chief storage carbohydrate in animals.

Gondwanaland. Southern half of Pangaea that broke away as a continent in the Triassic Period.

Great Valley. Long, narrow valley between the Blue Ridge and Ridge and Valley provinces of Appalachia.

greenhouse effect. Warming of earth's climate due to an increase of carbon dioxide and other pollutants in the atmosphere.

ground beetle. Common name for beetles of the family Carabidae.

ground cover. Short plants, such as grasses, ferns, and wildflowers, that form a layer on the ground in a forest.

habitat island. A patch, often on a mountaintop, of a distinct habitat type.

habitat segregation. Different species occupying different habitats, presumably because of natural selection to avoid competition.

hangingfly. Common name for some species of the insect order Mecoptera.

hard water. Water that, because of its high level of dissolved solids, can dissolve little solute.

heath. Common name for species in the plant family Ericaceae, which are shrubby, typically evergreen plants that thrive in open, poorly drained soils.

heliotropic. Plant that turns toward the sun.

hemipenis. Singular of hemipenes, the paired copulatory organs of snakes and lizards.

herb. A plant that does not develop overwintering woody tissue and therefore dies back to ground level in the autumn.

herbivore. Animal that eats plants.

hermaphrodite. An organism that has both male and female reproductive organs.

hibernaculum. Shelter occupied during winter by dormant animals.

hibernation. Passing winter in a state of depressed metabolism.

Holocene Epoch. Also known as the recent epoch, the last 11,000 years of the Neogene Period.

home range. The area over which an animal repeatedly moves in its normal activities.

homozygous. Having identical alleles at the corresponding locus of homologous chromosomes.

horizon. A layer of soil with unique, distinguishable features.

humus. Organic matter in soil.

hybrid. Offspring produced by genetically different parents.

Hylidae. Family of frogs commonly called tree frogs.

hypha. One of the threads that make up the body of a fungus.

hypothermia. Body temperature that is lower than normal.

inbreeding. Interbreeding of closely related individuals.

inbreeding depression. Low fitness caused by inbreeding.

indigenous. Species living naturally in a given area.

inducible defense. A plant's ability to limit losses to herbivores by deploying antiherbivore chemicals.

inflorescence. FLower cluster.

infrared radiation. Electromagnetic radiation beyond the visible spectrum at the red end.

injection flash. Light pulse produced by a firefly between two flashes of another individual.

in situ. In its natural place.

insularity. The degree to which a habitat patch manifests island-like features, such as small size and isolation.

insulation. Material that slows the movement of heat.

interspecific competition. Competition between individuals of different species.

interstadial. Period of temporary retreat by glacial ice.

iridium. Hard, heavy metallic element of the platinum group.

island biogeography. Branch of ecology that attempts to explain the number of species on a habitat island as an equilibrium between immigration, which is in part a function of isolation, and extinction, which is in part a function of island size.

isolate. Small isolated population, as on a habitat island.

Jurassic Period. Part of the Mesozoic Era between 213 and 144 million years ago.

kin selection. Differential reproductive success among lineages of closely related individuals because of differences in social behavior.

labellum. Middle part of an orchid's corolla.

Lampyridae. Family of insects that includes fireflies.

land-use planning. The process of deciding appropriate uses of land.

larderhoarding. Storing many food items in one place.

Laurasia. The northern supercontinent made of North America, Greenland, and Eurasia during the Mesozoic Era.

Laurasian faunal element. Animal groups that arose on Laurasia after it separated from Gondwanaland.

Laurentia. Continent made of North America, Greenland, and Scotland during the Cambrian and Ordovician periods.

Laurentide ice sheet. Large, thick sheet of glacial ice that covered northern North America during the Pleistocene Epoch.

leachate. Liquid draining from a solid mass.

leaf-out. The time in spring when leaves open.

Lepidoptera. Order of insects that includes moths and butterflies.

life history. The sequence of events in an organism's life cycle.

lipid. Type of organic molecule including fats and waxes.

lithophyte. Plant that grows on rocks.

lithosphere. A solid portion of Earth that includes the crust and part of the upper mantle.

litter. Uppermost layer of slightly decayed organic matter on the forest floor.

lungless salamander. Common name of small to medium-sized amphibian species in the family Plethodontidae.

magma. Molten rock material within the earth.

mantle. Part of earth's interior under the lithosphere and above the core.

mast. Nuts accumulated on the forest floor.

mast-yearing. The phenomenon of trees producing much mast only in occasional years.

Mecoptera. Insect order that includes hangingflies.

megafauna. A community of large-bodied mammals.

meiosis. Form of cell division that produces sperm and egg cells.

mesic. Moderately moist.

Mesozoic Era. Part of earth's history between 248 and 65 million years ago.

metamorphism. Compaction of rock by water, pressure, and heat.

microarthropod. Minute animal with exoskeleton and jointed legs, such as daphnia.

microhabitat. The specific parts of a habitat actually encountered by an individual.

microspermy. Production of huge numbers of minute seeds.

microtopography. Variation in altitude over a small area.

mid-oceanic ridge. A continuous ridge on the ocean floor where plates rift apart.

migration. Two-way, round-trip movement cued by seasonal changes.

mimicry. The evolution of an organism to look like another kind of living thing, presumably to discourage predation.

mineralized layer. Soil horizon below organic layers, composed of inorganic matter.

minnows. Common name of many fishes of the family Cyprinidae.

Miocene Epoch. Part of the Neogene Period between 24 and 5 million years ago.

mistake pollination. When a pollinating animal visits a flower that offers no reward.

mitochrondria. Organelle in which aerobic metabolism occurs.

mixed deciduous forest. General name for a large, complex vegetational unit dominated by deciduous trees.

mixed mesophytic forest. Subset of the mixed deciduous forest that develops on moist well-drained sites in unglaciated Appalachian plateaus.

mixed-species flock. Group of birds of several species.

monogamy. Situation in which each individual mates with only one of the opposite sex.

moonshine. Illegally distilled corn whiskey.

morph. A specific form.

mountain whites. Mountain-living descendants of original Appalachian homesteaders.

mountain love. Informal phrase for emotional bonding with the forested hills of Appalachia.

mutation. Change in genetic material that produces altered offspring.

Mullerian mimicry. Mutual likeness of two or more distasteful species that enhances predator rejection.

multicellular organism. Living thing made of two or more cells.

mutualism. Mutually beneficial association between members of different species.

mycorrhiza. Mutualistic association of a fungus and plant root.

natural selection. Change in the frequency of genetic traits because of differential reproduction and survival of individuals carrying those traits.

Neogene Period. Part of the Cenozoic Era between 24 and 1.6 million years ago.

neonate. Newborn animal.

neotropical migrant. Bird that breeds in North America and winters in Central or South America.

neurotoxin. Substance that is poisonous to nervous tissue.

neutral trait. Gene or trait that conveys no fitness consequences.

niche. Ecological role of a species in an environment, or the conditions within which the organism persists.

northern hardwood forest. Forest type located between the boreal and deciduous forests in a zone from Minnesota eastward to the Atlantic Coast; dominant species include sugar maple, beech, basswood, yellow birch, hemlock, and white pine.

nucleus. Organelle that controls much of the cell's activities.

nuptial gift. Food item offered by some male animals to stimulate sexual receptivity in females.

nutrient cycling. Recycling of elemental atoms, such as nitrogen and phosphorous, through an ecosystem.

oak-chestnut forest. Former forest type found in the Ridge and Valley and Blue Ridge provinces characterized by the dominance of oak species and American chestnut.

open winter. Winters that alternate between freeze and thaw.

Orchidaceae. Plant family that includes orchids; the largest plant family.

Ordovician Period. Part of the Paleozoic Era between 505 and 438 million years ago.

organelle. Structure in a cell with a specialized function.

osmosis. The diffusion of water through a selectively permeable membrane.

osmotic pressure. Force exerted by water during osmosis.

oviposition. Egglaying.

pH. A measure of acidity or alkalinity of a solution denoted as a number on a logarithmic scale running from 0 to 14 used to express the concentration of hydrogen ions, with 7 being neutral, 0 to 7 being acidic, and 7 to 14 being basic (alkaline).

Paleocene Epoch. Part of the Paleogene Period between 65 and 58 million years ago.

Paleozoic Era. Part of earth's history between 590 and 248 million years ago.

Pangaea. Supercontinent that broke apart 200 million years ago, leading to today's continents.

parallel evolution. Change in similar directions over many generations by different species.

parent stream. The stream yielding a tributary during stream capture.

parental care. Acts by an adult animal that enhance the survival of an offspring.

peck order. Form of social organization in which each individual pecks others lower in the hierarchy and is pecked by those higher.

pectoralis muscle. Chief flight muscle in breast of birds.

Percidae. Fish family that includes darters and perches.

petiole. Slender stem that supports the blade of a leaf.

phenolic. Resin made by plants, commonly containing antimicrobial properties.

Piedmont physiographic province. The gently rolling zone between the Coastal Plain and Blue Ridge provinces.

pheromone. Chemical used for communication between individuals.

photosynthesis. Process by which green plants capture the energy of sunlight to make carbohydrates.

physiognomy. External features of organisms such as size and shape.

physiographic province. Region characterized by distinct topography.

phytotoxin. Poisonous substance produced by a plant.

pioneer species. A plant or animal capable of establishing itself in a barren area and starting succession.

pit-and-mound relief. Ground topography characterized by earthen pits and mounds created by decay of fallen trees.

plastron. Ventral part of a turtle's shell.

plate. Rigid section of the lithosphere that moves over the Earth's upper mantle.

plate tectonics. Theory proposing that earth's outer shell consists of several plates that interact to produce earthquakes, volcanoes, and mountains.

Pleistocene Epoch. Part of the Quaternary Period between 1.8 million and 10,000 years ago.

Plethodon. Genus of woodland salamanders in the family Plethodontidae.

Plethodontidae. Family of lungless salamanders.

pollinator-limited. Said of plants whose fertilization rate is limited by the availability of pollinating animals.

polygyny. Mating system in which one male mates with two or more females.

polymorphism. Occurrence of several distinct forms of individuals in one population.

population. A group of individuals that interbreed, or the set of individuals of a species in a given area.

Precambrian Period. Part of earth's history 4.6 billion to 590 million years ago.

predator swamping. Sudden increase in the numbers of a prey species, presumably to overwhelm the predator's needs and insuring escape of at least some prey individuals.

proboscis. Snout, or long tubular parts of the oral region, of an invertebrate.

prokaryote. Organism whose cells contain no nucleus or other organelles.

proximate cause. Environmental cue that stimulates short-term change in an individual, as in photoperiod stimulating migration.

pseudoaposematic coloration. False warning coloration; conspicuous patterns on palatable organisms that mimic similar colors on noxious species.

Quaternary Period. Part of the Cenozoic Era between 1.6 million years ago and present.

recruitment. Process of birth and growth that adds new individuals to a population.

recruitment trail. Line of pheromone applied to a twig by one caterpillar that stimulates others to follow it, usually to fresh food.

red eft. Immature terrestrial stage of the red-spotted newt.

redd. Nest of a fish, especially trout and salmon.

reference group. Small group of people that serves as a person's psycho-social context.

refuging behavior. Clustering in a protected site.

refugium. Place where species persist during long-term climatic stress.

relict. Persistent remnant of an otherwise extinct group of organisms.

repertoire. Set of different songs vocalized by a male bird.

reproductive success. Relative to other individuals in the population, the number of offspring that reproduce.

reproductive isolation. Inability to produce fertile offspring because of genetic or morphologic incompatibilities.

resting coil. Tightly wound shape of a snake waiting for prey.

reverberation. Repeated reflection, for example, a repeating echo.

rhizome. Underground stem of a plant.

Ridge and Valley physiographic province. Region of the Appalachian Mountains characterized by long parallel ridges and intervening valleys.

rifting. Plates of earth's crust moving apart.

riparian. Terrestrial community alongside a watercourse.

root exudate. Chemicals that leach from plant roots into soil.

salamander. Moist-skinned, lizard-like amphibian.

Salmonidae. Fish family that includes trout and salmon.

satellite male. Male animal that lingers around dominant territorial ones, attempting to mate females attracted to the territory holder.

scatterhoarding. Storing a little food in many different sites.

sculpin. Common name for fish of the genus *Cottus* and family Cottidae.

secondary sex characeristics. Body traits unique to one sex that play no direct role in copulation, such as red plumage of male cardinal and beard of man.

sedge. Common name for grasslike herbs of the plant family Cyperaceae, often found in wet places.

sedimentary rock. Rock formed from fragments of other rock transported from its source, typically by water or wind, and deposited elsewhere.

seminal receptacle. Blind-ended sac in females of some animals that presumably stores sperm.

sepal. One of the modified leaves around the outside of a flower's petals.

sequential hermaphroditism. Condition in which an organism has the ability to change sex.

sere. One in a series of stages of ecological succession in a particular area.

serotiny. Ability of the cones of some pines to remain closed after maturity and open after being exposed to heat as in a forest fire.

sex ratio. Ratio of the number of individuals of one sex to that of the other sex.

sexual dimorphism. Differences between the sexes in outward body characteristics.

sexual selection. Choice by one sex for specific characteristics in individuals of the opposite sex, usually exercised during courtship.

Shenandoah Valley. Name of Great Valley as it runs through central Appalachia.

shivering. Rapid contraction and relaxation of muscles that generates heat.

shrew. Common name for small-bodied mammals of the family Soricidae, order Insectivora.

Silurian Period. Part of the Paleozoic Era between 438 and 408 million years ago.

size-advantage model. Hypothesis that explains fitness advantages associated with certain body sizes.

slime mold. Species in the phylum Myxomycetes that exist as mobile slimy masses, contain thousands of nuclei, and reproduce by spores.

soft water. Water with low level of dissolved salts.

spadix. Floral spike with fleshy axis.

spathe. Sheathing bract enclosing a spadix.

speciation. Process of forming new species.

species. Set of individual organisms with similar body structure and that can potentially interbreed.

species-area relationship. Theory that explains the number of species in an area as a function of the size of the area.

staminate flower. A flower with stamens (the male reproductive organ) but no pistils (the female reproductive organ).

standing crop. Instantaneous estimate of an organism's abundance, for instance, mass per hectare.

stem flow. Water flowing down a tree trunk.

stigma. Part of the pistil (female organ) of a flower that receives pollen.

stochastic. Random; involving a random movement at each point in time.

stratification. Process of forming layers.

stream capture. Stream piracy; the diversion of flow from one basin to another presumably by headward erosion of the more aggressive, capturing stream.

stratum. Layer of sedimentary rock.

subduction. Process by which oceanic lithosphere plunges into the mantle where two of earth's crustal plates collide.

subspecies. Taxonomic category that ranks below species; a morphologically distinguishable group whose members breed successfully with those of other subspecies of the same species.

succession. Replacement of populations in a habitat through a regular progression.

sunfleck. Patch of direct sunshine on the forest floor.

supercooling. Cooling a liquid below its normal freezing point without crystallization occurring.

superterritory. Area a male bird defends that is larger than needed to supply resources for the bird's family; presumably discourages potential competitors from settling in the area.

surface-to-volume ratio. Ratio of surface area to internal volume of a solid.

suture. Line of union.

symbiosis. Intimate, often obligatory, association of two species.

sympatry. Two species occurring in the same area.

syncline. Trough of folded rock bent into a U shape; opposite of anticline.

synergism. Action of different agents creating a total effect greater than the sum of the two effects taken independently.

talus. Accumulation of rock debris at the base of a cliff.

tannin. Phenolic substance in plants that presumably deters herbivores.

taxon. A taxonomic group of living things.

Tennessee Valley. Name of the Great Valley in southern Appalachia.

terrane. Crustal block whose geologic history is distinct from that of adjoining blocks.

territory. Defended area.

Tertiary Period. Part of the Cenozoic Era between 66.4 and 1.6 million years ago.

tetrodotoxin. Poison found in pufferfish and red-spotted newts.

thermal sum. Measure of heat accumulated over a time period.

throughfall. Water falling through the forest canopy.

thrust fault. Low-angle reverse fault caused by compression of colliding plates; can result in older strata overlying younger rocks.

topographic diversity. Degree of variation in surface shape.

torpor. State of inactivity.

torso. Central trunk of an animal.

trachea. Main tube passing air to and from lungs.

tradeoff. Costs and benefits of alternative actions.

transpiration. Evaporation of water from a plant leaf through a membrane or pores.

transvestite. Individual that exhibits behavior of a member of the opposite sex.

trellised drainage. System of streams in which nearly parallel tributaries run through valleys among folded strata.

Triassic Period. Part of the Mesozoic Era between 248 and 213 million years ago.

ultimate cause. Aspect of the environment that influences direction of natural selection.

understory. Set of plants deploying leaves at 5 to 15 feet high that form a forest's middle layer.

upliftng. Elevating landmasses caused by compression of colliding plates.

vacuole. Saclike organelle that stores water, food, or waste fluids.

viviparity. Giving birth to living young that were nurtured as embryos in the mother's body.

warning coloration. Conspicuous colors displayed by noxious organisms that advertise their toxicity to predators.

windthrow. Group of trees pushed over by a strong wind.

Wisconsin glacial period. Last glacial interval of the Pleistocene Epoch between 175,000 and 12,000 years ago.

woodland salamander. Common name for species in the salamander genus *Plethodon*.

xanthophyll. Yellow pigments in plants.

xeric. Dry.

Bibliography

(Sources are listed by chapter.)

1. Modus

Bake, W. A. 1977. *The Blue Ridge*. Birmingham, Ala.: Oxmoor House, Inc.

Brooks, M. 1965. *The Appalachians*. Grantsville, W.Va.: Seneca Books, Inc.

———. 1967. *The life of the mountains*. New York: McGraw-Hill Book Co.

———. 1971. The southern Appalachians. In *The distributional history of the biota of the southern Appalachians, Part 3: Vertebrates*, edited by P. C. Holt. Res. Div. Mono. 4, Blacksburg, Va.: Virginia Poly. Inst. and St. Univ.

Catlin, D. T. 1984. *A naturalist's Blue Ridge Parkway*. Knoxville: Univ. Tennessee Press.

Cody, M. L. 1974. Optimization in ecology. *Science* 183:1156-64.

Darwin, C. R. 1859. *The origin of species by means of natural selection*. New York: Random House, The Modern Library.

Dillard, A. 1974. *Pilgrim at Tinker Creek*. New York: Bantam Books.

Doolittle, J. 1975. *The southern Appalachians*. New York: Time-Life Books.

Evans, H. E. 1966. *Life on a little-known planet*. New York: Dell Publ. Co.

Hutchinson, G. E. 1965. *The ecological theater and the evolutionary play*. New Haven, Conn.: Yale Univ. Press.

Lack, D. 1954. The evolution of reproductive rates. In *Evolution as a process*, edited by J. S. Huxley, A. C. Hardy, and E. B. Ford. London: Allen and Unwin.

Ogburn, C. 1975. *The southern Appalachians, A wilderness quest*. New York: William Morrow and Co.

Porter, E., and E. Abbey. 1973. *Appalachian wilderness, The Great Smoky Mountains*. New York: Ballantine Books.

Trivers, R. 1985. *Social evolution*. Menlo Park, Calif.: Benjamin/Cummings Publ.

Williams, G. C. 1966. *Adaptation and natural selection*. Princeton, N.J.: Princeton Univ. Press.

2. Origins

Alvarez, W., L. W. Alvarez, F. Asaro, and H. V. Michel. 1984. The end of the Cretaceous: Sharp boundary or gradual transition? *Science* 223:1183-86.

Berggren, W. A., and J.A. van Couvering. 1984. *Catastrophes and earth history*. Princeton: Princeton Univ. Press.

Braun, E. L., Jr. 1950. *Deciduous forests of eastern North America*. New York: The Free Press, Macmillan.

Brooks, M. 1967. Cited in Chap. 1.

———. 1971. Cited in Chap. 1.

Catlin, D. T. 1984. Cited in Chap. 1.

Cook, F. A., L. D. Brown, and J. E. Oliver. 1980. The southern Appalachians and the growth of continents. *Sci. Amer.* 243:156-68.

Cracraft, J. 1974. Continental drift and vertebrate distribution. *Ann. Rev. Ecol. Syst.* 5:215-61.

Davis, M. B. 1983. Quaternary history of deciduous forests of eastern North America and Europe. *Ann. Missouri Bot. Gard.* 70:550-63.

Delcourt, H. R., and P. A. Delcourt. 1984. Ice age haven for hardwoods. *Natural History* 9:22-28.

Fenneman, N. M. 1938. *Physiography of the eastern United States.* New York: McGraw-Hill Book Co.

Frye, K. 1986. *Roadside geology of Virginia.* Missoula, Mont.: Mountain Press Publ. Co.

Ganapathy, R. 1980. A major meteorite impact on the earth 65 million years ago: Evidence from the Cretaceous-Tertiary boundary clay. *Science* 209:921-23.

Gathright, T. M., II. 1976. *Geology of the Shenandoah National Park, Virginia.* Virginia Div. Min. Res. Bull. 86.

Gore, R. 1985. Our restless planet, Earth. *Natl. Geogr.* (Aug):142-81.

Hack, J. T. 1969. The area, its geology: Cenozoic development of the southern Appalachians. In *The distributional history of the biota of the southern Appalachians, Part I: Invertebrates,* edited by P. C. Holt. Res. Div. Mono. 1. Blacksburg, Va.: Virginia Poly. Inst. and St. Univ.

Hamilton, W. 1983. Cretaceous and Cenozoic history of the northern continents. *Ann. Missouri Bot. Gard.* 70:440-58.

Harris, S. L. 1990. *Agents of chaos.* Missoula, Mont.: Mountain Press Publ. Co.

Hays, J. D., J. Imbrie, and N. J. Shackleton. 1976. Variations in the earth's orbit: Pacemaker of the ice ages. *Science* 194:1121-32.

Hsu, K. J., et al. 1982. Mass mortality and its environmental consequences. *Science* 216:249-56.

McKenzie, D. P. 1983. The earth's mantle. *Sci. Amer.* 249:66-78.

McPhee, J. 1983. *In suspect terrain.* New York: Farrar, Straus, and Giroux.

Peters, P. T. 1986. Appalachian genesis. *Wonderful West Virginia* 50:10-17.

Shimer, J. A. 1972. *Field guide to landforms in the United States.* New York: Macmillan Co.

Stanley, S. M. 1986. *Earth and life through time.* New York: W. H. Freeman.

Sutton, A., and M. Sutton. 1985. *Eastern forests.* New York: Knopf.

Tilton, J. L. 1926. Map 2, Hampshire Co., showing general and economic geology. Morgantown, W.Va.: West Virginia Geol. Surv.

Tapponnier, P. 1986. A tale of two continents. *Natural History* 11:56-64.

Van Diver, B. B. 1985. *Roadside Geology of New York.* Missoula, Mont.: Mountain Press Publ. Co.

———. 1990. *Roadside Geology of Pennsylvania.* Missoula, Mont.: Mountain Press Publ. Co.

Watts, W. A. 1970. The full-glacial vegetation of northwestern Georgia. *Ecology* 51:17-33.

———. 1979. Late Quaternary vegetation of central Appalachia and the New Jersey coastal plain. *Ecol. Mono.* 49:427-69.

———. 1980. The late Quaternary vegetation of the southeastern United States. *Ann. Rev. Ecol. Syst.* 11:387-409.

———. 1983. Vegetational history of the eastern United States 25,000 to 10,000 years ago. In *Late-Quaternary environments of the United States, Vol. 1, The late Pleistocene,* edited by S. C. Porter. Minneapolis: Univ. Minnesota Press.

Watts, W. A., and M. Stuiver. 1980. Late Wisconsin climate of northern Florida and the origin of species-rich deciduous forest. *Science* 210:325-27.

Weiner, J. 1986. *Planet Earth*. New York: Bantam Books.

3. *Forest Design*

Aber, J. D. 1979. Foliage-height profiles and succession in northern hardwood forests. *Ecology* 60:18-23.

Bazzaz, F. A. 1979. The physiological ecology of plant succession. *Ann. Rev. Ecol. Syst.* 10:351-71.

Braun. 1950. Cited in Chap. 2.

Christensen, N. L., and R. K. Peet. 1984. Convergence during secondary forest succession. *J. Ecol.* 72:25-36.

Core, E. L. 1966. *Vegetation of West Virginia*. Parsons, W.Va.: McClain Printing Co.

Good, N. F. 1968. A study of the natural replacement of chestnut in six stands in the highlands of New Jersey. *Bull. Torrey Bot. Club* 95:240-53.

Henry, J. D., and J. M. A. Swan. 1974. Reconstructing forest history from live and dead plant material—an approach to the study of forest succession in southwest New Hampshire. *Ecology* 55:772-83.

Keever, C. 1950. Causes of succession on old fields of the piedmont, North Carolina. *Ecol. Mono.* 20:229-50.

Krefting, L. W., and C. E. Ahlgren. 1974. Small mammals and vegetation changes after fire in a mixed conifer-hardwood forest. *Ecology* 55:1391-98.

McIntosh, R. P. 1970. Community, competition, and adaptation. *Quart. Rev. Biol.* 45:259-80.

Moore, J. C., T. V. St. John, and D. C. Coleman. 1985. Ingestion of vesicular-arbuscular mycorrhizal hyphae and spores by soil microarthropods. *Ecology* 66:1979-81.

Newell, S. J., and E. J. Tramer. 1978. Reproductive strategies in herbaceous plant communities during succession. *Ecology* 59:228-34.

Nicholson, S. A., J. T. Scott, and A. R. Breisch. 1979. Structure and succession in the tree stratum at Lake George, New York. *Ecology* 60:1240-54.

Niering, W. A., and R. H. Goodwin. 1974. Creation of relatively stable shrubland with herbicides: Arresting "succession" on rights-of-way and pastureland. *Ecology* 55: 784-95.

Odum, E. P. 1969. The strategy of ecosystem development. *Science* 164:262-70.

Pickett, S. T. A. 1976. Succession: An evolutionary interpretation. *Am. Nat.* 110:107-19.

Smith, A. P. 1973. Stratification of temperate and tropical forests. *Am. Nat.* 107:671-83.

Strausbaugh, P. D., and E. L. Core. n.d. *Flora of West Virginia*. Grantsville, W.Va.: Seneca Books, Inc.

Sutton and Sutton. 1985. Cited in Chap. 2.

Terborgh, J. 1985. The vertical component of plant species diversity in temperate and tropical forests. *Am. Nat.* 126:760-76.

Tinker, P. B., and A. Gildon. 1982. Mycorrhizal fungi and ion uptake. In *Metals and micronutrients, uptake and utilization by plants*, edited by D. A. Robb and W. S. Pierpoint. Phytochemical Soc. Europe Symp. Ser. No. 21. San Diego, Calif.: Academic Press.

White, P. S. 1979. Pattern, process, and natural disturbance in vegetation. *Bot. Rev.* 45:229-99.

Whittaker, R. H. 1956. Vegetation of the Great Smoky Mountains. *Ecol. Mono.* 26:1-80.

4. Creating Diversity

Braun. 1950. Cited in Chap. 2.

Brooks, M. 1948. Notes on the Cheat Mountain salamander. *Copeia* 1948:240-44.

———. 1955. An isolated population of the Virginia varying hare. *J.Wildl. Mgmt.* 19:54-61.

Deeney, E. S., Jr. 1976. Time-worn highlands and coastal plain. In *Our continent: A natural history of North America*. Washington, D.C.: National Geographic Society.

Echelle, A. A., A. F. Echelle, M. H. Smith, and L. G. Hill. 1975. Analysis of genic continuity in a headwater fish, *Etheostoma radiosum* (Percidae). *Copeia* 1975:197-204.

Echelle, A. A., A. F. Echelle, and B. A. Taber. 1976. Biochemical evidence for congeneric competition as a factor restricting gene flow between populations of a darter (Percidae: *Etheostoma*). *Copeia* 1976:228-35.

Green, N. B., and T. K. Pauley. 1987. *Amphibians and reptiles in West Virginia*. Pittsburg: Univ. Pittsburgh Press.

Hocutt, C. H. 1979. Drainage evolution and fish dispersal in the central Appalachians. *Geol. Soc. Am. Bull.*, Part II 90:197-234.

Hocutt, C. H., R. F. Denoncourt, and J. R. Stauffer Jr. 1978. Fishes of the Greenbrier River, West Virginia, with drainage history of the central Appalachians. *J. Biogeogr.* 5:59-80.

Jenkins, R. E., E. A. Lachner, and F. J. Schwartz. 1971. In *The distributional history of the biota of the southern Appalachians, Part III: Vertebrates*, edited by P. C. Holt. Res. Div. Mono. I. Blacksburg, Va.: Virginia Poly. Inst. and St. Univ.

Jopson, H. G. M. 1971. The origin of the reptile fauna of the southern Appalachinas. In *The distributional history of the biota of the southern Appalachians, Part III: Vertebrates*, edited by P. C. Holt. Res. Div. Mono. 4. Blacksburg, Va.: Virginia Poly. Inst. and St. Univ.

Kendeigh, S. C. 1974. *Ecology, with special reference to animals and man*. Englewood Cliffs, N.J.: Prentice-Hall.

Knight, R. L., and M. W. Call. 1980. *The common raven*. Tech. Note 344. U.S. Dept. Interior, Bur. Land Mgmt.

Little, E. L. Jr. 1971. Endemic, disjunct and northern trees in the southern Appalachians. In *The distributional history of the biota of the southern Appalachians, Part II: Flora*, edited by P. C. Holt. Res. Div. Mono. 2. Blacksburg, Va.: Virginia Poly. Inst. and St. Univ.

Mathews, R. C., Jr., and A. C. Echternacht. 1984. Herpetofauna of the spruce-fir ecosystem in the southern Appalachian mountain regions, with emphasis on the Great Smoky Mountains National Park. In The southern Appalachian spruce-fir ecosystem: Its biology and threats, edited by P. S. White. *Research/Resources Mgmt. Report SER-71*. U.S. Dept. Interior, Natl. Park Serv.

Matthews, W. J., R. E. Jenkins, and J. T. Styron Jr. 1982. Systematics of two forms of blacknose dace, *Rhinichthys atratulus* (Pisces: Cyprinidae) in a zone of syntopy, with a review of the species group. *Copeia* 1982:902-20.

Mohlenbrock, R. H. 1985. Alpine Garden, New Hampshire. *Natural History* 7:22-27.

Oosting, H. J., and W. D. Billings. 1951. A comparison of virgin spruce-fir forest in the northern and southern Appalachian system. *Evolution* 32:84-103.

Page, L. M. 1983. *Handbook of darters*. Neptune City, N.J.: TFH Publications, Inc.

Rabenold, K. N. 1978. Foraging strategies, diversity, and seasonality in bird communities of Appalachian spruce-fir forests. *Ecol. Mono.* 48:397-424.

Sharp, A. J. 1971. Epilogue. In *The distributional history of the biota of the southern Appalachians, Part II: Flora*, edited by P. C. Holt. Res. Div. Mono. 2. Blacksburg, Va.: Virginia Poly. Inst. and St. Univ.

Stauffer, J. R. Jr., C. H. Hocutt, and D. S. Lee. 1978. The zoogeography of the freshwater fishes of the Potomac River basin. In *The freshwater Potomac: Aquatic communities and environmental stresses*, edited by K. C. Flynn and W. T. Mason. Rockville, Md.: Interstate Comm. Potomac R. Basin.

Stauffer, J. R. Jr., B. M. Burr, C. H. Hocutt, and R. E. Jenkins. 1982. Checklist of the fishes of the central and northern Appalachian Mountains. *Proc. Biol. Soc. Washington* 95:27-47.

Tilley, S. G., and P. M. Schmerdtfeger. 1981. Electrophoretic variation in Appalachian populations of the *Desmognathus fuscus* complex (Amphibia: Plethodontidae). *Copeia* 1981:109-19.

Wake, D. B., and J. F. Lynch. 1976. The distribution, ecology, and evolutionary history of plethodontid salamanders in tropical America. *Sci. Bull. 25*. Los Angeles, Calif.: Natural History Museum.

White, P. S. 1984. The southern Appalachian spruce-fir ecosystem, An introduction. In The southern Appalachian spruce-fir ecosystem: Its biology and threats, edited by P.W. White. *Research/Resources Mgmt. Report SER-71*. U.S. Dept. Interior, Natl. Park Serv.

Woods, F. W., and R. E. Shanks. 1959. Natural replacement of chestnut by other species in the Great Smoky Mountains National Park. *Ecology* 40:349-61.

Zobel, D. B. 1969. Factors affecting the distribution of *Pinus pungens*, an Appalachian endemic. *Ecol. Mono.* 39:271-301.

5. Catastrophe and the Appalachian Quilt

Barden, L. S. 1979. Serotiny and seed viability of *Pinus pungens* in the southern Appalachians. *Castanea* 44:44-47.

———. 1979. Tree replacement in small canopy gaps of a *Tsuga canadensis* forest in the southern Appalachians, Tennessee. *Oecologia* 44:141-42.

———. 1980. Tree replacement in a cove hardwood forest of the southern Appalachians. *Oikos* 35:16-19.

———. 1981. Forest development in canopy gaps of a diverse hardwood forest of the southern Appalachian Mountains. *Oikos* 37:205-9.

———. 1983. Size, age, and growth rate of trees in canopy gaps of a cove hardwood forest in the southern Appalachians. *Castanea* 48:19-23.

Beatty, S. W. 1984. Influence of microtopography and canopy species on spatial patterns of forest understory plants. *Ecology* 65:1406-19.

Bormann, F. H., and G. E. Likens. 1979. Catastrophic disturbance and the steady state in northern hardwood forests. *Am. Sci.* 67:660-69.

Bratton, S. P. 1976. Resource division in an understory herb community: Responses to temporal and microtopographic gradients. *Am. Nat.* 110:679-93.

Canham, C. D., and O. L. Loucks. 1984. Catastrophic windthrow in the presettlement forests of Wisconsin. *Ecology* 65:803-9.

Day, F. P. Jr., and C. D. Monk. 1974. Vegetation patterns on a southern Appalachian watershed. *Ecology* 55:1064-74.

Fox, J. F. 1977. Alternation and coexistence of tree species. *Am. Nat.* 111:69-89.

Gant, R. E., and E. E. C. Clebsch. 1975. The allelopathic influences of *Sassafras albidum* in old-field succession in Tennessee. *Ecology* 56:604-15.

Gemborys, S. R. 1974. The structure of hardwood forest ecosystems of Prince Edward County, Virginia. *Ecology* 55:614-21.

Gleick, J. 1987. *Chaos: Making a new science*. New York: Viking Press.

Harmon, M. E. 1984. Survival of trees after low-intensity surface fires in Great Smoky Mountains National Park. *Ecology* 65:796-802.

Harmon, M. E., S. P. Bratton, and P. S. White. 1983. Disturbance and vegetation response in relation to environmental gradients in the Great Smoky Mountains. *Vegetatio* 55:129-39.

Jones, E. W. 1945. The structure and reproduction of the virgin forest of the north temperate zone. *New Phytol.* 44:130-48.

Leak, W. B. 1975. Age distribution in virgin red spruce and northern hardwoods. *Ecology* 56:1451-54.

Lorimer, C. G. 1977. The presettlement forest and natural disturbance cycle of northeastern Maine. *Ecology* 58:139-48.

———. 1980. Age structure and disturbance history of a southern Appalachian virgin forest. *Ecology* 61:1169-84.

McCormick, J. F., and R. B. Platt. 1980. Recovery of an Appalachian forest following the chestnut blight, or Catherine Keever—you were right! *Am. Midl. Nat.* 104:264-73.

McEvoy, T. J., T. L. Sharik, and D. W. Smith. 1980. Vegetative structure of an Appalachian oak forest in southwestern Virginia. *Am. Midl. Nat.* 103:96-105.

Muller, C. H. 1966. The role of chemical inhibition (allelopathy) in vegetation composition. *Bull. Torrey Bot. Club* 93:332-51.

———. 1970. The role of allelopathy in the evolution of vegetation. In *Biochemical evolution, Proc. 29th Ann. Biol. Coll.*, 1968, edited by K. L. Chambers, Corvallis: Oregon St. Univ. Press.

Oliver, C. D., and E. P. Stephens. 1977. Reconstruction of a mixed-species forest in central New England. *Ecology* 58:562-72.

Putz, F. E., G. G. Parker, and R. M. Archibald. 1984. Mechanical abrasion and intercrown spacing. *Am. Midl. Nat.* 112:24-28.

Racine, C. H. 1971. Reproduction of three species of oak in relation to vegetational and environmental gradients in the southern Blue Ridge. *Bull. Torrey Bot. Club* 98:297-310.

Reiners, W. A., and G. E. Lang. 1979. Vegetational patterns and processes in the balsam fir zone, White Mountains, New Hampshire. *Ecology* 60:403-17.

Rogers, R. S. 1980. Hemlock stands from Wisconsin to Nova Scotia: Transitions in understory composition along a floristic gradient. *Ecology* 61:178-93.

———. 1983. Small-area coexistence of vernal forest herbs: Does functional similarity of plants matter? *Am. Nat.* 121:835-50.

———. 1985. Local coexistence of deciduous-forest groundlayer species growing in different seasons. *Ecology* 66:701-7.

Schemske, D. W., M. F. Willson, M. N. Melampy, L. J. Miller, L. Verner, K. M. Schemske, and L. D. Best. 1978. Flowering ecology of some spring woodland herbs. *Ecology* 59:351-66.

Sousa, W. P. 1984. The role of disturbance in natural communities. *Ann. Rev. Ecol. Syst.* 15:353-91.

Turner, B. H., and E. Quarterman. 1975. Allelochemic effects of *Petalostemon gattingeri* on the distribution of *Arenaria patula* in cedar glades. *Ecology* 56:924-32.

VanVoris, P., R. V. O'Neill, W. R. Emanuel, and H. H. Shugart. 1980. Functional complexity and ecosystem stability. *Ecology* 61:1352-60.

White, P. S., M. D. MacKenzie, and R. T. Busing. 1985. Natural disturbance and gap phase dynamics in southern Appalachian spruce-fir forests. *Can. J. For. Res.* 15:233-40.

Whitney, G. G. 1984. Fifty years of change in the arboreal vegetation of Hart's Content, an old-growth hemlock-white pine-northern hardwood stand. *Ecology* 65:403-8.

Whittaker, R. H., and P. P. Feeny. 1971. Allelochemics: Chemical interactions between species. *Science* 171:757-70.

Williamson, G. B. 1975. Pattern and seral composition in an old-growth beech-maple forest. *Ecology* 56:727-31.

6. Balds

Barden, L. S. 1978. Regrowth of shrubs in grassy balds of the southern Appalachians after prescribed burning. *Castanea* 43:238-46.

Billings, W. D., and A. F. Mark. 1957. Factors involved in the persistence of montane treeless balds. *Ecology* 38:140-42.

Braun. 1950. Cited in Chap. 2.

Catlin. 1984. Cited in Chap. 1.

Wells, B. W. 1937. Southern Appalachian grass balds. *Elisha Mitchell Sci. Soc. J.* 53:1-26.

Whittaker, R. H. 1956. Vegetation of the Great Smoky Mountains. *Ecol. Mono.* 26:1-80.

7. The Asian Connection

Boufford, D. E., and S. A. Sponberg. 1983. Eastern Asian-eastern North American phytogeographical relationships—A history from the time of Linnaeus to the twentieth century. *Ann. Missouri Bot. Gard.* 70:423-39.

Braun. 1950. Cited in Chap. 2.

Cheng, Z. 1983. A comparative study of the vegetation in Hubei Province, China, and in the Carolinas of the United States. *Ann. Missouri Bot. Gard.* 70:571-75.

Davis. 1983. Cited in Chap. 2.

Hamilton. 1983. Cited in Chap. 2.

Hsu, J. 1983. Late Cretaceous and Cenozoic vegetation in China, emphasizing their connections with North America. *Ann. Missouri Bot. Gard.* 70:490-508.

Kato, M., and K. Iwatsuki. 1983. Phytogeographic relationships of pteridophytes between temperate North America and Japan. *Ann. Missouri Bot. Gard.* 70:724-33.

Little, E. L. Jr. 1983. North American trees with relationships in eastern Asia. *Ann. Missouri Bot. Gard.* 70:605-15.

Parks, C. R., N. G. Miller, J. F. Wendel, and K. M. McDougal. 1983. Genetic divergence within the genus *Liriodendron* (Magnoliaceae). *Ann. Missouri Bot. Gard.* 70:658-66.

Sing-chi, C. 1983. A comparison of orchid floras of temperate North America and eastern Asia. *Ann. Missouri Bot. Gard.* 70:713-23.

White, P. S. 1983. Eastern Asian-eastern North American floristic relations: The plant community level. *Ann. Missouri Bot. Gard.* 70:734-47.

Ying, T. 1983. The floristic relationships of the temperate forest regions of China and the United States. *Ann. Missouri Bot. Gard.* 70:597-604.

Zhengyi, W. 1983. On the significance of the Pacific intercontinental discontinuity. *Ann. Missouri Bot. Gard.* 70:577-90.

8. *The Improbable Lady's Slipper*

Dafni, A. 1984. Mimicry and deception in pollination. *Ann. Rev. Ecol. Syst.* 15:259-78.

Dodson, C. H. 1966. Studies in orchid pollination—*Cypripedium*, *Phragmipedium* and allied genera. *Am. Orchid Soc. Bull.* 35:125-28.

Dressler, R. L. 1981. *The orchids: Natural history and classification.* Cambridge, Mass.: Harvard Univ. Press.

Luer, C. A. 1975. *The native orchids of the United States and Canada excluding Florida.* New York: New York Bot. Gard.

Stoutamire, W. P. 1964. Seeds and seedlings of native orchids. *The Michigan Botanist* 3:107-19.

———. 1967. Flower biology of the lady's slippers. *The Michigan Botanist* 6:159-75.

———. 1971. Pollination in temperate American orchids. In *Proc. 6th World Orchid Conf., Sydney, Australia, 1969*, edited by M. J. Corrigan. Sydney, Aust.: Halstead Press.

———. 1974. Relationships of the purple-fringed orchids *Platanthera psycodes* and *P. grandiflora*. *Brittonia* 26:42-58.

———. 1978. Pollination of *Tipularia discolor*, an orchid with modified symmetry. *Am. Orchid Soc. Bull.* 47:413-15.

———. 1983. Early growth in North American terrestrial orchid seedlings. In *Proc. Symp. II and Lectures, North American Terrestrial Orchids*, edited by E. H. Plaxton. Southfield, Mich.: Michigan Orchid Society.

Waters, V. H., and C. C. Waters. 1973. A survey of the slipper orchids. Shelby, N.C.: Carolina Press.

9. *Sexual Decisions of Jack-in-the-Pulpit*

Bierzychudek, P. 1981. Pollinator limitation of plant reproductive effort. *Am. Nat.* 117:838-40.

———. 1982. The demography of jack-in-the-pulpit, a forest perennial that changes sex. *Ecol. Mono.* 52:335-51.

———. 1984. Assessing "optimal" life histories in a fluctuating environment: The evolution of sex-changing by jack-in-the-pulpit. *Am. Nat.* 123:829-40.

———. 1984. Determinants of gender in jack-in-the-pulpit: The influence of plant size and reproductive history. *Oecologia* 65:14-18.

Charnov, E. L. 1982. *The theory of sex allocation*. Princeton, N.J.: Princeton Univ. Press.

Ghiselin, M. T. 1969. The evolution of hermaphroditism among animals. *Quart. Rev. Biol.* 44:189-208.

Gould, S. J. 1985. *The flamingo's smile*. New York: W.W. Norton and Co.

Lovett Doust, J., and P. B. Cavers. 1982. Sex and gender dynamics in jack-in-the-pulpit, *Arisaema triphyllum* (L.) Schott (Araceae). *Ecology* 63:797-808.

Maekawa, T. 1924. On the phenomena of sex transition in *Arisema japonica*. *Hokkaido Imp. Univ. J. Coll. Agr.* 13:217-305.

Policansky, D. 1981. Sex choice and the size advantage model in jack-in-the-pulpit (*Arisema triphyllum*). *Proc. Natl. Acad. Sci.* 78:1306-08.

———. 1982. Sex change in plants and animals. *Ann. Rev. Ecol. Syst.* 13:471-95.

Schaffner, J. H. 1922. Control of sexual state in *Arisaema triphyllum* and *A. dracontium*. *Am. J. Bot.* 9:72-78.

10. *Nuptial Gift of the Hangingfly*

Thornhill, R. 1976. Sexual selection and nuptial feeding behavior in *Bittacus apicalis* (Insecta: Mecoptera). *Am. Nat.* 110:529-48.

———. 1977. The comparative predatory and sexual behavior of hangingflies (Mecoptera: Bittacidae). *Occ. Pap. Mus. Zool. Univ. Michigan, No. 677.*

———. 1979. Adaptive female-mimicking behavior in a scorpionfly. *Science* 205:412-14.

———. 1980. Mate choice in *Hylobittacus apicalis* (Insecta: Mecoptera) and its relation to some models of female choice. *Evolution* 34:519-38.

———. 1980. Sexual selection in the black-tipped hangingfly. *Sci. Am.* 242 (6):162-72.

11. *Femmes Fatales of Twilight*

Carlson, A. D., and J. Copeland. 1978. Behavioral plasticity in the flash communication systems of fireflies. *Amer. Sci.* 66:340-46.

Lall, A. B., H. H. Seliger, W. H. Biggley, and J. E. Lloyd. 1980. Ecology of colors of firefly bioluminescence. *Science* 210:560-62.

Lloyd, J. E. 1980. Male *Photuris* fireflies mimic sexual signals of their females' prey. *Science* 210:669-71.

———. 1981. Firefly mate-rivals mimic their predators and vice versa. *Nature* 290:498-500.

———. 1981. Mimicry in the sexual signals of fireflies. *Sci. Am.* 245 (1): 138-45.

———. 1983. Bioluminescence and communication in insects. *Ann. Rev. Entomol.* 28:131-60.

———. 1984. On deception, a way of all flesh, and firefly signalling and systematics. In Vol. 1 of *Oxford Survey of Evolutionary Biology* 1:48-84, edited by R. Dawkins and M. Ridley. London: Oxford Univ. Press.

———. 1984. Occurrence of aggressive mimicry in fireflies. *The Florida Entomologist* 67:368-76.

Lloyd, J. E., and S. R. Wing. 1983. Nocturnal aerial predation of fireflies by light-seeking fireflies. *Science* 222:634-35.

McElroy, W. D., and H. H. Seliger. 1962. Biological luminescence. In *The living cell, readings from Scientific American*. San Francisco: W. H. Freeman.

Thornhill, R., and J. Alcock. 1983. *The evolution of insect mating systems*. Cambridge, Mass.: Harvard Univ. Press.

12. Small Fishes in Shallow Headwaters

Angermeier, P. L. 1982. Resource seasonality and fish diets in an Illinois stream. *Env. Biol. Fish.* 7:251-64.

Beauchamp, G. K., K. Yamazaki, and E. A. Boyse. 1985. The chemosensory recognition of genetic individuality. *Sci. Am.* 253:86-92.

Cerri, R. D. 1983. The effect of light intensity on predator and prey behaviour in a cyprinid fish: Factors that influence prey risk. *Anim. Behav.* 31:736-42.

Cerri, R. D., and D. F. Fraser. 1983. Predation and risk in foraging minnows: Balancing conflicting demands. *Am. Nat.* 121:552-61.

Cooper, J. C., and A. D. Hasler. 1976. Electrophysiological studies of morpholine-imprinted coho salmon (*Oncorhynchus kisutch*) and rainbow trout (*Salmo gairdneri*). *J. Fish. Res. Bd. Can.* 33:688-94.

Fraser, D. F. 1983. An experimental investigation of refuging behaviour in a minnow. *Can. J. Zool.* 61:666-72.

Fraser, D. F., and R. D. Cerri. 1982. Experimental evaluation of predator-prey relationships in a patchy environment: Consequences for habitat use patterns in minnows. *Ecology* 63:307-13.

Fraser, D. F., and E. E. Emmons. 1984. Behavioral response of juvenile blacknose dace (*Rhinichthys atratulus*) to varying densities of predatory creek chub (*Semotilus atromaculatus*). *Can. J. Fish. Aquat. Sci.* 41:364-70.

Fraser, D. F., and T. E. Sise. 1980. Observations on stream minnows in a patchy environment: A test of a theory of habitat distribution. *Ecology* 61:790-97.

Gee, J. H. 1974. Behavioral and developmental plasticity of buoyancy in the longnose, *Rhinichthys cataractae*, and blacknose, *R. atratulus*, dace (Cyprinidae). *J. Fish. Res. Bd. Can.* 31:35-41.

Gerking, S. D. 1950. Stability of a stream fish population. *J. Wildl. Mgmt.* 14:193-202.

———. 1953. Evidence for the concepts of home range and territory in stream fishes. *Ecology* 34:347-65.

———. 1959. The restricted movement of fish populations. *Biol. Rev.* 34:221-42.

Hasler, A. D. 1966. *Underwater guideposts*. Cambridge, Mass.: Univ. Wisconsin Press.

Liley, N. R. 1982. Chemical communication by fish. *Can. J. Fish. Aquat. Sci.* 39:22-35.

Page, L. M. 1983. Cited in Chap. 4.

Reed, R. J. 1968. Mark and recapture studies of eight species of darters (Pisces: Percidae) in three streams of northwestern Pennsylvania. *Copeia* 1968:172-75.

Schlosser, I. J. 1982. Fish community structure and function along two habitat gradients in a headwater stream. *Ecol. Mono.* 52:395-414.

Scholz, A. T., R. M. Horrall, J. C. Cooper, and A. D. Hasler. 1976. Imprinting to chemical cues: The basis for home stream selection in salmon. *Science* 192:1247-49.

Smith, R. J. F. 1973. Testosterone eliminates alarm substance in male fathead minnows. *Can. J. Zool.* 51:875-76.

———. 1977. Chemical communication as adaptation: Alarm substance of fish. In *Chemical signals in vertebrates*, edited by D. Muller-Schwarze and M. M. Mozell. New York: Plenum Publ. Corp.

————. 1979. Alarm reaction of Iowa and johnny darters (*Etheostoma*, Percidae, Pisces) to chemicals from injured conspecifics. *Can. J. Zool.* 57:1278-82.

————. 1982. Reaction of *Percina nigrofasciata, Ammocrypta beani,* and *Etheostoma beani* (Percidae, Pisces) to conspecific and intergeneric skin extracts. *Can. J. Zool.* 60:1067-72.

Smith, R. J. F., and J. D. Smith. 1983. Seasonal loss of alarm substance cells in *Chrosomus neogaetus, Notropis venustus,* and *N. whipplei. Copeia* 1983:822-26.

Thunberg, B. E. 1971. Olfaction in parent stream selection by the alewife (*Alosa pseudoharengus*). *Anim. Behav.* 19:217-25.

13. *Darter Daddies*

Atz, J. W. 1940. Reproductive behavior in the eastern johnny darter, *Boleosoma nigrum olmstedi. Copeia* 1940:100-6.

Brown, L. 1981. Patterns of female choice in mottled sculpins (Cottidae, Teleostei). *Anim. Behav.* 29:375-82.

Brown, L., and J. F. Downhower. 1982. Polygamy in the mottled sculpins (*Cottus bairdi*) of southwestern Montana (Pisces: Cottidae). *Can. J. Zool.* 60:1973-80.

Clutton-Brock, T. H. 1991. *The evolution of parental care.* Princeton: Princeton Univ. Press.

Constantz, G. D. 1979. Social dynamics and parental care in the tessellated darter. *Proc. Acad. Nat. Sci. Phila.* 131:131-38.

————. 1985. Allopaternal care in the tessellated darter (Pisces: Percidae). *Env. Biol. Fish.* 14:175-83.

Downhower, J. F., and L. Brown. 1979. Seasonal changes in the social structure of a mottled sculpin (*Cottus bairdi*) population. *Anim. Behav.* 27:451-58.

————. 1980. Mate preferences of female mottled sculpins, *Cottus bairdi. Anim. Behav.* 28:728-34.

————. 1981. The timing of reproduction and its behavioral consequences for mottled sculpins, *Cottus bairdi.* In *Natural selection and social behavior,* edited by R. D. Alexander and D. W. Tinkle. New York: Chiron Press.

Downhower, J. F., L. Brown, R. Pederson, and G. Staples. 1983. Sexual selection and sexual dimorphism in mottled sculpins. *Evolution* 37:96-103.

Kuehne, R. A., and R. W. Barbour. 1983. *The American darters.* Lexington: Univ. Press Kentucky.

Page, L. M. 1983. Cited in Chap. 4.

Thomas, L. 1980. Altruism. In *Late night thoughts on listening to Mahler's ninth symphony.* New York: Viking Press.

14. *To the Brook Trout, with Esteem*

Cooper, E. L. 1967. Growth and longevity of brook trout (*Salvelinus fontinalis*) in populations subjected to light exploitation. *Trans. Am. Fish. Soc.* 96:383-86.

————. 1983. *Fishes of Pennsylvania and the northeastern United States.* University Park, Pa.: Penn. St. Univ. Press.

Cooper, E. L., and R. C. Scherer. 1967. Annual production of brook trout (*Salvelinus fontinalis*) in fertile and infertile streams of Pennsylvania. *Proc. Pa. Acad. Sci.* 41:65-70.

Gradall, K. S., and W. A. Swenson. 1982. Responses of brook trout and creek chubs to turbidity. *Trans. Am. Fish. Soc.* 111:392-95.

Hanson, D. L., and T. F. Waters. 1974. Recovery of standing crop and production rate of a brook trout population in a flood-damaged stream. *Trans. Am. Fish. Soc.* 103:431-39.

Lennon, R. E. 1967. Brook trout of Great Smoky Mountains National Park. *U.S. Bur. Sport Fish. and Wildl., Tech. Paper 15.*

McCormick, S. D., and R. J. Naiman. 1984. Osmoregulation in the brook trout, *Salvelinus fontinalis*—II. Effects of size, age and photoperiod on seawater survival and ionic regulation. *Comp. Biochem. Physiol.* 79A:17-28.

McNicol, R. E., and D. L. G. Noakes. 1981. Territories and territorial defense in juvenile brook charr, *Salvelinus fontinalis* (Pisces: Salmonidae). *Can. J. Zool.* 59:22-28.

———. 1984. Environmental influences on territoriality of juvenile brook charr, *Salvelinus fontinalis*, in a stream environment. *Env. Biol. Fish.* 10:29-42.

Menendez, R. 1976. Chronic effects of reduced pH on brook trout. *J. Fish. Res. Bd. Can.* 33:118-23.

Naiman, R. J., S. D. McCormick, W. L. Montgomery, and R. Morin. Unpubl. ms. Anadromous brook trout, *Salvelinus fontinalis*: Opportunities and constraints for population enhancement. 40 p.

Neves, R. J., and G. B. Pardue. 1983. Abundance and production of fishes in a small Appalachian stream. *Trans. Am. Fish. Soc.* 112:21-26.

Power, G. 1980. The brook charr, *Salvelinus fontinalis*. In *Charrs: Salmonid fishes of the genus* Salvelinus, edited by E.K. Balon. The Hague: Dr. W. Junk Publ.

Waters, T. F. 1982. Annual production of a stream brook charr population and by its principal invertebrate food. *Env. Biol. Fish.* 7:165-70.

——— 1983. Replacement of brook trout by brown trout over 15 years in a Minnesota stream: Production and abundance. *Trans. Am. Fish. Soc.* 112:137-46.

Whitworth, W. E., and R. J. Strange. 1983. Growth and production of sympatric brook and rainbow trout in an Appalachian stream. *Trans. Am. Fish. Soc.* 112:469-75.

Wydoski, R. S., and E. L. Cooper. 1966. Maturation and fecundity of brook trout from infertile streams. *J. Fish. Res. Bd. Can.* 23:623-49.

15–17. A Lungless Salamander Trilogy

Brodie, E. D. Jr., and R. R. Howard. 1973. Experimental study of Batesian mimicry in the salamanders *Plethodon jordani* and *Desmognathus ochrophaeus*. *Am. Midl. Nat.* 90:38-46.

Bruce, R. C. 1980. A model of the larval period of the spring salamander, *Gyrinophilus porphyriticus*, based on size-frequency distributions. *Herpetologica* 36:78-86.

———. 1982. Larval periods and metamorphosis in two species of salamanders of the genus *Eurycea*. *Copeia* 1982:117-27.

———. 1982. Egg-laying, larval periods, and metamorphosis of *Eurycea bislineata* and *E. junaluska* at Santeetlah Creek, North Carolina. *Copeia* 1982:755-62.

———. 1985. Larval period and metamorphosis in the salamander *Eurycea bislineata*. *Herpetologica* 41:19-28.

———. 1985. Larval periods, population structure and the effects of stream drift in larvae of the salamanders *Desmognathus quadramaculatus* and *Leurognathus marmoratus* in a southern Appalachian stream. *Copeia* 1985:847-54.

Danstedt, R. T., Jr. 1975. Local geographic variation in demographic parameters and body size of *Desmognathus fuscus* (Amphibia: Plethodontidae). *Ecology* 56: 1054-67.

David, R. S., and R. G. Jaeger. 1981. Prey location through chemical cues by a terrestrial salamander. *Copeia* 1981:435-40.

Dunn, E. R. 1927. A new mountain race of *Desmognathus*. *Copeia* 1927:84-86.

Feder, M. E. 1983. Integrating the ecology and physiology of plethodontid salamanders. *Herpetologica* 39:291-310.

Forester, D. C. 1979. The adaptiveness of parental care in *Desmognathus ochrophaeus* (Urodela: Plethodontidae). *Copeia* 1979:332-41.

———. 1981. Parental care in the salamander *Desmognathus ochrophaeus*: Female activity pattern and trophic behavior. *J. Herpetol.* 15:29-34.

Fraser, D. F. 1976. Coexistence of salamanders in the genus *Plethodon*: A variation of the Santa Rosalia theme. *Ecology* 57:238-51.

———. 1976. Empirical evaluation of the hypothesis of food competition in salamanders of the genus *Plethodon*. *Ecology* 57:459-71.

Grobman, A. B. 1944. The distribution of salamanders of the genus *Plethodon* in eastern United States and Canada. *Ann. New York Acad. Sci.* 45:261-316.

Hairston, N. G. 1980. The experimental test of an analysis of field distributions: Competition in terrestrial salamanders. *Ecology* 61:817-26.

———. 1980. Species packing in the salamander genus *Desmognathus*: What are the interspecific interactions involved? *Am. Nat.* 115:354-66.

———. 1981. An experimental test of a guild: Salamander competition. *Ecology* 62:65-72.

———. 1983. Alpha selection in competing salamanders: Experimental verification of an *a priori* hypothesis. *Am. Nat.* 122:105-13.

———. 1986. Species packing in *Desmognathus* salamanders: Experimental demonstration of predation and competition. *Am. Nat.* 127:266-91.

Highton, R. 1962. Geographic variation in the life history of the slimy salamander. *Copeia* 1962:597-613.

———. 1972. Distributional interactions among eastern North American salamanders of the genus *Plethodon*. In *The distributional history of the biota of the southern Appalachians, Part III: Vertebrates*, edited by P.C. Holt. Res. Div. Mono. 4. Blacksburg, Va.: Virginia Poly. Inst. and St. Univ.

Highton, R., and R. D. Worthington. 1967. A new salamander of the genus *Plethodon* from Virginia. *Copeia* 1967:617-26.

Jaeger, R. G. 1971. Competitive exclusion as a factor influencing the distributions of two species of terrestrial salamanders. *Ecology* 52:632-37.

———. 1971. Moisture as a factor influencing the distributions of two species of terrestrial salamanders. *Oecologia* 6:191-207.

———. 1972. Food as a limited resource in competition between two species of terrestrial salamanders. *Ecology* 53:535-46.

———. 1978. Plant climbing by salamanders: Periodic availability of plant-dwelling prey. *Copeia* 1978:686-91.

———. 1979. Seasonal spatial distributions of the terrestrial salamander *Plethodon cinereus*. *Herpetologica* 35:90-93.

———. 1980. Density-dependent and density-independent causes of extinction of a salamander population. *Evolution* 34:617-21.

———. 1980. Fluctuations in prey availability and food limitation for a terrestrial salamander. *Oecologia* 44:335-41.

———. 1980. Microhabitats of a terrestrial forest salamander. *Copeia* 1980:265-68.

———. 1981. Birds as inefficient predators on terrestrial salamanders. *Am. Nat.* 117:835-37.

———. 1981. Dear enemy recognition and the costs of aggression between salamanders. *Am. Nat.* 117:962-74.

———. 1984. Agonistic behavior of the red-backed salamander. *Copeia* 1984:309-14.

Jaeger, R. G., and W. F. Gergits. 1979. Intra- and interspecific communication in salamanders through chemical signals on the substrate. *Anim. Behav.* 27:150-56.

Jaeger, R. G., D. E. Barnard, and R. G. Joseph. 1982. Foraging tactics of a terrestrial salamander: Assessing prey density. *Am. Nat.* 119:885-90.

Jaeger, R. G., D. Kalvarsky, and N. Shimizu. 1982. Territorial behaviour of the red-backed salamander: Expulsion of intruders. *Anim. Behav.* 30:490-96.

Kaplan, R. H., and M. L. Crump. 1978. The non-cost of brooding in *Ambystoma opacum*. *Copeia* 1978:99-103.

Keen, W. H. 1982. Habitat selection and interspecific competition in two species of plethodontid salamanders. *Ecology* 63:94-102.

———. 1984. Influence of moisture on the activity of a plethodontid salamander. *Copeia* 1984:684-88.

Keen, W. H., and S. Sharp. 1984. Responses of a plethodontid salamander to conspecific and congeneric intruders. *Anim. Behav.* 32:58-65.

Kleeberger, S. R. 1984. A test of competition in two sympatric populations of desmognathine salamanders. *Ecology* 65:1846-56.

Labanick, G. M., and R. A. Brandon. 1981. An experimental study of Batesian mimicry between the salamanders *Plethodon jordani* and *Desmognathus ochrophaeus*. *J. Herpetol.* 15:275-81.

Simon, G. S., and D. M. Madison. 1984. Individual recognition in salamanders: cloacal odours. *Anim. Behav.* 32:1017-20.

Southerland, M. T. 1986. Coexistence of three congeneric salamanders: The importance of habitat and body size. *Ecology* 67:721-28.

Tilley, S. G. 1972. Aspects of parental care and embryonic development in *Desmognathus ochrophaeus*. *Copeia* 1972:532-40.

———. 1974. Structures and dynamics of populations of the salamander *Desmognathus ochrophaeus* Cope in different habitats. *Ecology* 55:808-17.

Tilley, S. G., B. L. Lundrigan, and L. P. Brower. 1982. Erythrism and mimicry in the salamander *Plethodon cinereus*. *Herpetologica* 38:409-17.

Wells, K. D. 1980. Spatial associations among individuals in a population of slimy salamanders (*Plethodon glutinosus*). *Herpetologica* 36:271-75.

Wilbur, H. M. 1972. Competition, predation, and the structure of the *Ambystoma-Rana sylvatica* community. *Ecology* 53:3-21.

———. 1977. Propagule size, number, and dispersion pattern in *Ambystoma* and *Ascelpias*. *Am. Nat.* 111:43-68.

Wrobel, D. J., W. F. Gergits, and R. G. Jaeger. 1980. An experimental study of interference competition among terrestrial salamanders. *Ecology* 61:1034-39.

18. *Love among the Frogs*

Berven, K. A. 1981. Mate choice in the wood frog, *Rana sylvatica*. *Evolution* 35:707-22.

Dillard. 1974. Cited in Chap. 1.

Fellers, G. M. 1975. Behavioral interactions in North American treefrogs (Hylidae). *Chesapeake Sci.* 16:218-19.

———. 1979. Aggression, territoriality, and mating behaviour in North American treefrogs. *Anim. Behav.* 27:107-19.

———. 1979. Mate selection in the gray treefrog, *Hyla versicolor*. *Copeia* 1979:286-90.

Gatz, A. J. Jr. 1981. Size selective mating in *Hyla versicolor* and *Hyla crucifer*. *J. Herpetology* 15:14-16.

Howard, R. D. 1980. Mating behaviour and mating success in wood frogs, *Rana sylvatica*. *Anim. Behav.* 28:705-16.

Howard, R. D., and A. G. Kluge. 1985. Proximate mechanisms of sexual selection in wood frogs. *Evolution* 39:260-77.

Orians, G. H. 1969. On the evolution of mating systems in birds and mammals. *Am. Nat.* 103:589-603.

Perrill, S. A. 1984. Male mating behavior in *Hyla regilla*. *Copeia* 1984:727-32.

Perrill, S. A., H. C. Gerhardt, and R. Daniel. 1978. Sexual parasitism in the green tree frog (*Hyla cinerea*). *Science* 200:1179-80.

———. 1982. Mating strategy shifts in male green treefrogs (*Hyla cinerea*): An experimental study. *Anim. Behav.* 30:43-48.

Roble, S. M. 1985. Observations on satellite males in *Hylachrysoscelis*, *Hyla picta*, and *Pseudacris triseriata*. *J. Herpetol.* 19:432-36.

Waldman, B. 1982. Adaptive significance of communal oviposition in wood frogs, *Rana sylvatica*. *Behav. Ecol. Sociobiol.* 10:169-74.

Waldman, B., and M. J. Ryan. 1983. Thermal advantages of communal egg mass deposition in wood frogs (*Rana sylvatica*). *J. Herpetol.* 17:70-72.

Wells, K. D. 1977. The social behaviour of anuran amphibians. *Anim. Behav.* 25:666-93.

19. *Box Turtle's Independence*

Dolbeer, R. A. 1969. A study of population density, seasonal movements and weight changes, and winter behavior of the eastern box turtle, *Terrapene c. carolina* L., in eastern Tennessee. Master's thesis, University of Tennessee.

———. 1971. Winter behavior of the eastern box turtle, *Terrapene c. carolina*, in eastern Tennessee. *Copeia* 1971:758-60.

Nichols, J. T. 1939. Data on size, growth, and age in the box turtle, *Terrapene carolina*. *Copeia* 1939:14-20.

Obbard, M. E., and R. J. Brooks. 1981. A radio-telemetry and mark-recapture study of activity in the common snapping turtle, *Chelydra serpentina*. *Copeia* 1981:630-37.

Schwartz, C. W., and E. R. Schwartz. 1974. *The three-toed box turtle in central Missouri: Its population, home range, and movements*. Terrestrial Ser. No. 5. Jefferson City, Mo.: Missouri Dept. Conserv.

Schwartz, E. R., C. W. Schwartz, and A. R. Kiester. 1984. *The three-toed box turtle in central Missouri, Part II: A nineteen-year study of home range, movements and population*. Terrestrial Ser. No. 12. Jefferson City, Mo.: Missouri Dept. Conserv.

Stickel, L. F. 1950. Populations and home range relationships of the box turtle, *Terrapene c. carolina* (Linnaeus). *Ecol. Mono.* 20:351-78.

Strass, P. K., K. J. Miles, B. S. McDonald, and I. L. Brisbin. 1982. An assessment of factors associated with the daytime use of resting forms by eastern box turtles (*Terrapene carolina carolina*). *J. Herpetol.* 16:320-22.

Wiens, J. A. 1977. On competition and variable environments. *Am. Sci.* 65:590-97.

Williams, E. C. Jr. 1961. A study of the box turtle, *Terrapene carolina carolina* (L.), population in Allee Memorial Woods. *Proc. Indiana Acad. Sci.* 71:399-406.

20. Copperhead's Year

Brown, W.S. 1982. Overwintering body temperatures of timber rattlesnakes (*Crotalus horridus*) in northeastern New York. *J. Herpetol.* 16:145-50.

Fitch, H. S. 1960. Autecology of the copperhead. *Univ. Kansas Publ. Mus. Nat. History* 13:85-228.

Hubbell, S. 1986. *A country year: Living the questions*. New York: Random House.

Reinert, H. K. 1984. Habitat separation between sympatric snake populations. *Ecology* 65:478-86.

Shine, R., and J. J. Bull. 1977. Skewed sex ratios in snakes. *Copeia* 1977:228-34.

———. 1979. The evolution of live-bearing in lizards and snakes. *Am. Nat.* 113:905-23.

Smith, R. L., ed. 1985. *Sperm competition and the evolution of animal mating systems*. New York: Academic Press.

21. Oaks and Squirrels

Allen, D. L. 1942. Populations and habits of the fox squirrel in Allegan County, Michigan. *Am. Midl. Nat.* 27:338-79.

Baker, R. H. 1944. An ecological study of tree squirrels in eastern Texas. *J. Mammal.* 25:8-24.

Brown, L. G., and L. E. Yaeger. 1945. Fox and gray squirrels in Illinois. *Ill. Nat. Hist. Surv.* 23:449-532.

Cahalane, V. H. 1942. Caching and recovery of food by the western fox squirrel. *J. Wildl. Mgmt.* 6:338-52.

Fitzwater, W. D., and W. J. Frank. 1944. Leaf nests of gray squirrels in Connecticut. *J. Mammal.* 25:160-70.

Janzen, D. H. 1971. Seed predation by animals. *Ann. Rev. Ecol. Syst.* 2:465-92.

Lewis, A. R. 1980. Patch use by gray squirrels and optimal foraging. *Ecology* 61:1371-79.

Moller, H. 1983. Foods and foraging behavior of red (Sciurus vulgaris) and grey (Sciurus carolinensis) squirrels. Mammal Rev. 13:81-98.

Shettleworth, S. J. 1983. Memory in food-hoarding birds. Sci. Am. 248 (3): 102-10.

Stapanian, M. A., and C. C. Smith. 1978. A model for seed scatterhoarding: Coevolution of fox squirrels and black walnuts. Ecology 59:884-96.

———. 1984. Density-dependent survival of scatterhoarded nuts: An experimental approach. Ecology 65:1387-96.

Thompson, D. C. 1978. Regulation of a northern grey squirrel (Sciurus carolinensis) population. Ecology 59:708-15.

Uhlig, H. G. 1956. The gray squirrel in West Virginia. Pittman-Robertson Project 31-R, Conserv. Comm. of West Virginia Bull. No. 3. Charleston, W.Va.

Weigl, P. D., and E. V. Hanson. 1980. Observational learning and the feeding behavior of the red squirrel, Tamiasciurus hudsonicus: The ontogeny of optimization. Ecology 61:213-18.

22. Highlanders

Catlin. 1984. Cited in Chap. 1.

Caudill, H. M. 1962. Night comes to the Cumberlands. Boston: Little, Brown and Co.

Day, G. M. 1953. The Indian as an ecological factor in the northeastern forest. Ecology 34:329-46.

Dillard. 1974. Cited in Chap. 1.

Fell, B. 1983. Christian messages in Old Irish script deciphered from rock carvings in West Virginia. Wonderful West Virginia 47 (1): 12-19.

Kephart, H. 1976. Our southern highlanders. Knoxville: Univ. Tennessee Press.

MacNeil, M. 1975. A Shenandoah story. A song and narrative on the record album Shenandoah Spring. Westview Music, BMI. (Available from Skyline Records, Rt. 1, Box 57, Swoope, VA 24479.)

McMichael, E. V. 1968. Introduction to West Virginia archeology. Educ. Ser. Morgantown, W.Va.: West Virginia Geol. and Econ. Surv.

McPhee. 1983. Cited in Chap. 2.

Miles, E. B. [1905] 1975. The spirit of the mountains. Knoxville: Univ. Tennessee Press.

Moize, E. A. 1985. Daniel Boone, first hero of the frontier. Natl. Geogr. 168 (6): 812-41.

Moore, J. A. 1985. Science as a way of knowing—Human ecology. Amer. Zool. 25:483-637.

Pyle, R. L. 1983. A message from the past. Wonderful West Virginia 47 (1): 3-6.

Pyne, S. J. 1983. Indian fires. Natural History 92 (2): 6-11.

Scherman, T. 1985. A man who mined musical gold in the southern hills. Smithsonian 16 (1): 173-96.

Thornborough, L. 1937. The Great Smoky Mountains. New York: Thomas Y. Crowell Co.

Weller, J. E. 1965. Yesterday's people: Life in contemporary Appalachia. Lexington: Univ. Press Kentucky.

Wigginton, E. 1972. The foxfire book. Garden City, N.Y.: Anchor Press-Doubleday.

———. 1975. Foxfire 3. Garden City, N.Y.: Anchor Press-Doubleday.

23. Autumn Leaves

Kimball, J. W. 1983. *Biology*, Fifth ed. Menlo Park, Calif.: Benjamin/Cummings Publ.

Northington, D. K., and J. R. Goodin. 1984. *The botanical world*. St. Louis, Mo.: Times Mirror/Mosby College Publ.

Raven, P. H., and H. Curtis. 1970. *Biology of Plants*. N.Y.: Worth Publ.

24. Window on Bird Politics

Baker, C. M., C. S. Belcher, L. G. Deutsch, G. L. Sherman, and D. B. Thompson. 1981. Foraging success in *Junco* flocks and the effects of social hierarchy. *Anim. Behav.* 29:137-42.

Baker, M. C., and S. F. Fox. 1978. Dominance, survival and enzyme polymorphism in dark-eyed juncos, *Junco hyemalis*. *Evolution* 32:697-711.

Balph, M. H. 1977. Winter social behaviour of dark-eyed juncos: Communication, social organization and ecological implications. *Anim. Behav.* 25:859-884.

Balph, M. H., D. F. Balph, and H. C. Romesburg. 1979. Social status signalling in winter flocking birds: An examination of current hypotheses. *Auk* 96:78-93.

Barash, D. P. 1974. An advantage of winter flocking in the black-capped chickadee, *Parus atricapillus*. *Ecology* 55:674-76.

Berner, T. O., and T. C. Grubb Jr. 1985. An experimental analysis of mixed-species flocking in birds of deciduous woodland. *Ecology* 66:1229-36.

Brawn, J. D., and F. B. Samson. 1983. Winter behavior of tufted titmice. *Wilson Bull.* 95:222-32.

Caraco, T. 1982. Flock size and the organization of behavioral sequences in juncos. *Condor* 84:101-5.

Caraco, T., and S. L. Lima. 1985. Foraging juncos: Interaction of reward mean and variability. *Anim. Behav.* 33:216-24.

Caraco, T., S. Martindale, and H. R. Pulliam. 1980. Avian flocking in the presence of a predator. *Nature* 285:400-401.

Charnov, E. L., and J. R. Krebs. 1975. The evolution of alarm calls: Altruism or manipulation? *Am. Nat.* 109:107-12.

Czikeli, H. 1983. Agonistic interactions within a winter flock of slate-coloured juncos (*Junco hyemalis*): Evidence for the dominants' strategy. *Z. Tierpsychol.* 61:61-66.

Fretwell, S. 1969. Dominance behaviour and winter habitat distribution in juncos (*Junco hyemalis*). *Bird-Banding* 40:1-25.

Glase, T. C. 1973. Ecology of social organization in the black-capped chickadee. *Living Bird* 12:235-67.

Hamilton, W. D. 1971. Geometry for the selfish herd. *J. Theor. Biol.* 31:295-311.

Hartzler, J. E. 1970. Winter dominance relationships in black-capped chickadees. *Wilson Bull.* 82:427-34.

Ketterson, E. D. 1979. Aggressive behavior in wintering dark-eyed juncos: Determinants of dominance and their possible relation to geographic variation in the sex-ratio. *Wilson Bull.* 91:371-83.

———. 1979. Status signalling in dark-eyed juncos. *Auk* 96:94-99.

Lima, S. L. 1984. Downy woodpecker foraging behavior: Efficient sampling in simple stochastic environments. *Ecology* 65:166-74.

Loery, G., and J. D. Nichols. 1985. Dynamics of a black-capped chickadee population, 1958-1983. *Ecology* 66:1195-1203.

Morse, D. H. 1970. Ecological aspects of some mixed-species foraging flocks of birds. *Ecol. Mono.* 40:130-68.

Roberts, R. C. 1979. The evolution of avian food-storing behavior. *Am. Nat.* 114:418-38.

Rowher, S., and P. W. Ewald. 1981. The cost of dominance and advantages of subordination in a badge signalling system. *Evolution* 35:441-54.

Schneider, K. J. 1984. Dominance, predation, and optimal foraging in white-throated sparrows. *Ecology* 65:1820-27.

Smith, S. M. 1984. Flock switching in chickadees: Why be a winter floater? *Am. Nat.* 123:81-98.

———. 1985. The tiniest established permanent floater crap game in the northeast. *Natural History* 3:43-47.

———. 1991. *The black-capped chickadee.* Ithaca, N.Y.: Cornell Univ. Press.

Sullivan, K. 1985. Selective alarm calling by downy woodpeckers in mixed-species flocks. *Auk* 102:184-87.

Watt, D. J., C. J. Ralph, and C. T. Atkinson. 1984. The role of plumage polymorphism in dominance relationships of the white-throated sparrow. *Auk* 101:110-20.

25. *Thwarting Swords of Ice*

Carey, C., and R.L. Marsh. 1981. Shivering finches. *Natural History* 90:58-63.

Dethier, V. G. 1980. *The world of the tent-makers: A natural history of the eastern tent caterpillar.* Amherst: Univ. Massachusetts Press.

Emery, A. R., A. H. Berst, and K. Kodaira. 1972. Under-ice observations of wintering sites of lepoard frogs. *Copeia* 1972:123-26.

Fitzpatrick, L. C. 1976. Life history patterns of storage and utilization of lipids for energy in amphibians. *Amer. Zool.* 16:725-32.

George, M. F., S. G. Hong, and M. J. Burke. 1977. Cold hardiness and deep supercooling of hardwoods: Its occurrence in provenance collections of red oak, yellow birch, black walnut, and black cherry. *Ecology* 58:674-80.

Hamilton, W. J., Jr. 1934. The life history of the rufescent woodchuck, *Marmota monax rufescens* Howell. *Ann. Carnegie Museum* 23:85-178.

Heinrich, B., and T. P. Mommsen. 1985. Flight of winter moths near 0°C. *Science* 228:177-79.

Marchand, P. J. 1987. *Life in the cold.* Hanover, N.H.: University Press New England.

Moen, A. N. 1968. Energy exchange of white-tailed deer, western Minnesota. *Ecology* 49:676-82.

———. 1976. Energy conservation by white-tailed deer in the winter. *Ecology* 57:192-98.

Moen, A. N., and C. W. Severinghaus. 1984. Hair depths of the winter coat of white-tailed deer. *J. Mammal.* 65:497-99.

Schmid, W. D. 1982. Survival of frogs in low temperatures. *Science* 215:697-98.

Schmidt-Nielsen, K. 1981. Countercurrent systems in animals. *Sci. Am.* 244:118-28.

Sutton and Sutton. 1985. Cited in Chap. 2.

Thorkelson, J., and R. K. Maxwell. 1974. Design and testing of a heat transfer model of a raccoon (*Procyon lotor*) in a closed tree den. *Ecology* 55:29-39.

Ultsch, G. R., R. W. Hanley, and T. R. Bauman. 1985. Responses to anoxia during simulated hibernation in northern and southern painted turtles. *Ecology* 66:388-95.

Walker, J. 1986. The amateur scientist: Exotic patterns appear in water when it is freezing or melting. *Sci. Am.* 255 (1): 114-19.

26. Spring Tensions

Catlin. 1984. Cited in Chap. 1.

Schemske et al. 1978. Cited in Chap. 5.

27. Dawn Chorus

Baker, M. C., and M. A. Cunningham. 1985. The biology of bird-song dialects. *Behav. and Brain Sci.* 8:85-100.

Baptista, L. F., and L. Petrinovich. 1984. Social interaction, sensitive phases and the song template hypothesis in the white-crowned sparrow. *Anim. Behav.* 32:172-81.

Best, L. B. 1977. Territory quality and mating success in the field sparrow (*Spizella pusilla*). *Condor* 79:192-204.

Brooks, R. J., and J. B. Falls. 1975. Individual recognition in white-throated sparrows. I. Discrimination of songs of neighbors and strangers. *Can. J. Zool.* 53:879-88.

———. 1975. Individual recognition by song in white-throated sparrows. III. Song features used in individual recognition. *Can. J. Zool.* 53:1749-61.

Brown, J. H., and G. H. Orians. 1970. Spacing patterns in mobile animals. *Ann. Rev. Ecol. Syst.* 1:239-62.

Brown, J. L. 1964. The evolution of diversity in avian territorial systems. *Wilson Bull.* 76:160-69.

——— 1969. Territorial behavior and population regulation in birds. *Wilson Bull.* 81:293-329.

Burger, J. 1981. Super territories: A comment. *Am. Nat.* 118:578-80.

Carey, M., and V. Nolan Jr. 1975. Polygyny in indigo buntings. *Science* 190:1296-97.

Emlen, S. T. 1971. The role of song in individual recognition in the indigo bunting. *Z. Tierpsychol.* 28:241-46.

Falls, J. B., and R. J. Brooks. 1975. Individual recognition by song in white-throated sparrows. II. Effects of location. *Can. J. Zool.* 53:1412-20.

Fergus, C. 1984. *The wingless crow.* Harrisburg, Pa.: Penn. Game Comm.

Ficken, M. S. 1981. What is the song of the black-capped chickadee? *Condor* 83:384-86.

Ficken, M. S., and C. M. Weise. 1984. A complex call of the black-capped chickadee (*Parus atricapillus*). I. Microgeographic variation. *Auk* 101:349-60.

Ficken, M. S., R. W. Ficken, and K. M. Apel. 1985. Dialects in a call associated with pair interactions in the black-capped chickadee. *Auk* 102:145-51.

Ficken, R. W., M. S. Ficken, and J. P. Hailman. 1974. Temporal pattern shifts to avoid acoustic interference in singing birds. *Science* 183:762-63.

Ficken, R. W., J. W. Popp, and P. E. Matthiae. 1985. Avoidance of acoustic interference by ovenbirds. *Wilson Bull.* 97:569-71.

Greenlaw, J. S. 1978. The relation of breeding schedule and clutch size to food supply in the rufous-sided towhee. *Condor* 80:24-33.

Henwood, K., and A. Fabrick. 1979. A quantitative analysis of the dawn chorus: Temporal selection for communicatory optimization. *Am. Nat.* 114:260-74.

Hogstedt, G. 1980. Evolution of clutch size in birds: Adaptive variation in relation to territory quality. *Science* 210:1148-50.

Kroodsma, D. E. 1985. Development and use of two song forms by the eastern phoebe. *Wilson Bull.* 97:21-29.

———. 1976. Reproductive development in a female songbird: Differential stimulation by quality of male song. *Science* 192:574-75.

———. 1977. Correlates of song organization among North American wrens. *Am. Nat.* 111:995-1008.

Marler, P., and S. Peters. 1982. Long-term storage of learned birdsongs prior to production. *Anim. Behav.* 30:479-82.

Marler, P., and R. Pickert. 1984. Species-universal microstructure in the learned song of the swamp sparrow (*Melospiza georgiana*). *Anim. Behav.* 32:673-89.

Marler, P., and V. Sherman. 1985. Innate differences in singing behaviour of sparrows reared in isolation from adult conspecific song. *Anim. Behav.* 33:57-71.

McGregor, P. K., J. R. Krebs, and C. M. Perrins. 1981. Song repertoires and lifetime reproductive success in the great tit (*Parus major*). *Am. Nat.* 118:149-59.

Morton, E. S. 1975. Ecological sources of selection on avian sounds. *Am. Nat.* 109:17-34.

Murray, B. G. Jr. 1971. The ecological consequences of interspecific territorial behavior in birds. *Ecology* 52:414-23.

Orians, G. H., and M. F. Willson. 1964. Interspecific territories of birds. *Ecology* 45:736-45.

Payne, R. B. 1981. Population structure and social behavior: Models for testing the ecological significance of song dialects in birds. In *Natural selection and social behavior*, edited by R. D. Alexander and D.W. Tinkle. New York: Chiron Press.

———. 1982. Ecological consequences of song matching: Breeding success and intraspecific mimicry in indigo buntings. *Ecology* 63:401-11.

———. 1983. The social context of song mimicry: Song-matching dialects in indigo buntings (*Passerina cyanea*). *Anim. Behav.* 31:788-805.

Petrinovich, L., and L. F. Baptista. 1984. Song dialects, mate selection, and breeding success in white-crowned sparrows. *Anim. Behav.* 32:1078-88.

Petrinovich, L., and T. L. Patterson. 1981. The responses of white-crowned sparrows to songs of different dialects and subspecies. *Z. Tierpsychol.* 57:1-14.

Popp, J. W., R. W. Ficken, and J. A. Reinartz. 1985. Short-term avoidance of interspecific acoustic interference among forest birds. *Auk* 102:744-48.

Rice, J. 1978. Ecological relationships of two interspecifically territorial vireos. *Ecology* 59:526-538.

Richards, G. D., and R. H. Wiley. 1980. Reverberations and amplitude fluctuations in the propagation of sound in a forest: Implications for animal communication. *Am. Nat.* 115:381-399.

Ryan, M. J., and E. A. Brenowitz. 1985. The role of body size, phylogeny, and ambient noise in the evolution of bird song. Am. Nat. 126:87-100.

Schoener, T. W. 1968. Sizes of feeding territories among birds. Ecology 49:123-41.

Searcy, W. A. 1984. Song repertoire size and female preferences in song sparrows. Behav. Ecol. Sociobiol. 14:281-86.

Searcy, W. A., and P. Marler. 1984. Interspecific differences in the response of female birds to song repertoires. Z. Tierpsychol. 66:128-42.

Searcy, W. A., P. D. McArthur, and K. Yasukawa. 1985. Song repertoire size and male quality in song sparrows. Condor 87:222-28.

Smith, W. J. 1977. The behavior of communicating: an ethological approach. Cambridge, Mass.: Harvard Univ. Press.

Trainer, J. M. 1983. Changes in song dialect distrbutions and microgeographic variation in song of white-crowned sparrows (Zonotrichia leucophrys nuttalli). Auk 100:568-82.

Verner, J. 1977. On the adaptive significance of territoriality. Am. Nat. 111:769-75.

Weeden, J. S., and J. B. Falls. 1959. Differential responses of male ovenbirds to recorded songs of neighboring and more distant individuals. Auk 76:343-51.

Yasukawa, K., and W. A. Searcy. 1985. Song repertoires and density assessment in red-winged blackbirds: Further tests of the Beau Geste hypothesis. Behav. Ecol. Sociobiol. 16:171-75.

28. Trees and Caterpillars

Baldwin, I. T., and J. C. Schultz. 1983. Rapid changes in tree leaf chemistry induced by damage: Evidence for communication between plants. Science 221:277-79.

Belsky, A. J. 1986. Does herbivory benefit plants? A review of the evidence. Am. Nat. 127:870-92.

Dethier. 1980. Cited in Chap. 25.

Edwards, P. J., and S. D. Wratten. 1982. Wound-induced changes in palatability in birch (Betula pubescens Ehrh. ssp. pubescens). Am. Nat. 120:816-18.

Fitzgerald, T. D. 1983. Caterpillar on a silken thread. Natural History 92:56-63.

Fowler, S. V., and J. H. Lawton. 1985. Rapidly induced defenses and talking trees: The devil's advocate position. Am. Nat. 126:181-95.

Haukioja, E. 1980. On the role of plant defences in the fluctuation of herbivore populations. Oikos 35:202-13.

Haukioja, E., and S. Neuvonen. 1985. Induced long-term resistance of birch foliage against defoliators: Defensive or incidental? Ecology 66:1303-08.

Haukioja, E., and P. Niemela. 1977. Retarded growth of a geometrid larva after mechanical damage to leaves of its host tree. Ann. Zool. Fennici 14:48-52.

———. 1979. Birch leaves as a resource for herbivores: Seasonal occurrence of increased resistance in foliage after mechanical damage of adjacent leaves. Oecologia 39:151-59.

Haukioja, E., J. Suomela, and S. Neuvonen. 1985. Long-term inducible resistance in birch foliage: Triggering cues and efficacy on a defoliator. Oecologia 65:363-69.

Heichel, G. H., and N. C. Turner. 1984. Branch growth and leaf numbers of red maple (Acer rubrum L.) and red oak (Quercus rubra L.): Response to defoliation. Oecologia 62:1-6.

Holmes, R. T., J. C. Schultz, and P. Nothnagle. 1979. Bird predation on forest insects: An exclosure experiment. *Science* 206:462-63.

Lewis, W. H., R .L. Oliver, and T. K. Luikart. 1971. Multiple genotypes in individuals of *Claytonia virginiana*. *Science* 172:564-65.

Morse, D. H. 1971. The insectivorous bird as an adaptive strategy. *Ann. Rev. Ecol. Syst.* 2:177-200.

Neuvonen, S., and E. Haukioja. 1984. Low nutritive quality as defence against herbivores: Induced responses in birch. *Oecologia* 63:71-74.

Rosenthal, G. A. 1986. The chemical defenses of higher plants. *Sci. Am.* 254:94-99.

Schultz, J. C., and I. T. Baldwin. 1982. Oak leaf quality declines in response to defoliation by gypsy moth larvae. *Science* 217:149-50.

Sork, V. 1983. Mast-fruiting in hickories and availability of nuts. *Am. Midl. Nat.* 109:81-88.

White, J. 1979. The plant as a metapopulation. *Ann. Rev. Ecol. Syst.* 10:109-45.

Whitham, T. G., A. G. Williams, and A. M. Robinson. 1984. The variation principle: Individual plants as temporal and spatial mosaics of resistance to rapidly evolving pests. In *A new ecology: Novel approaches to interactive systems*, edited by P. W. Price, C. N. Slobodchikoff, and W. S. Gaud. New York: Wiley.

Whittaker and Feeny. 1971. Cited in Chap. 5.

29. The Remnant Archipelago

Connor, E. F., and E. D. McCoy. 1979. The statistics and biology of the species-area relationship. *Am. Nat.* 113:791-833.

Crowe, T. M. 1979. Lots of weeds: Insular phytogeography of vacant urban lots. *J. Biogeogr.* 6:169-81.

Diamond, J. M. 1975. The island dilemma: Lessons of modern biogeographic studies for the design of nature reserves. *Biol. Conserv.* 7:129-46.

———. 1976. Island biogeography and conservation: Strategy and limitations. *Science* 193:1027-29.

Engel, J. R. 1985. Renewing the bond of mankind and nature: Biosphere reserves as sacred space. *Orion* 4:52-59.

Franklin, J. F. 1977. The biosphere reserve program in the United States. *Science* 195:262-67.

Franklin, I. R. 1980. Evolutionary change in small populations. In *Conservation biology*, edited by M. E. Soulé and B. A. Wilcox. Sunderland, Mass.: Sinauer Assoc.

Gregg, W. P. Jr. 1983. MAB and its biosphere reserves project: A new dimension in global conservation. In *Papers from the 1982 Strategy Conference*. The George Wright Forum.

Harris, L. D. 1984. *The fragmented forest.* Chicago: Univ. of Chicago Press.

Howe, R. W. 1984. Local dynamics of bird assemblages in small forest habitat islands in Australia and North America. *Ecology* 65:1585-1601.

IUCN Conservation Monitoring Centre. 1983. *MAB information system biosphere reserves.* Compilation 3. September.

Kindlmann, P. 1983. Do archipelagos really preserve fewer species than one island of the same total area? *Oecologia* 59:141-44.

Kroodsma, R. L. 1984. Effect of edge on breeding forest bird species. *Wilson Bull.* 96:426-36.

MacArthur, R. H., and E. O. Wilson. 1967. *The theory of island biogeography*. Princeton, N.J.: Princeton Univ. Press.

Margules, C., A. J. Higgs, and R. W. Rafe. 1982. Modern biogeographic theory: Are there any lessons for nature reserve design? *Biol. Conserv.* 24:115-28.

Niering, W. A., and R. H. Goodwin. 1974. Creation of relatively stable shrublands with herbicides: Arresting "succession" on rights-of-way and pastureland. *Ecology* 55:784-95.

O'Brien, S. J., D. E. Wildt, and M. Bush. 1986. The cheetah in genetic peril. *Sci. Am.* 254 (5): 84-92.

O'Brien, S. J. et al. 1985. Genetic basis for species vulnerability in the cheetah. *Science* 227:1428-34.

Riebesell, J. F. 1982. Arctic-alpine plants on mountaintops: Agreement with island biogeography theory. *Am. Nat.* 119:657-74.

Shaffer, M. L. 1981. Minimum population sizes for species conservation. *BioScience* 31:131-34.

Simberloff, D. S., and L. G. Abele. 1976. Island biogeography theory and conservation practice. *Science* 191:285-86.

———. 1982. Refuge design and island biogeographic theory: Effects of fragmentation. *Am. Nat.* 120:41-50.

Soulé, M. E. 1980. Thresholds for survival: Maintaining fitness and evolutionary potential. In *Conservation biology*, edited by M. E. Soulé and B. A. Wilcox. Sunderland, Mass.: Sinauer Assoc.

Soulé, M., ed.. 1987. *Viable populations for conservation*. New York: Cambridge Univ. Press.

Tallamy, D. W. 1983. Equilibrium biogeography and its application to insect host-parasite systems. *Am. Nat.* 121:244-54.

Terborgh, J., and B. Winter. 1980. Some causes of extinction. In *Conservation biology*, edited by M. E. Soulé and B. A. Wilcox. Sunderland, Mass.: Sinauer Assoc.

Washburn, J. O. 1984. The gypsy moth and its parasites in North America: A community in equilibirum? *Am. Nat.* 124:288-92.

Wilcove, D. S. 1985. Nest predation in forest tracts and the decline of migratory songbirds. *Ecology* 66:1211-14.

Wilcove, D. S., and R. F. Whitcomb. 1983. Gone with the trees. *Natural History* 9:82-91.

Wilcox, B. A. 1980. Insular ecology and conservation. In *Conservation biology*, edited by M. E. Soulé and B. A. Wilcox. Sunderland, Mass.: Sinauer Assoc.

Wilcox, B. A., and D. D. Murphy. 1985. Conservation strategy: The effects of fragmentation on extinction. *Am. Nat.* 125:879-87.

Wilson, E. O., and E. O. Willis. 1975. Applied biogeography: The design of nature preserves. In *Ecology and evolution of communities*, edited by M. L. Cody and J.M. Diamond. Cambridge, Mass.: Belknap Press.

———. n.d. Parks, bioreserves, and recreation.

Wauer, R. H. n.d. Resource management in biosphere reserves.

30. Abuse, Resurrection, Hope

Baes, C. F. III, and S. B. McLaughlin. 1984. Trace elements in tree rings: Evidence of recent and historical air pollution. *Science* 224:494-97.

Boring, L. R., C. D. Monk, and W. T. Swank. 1981. Early regeneration of a clear-cut southern Appalachian forest. *Ecology* 62:1244-53.

Bratton, S. P. 1975. The effect of the European wild boar, *Sus scrofa*, on gray beech forest in the Great Smoky Mountains. *Ecology* 56:1356-66.

Campbell, R. W. 1979. Gypsy moth: Forest influence. *Agric. Info. Bull. No. 423*. U.S. Dept. Agric., Forest Serv. Washington, D.C.: GPO. (Stock No. 001-000-03928-8. 44 p.)

Carrick, T. R. 1979. The effect of acid water on the hatching of salmonid eggs. *J. Fish Biol.* 14:165-72.

Chiras, D. D. 1991. *Environmental science: Action for a sustainable future*. Menlo Park, Calif.: Benjamin/Cummings Publ.

Cronan, C. S., and W. A. Reiners. 1983. Canopy processing of acidic precipitation by coniferous and hardwood forests in New England. *Oecologia* 59:216-23.

Fritz, E. S. 1980. *Potential impacts of low pH on fish and fish populations*. U.S. Dept. Interior, Fish and Wildl. Serv. Washington, D.C.: GPO. (FSW/OBS-80/40.2. 14 p.)

Fromm, P. O. 1980. A review of some physiological and toxicological responses of freshwater fish to acid stress. *Env. Biol. Fish.* 5:79-93.

Galloway, J. N., G. E. Likens, and M. E. Hawley. 1984. Acid precipitation: Natural versus anthropogenic components. *Science* 226:829-30.

Glenn, L. C. 1911. Denudation and erosion in the southern Appalachian region and the Monongahela basin. *U.S. Geol. Surv. Prof. Paper 72*. U.S. Dept. Interior.

Gorham, E., F. B. Martin, and J. T. Litzau. 1984. Acid rain: Ionic correlations in the eastern United States, 1980-1981. *Science* 225:407-9.

Haines, B., M. Stefani, and F. Hendrix. 1980. Acid rain: Threshold of leaf damage in eight plant species from a southern Appalachian forest succession. *Water, Air, and Soil Pollution* 14:403-7.

Haines, T. A. 1981. Acidic precipitation and its consequences for aquatic ecosystems: A review. *Trans. Am. Fish. Soc.* 110:669-707.

Johnson, A. H., T. G. Siccama, R. S. Turner, and D. G. Lord. 1984. Assessing the possibility of a link between acid precipitation and decreased growth rates of trees in the northeastern United States. In *Direct and indirect effects of acidic deposition on vegetation*, edited by R. A. Linthurst. Boston: Butterworth Publ.

Johnson, N. M., G. E. Likens, M. C. Feller, and C. T. Driscoll. 1984. Acid rain and soil chemistry. *Science* 225:1424-25.

LaBastille, A. 1987. *Beyond Black Bear Lake*. New York: W.W. Norton and Co.

Leonard, D. E. 1981. Bioecology of the gypsy moth. In *The gypsy moth: Research toward integrated pest management*, edited by C. C. Doane and M. L. McManus. U.S. Dept. Agric., Forest Service Tech. Bull. 1584. Washington, D.C.: GPO.

Leopold, A. 1966. *A Sand County almanac*. New York: Ballantine Books.

Likens, G. E., R. F. Wright, J. N. Galloway, and T. J. Butler. 1979. Acid rain. *Sci. Am.* 241 (4): 43-51.

Mason, C. J., and M. L. McManus. 1981. Larval dispersal of the gypsy moth. In *The gypsy moth: Research toward integrated pest management*, edited by C. C. Doane and M. L. McManus. U.S. Dept. Agric., Forest Service Tech. Bull. 1584. Washington, D.C.: GPO.

Pierce, B. A., J. B. Hoskins, and E. Epstein. 1984. Acid tolerance in Connecticut wood frogs (*Rana sylvatica*). *J. Herpetol.* 18:159-67.

Pough, F. H. 1976. Acid precipitation and embryonic mortality of spotted salamanders, *Ambystoma maculatum*. *Science* 192:68-70.

Rahn, K. A., and D. H. Lowenthal. 1986. The acid rain whodunit. *Natural History* 95: 62-65.

Schofield, C. L. 1976. Acid precipitation: Effects on fish. *Ambio* 5:228-30.

Smith, C. W. G. 1986. What's killing the sugar maples? *Country Journal* (March):46-49.

Smith, H. R., and R. A. Lautenschlager. 1981. Gypsy moth predators. In *The gypsy moth: Research toward integrated pest management*, edited by C. C. Doane and M. L. McManus. U.S. Dept. Agric., Forest Service Tech. Bull. 1584. Washington, D.C.: GPO.

Swain, R. B. 1983. *Field days*. New York: Charles Scribner's Sons.

Index

George and Leah inspect a red-eyed vireo's nest near their home in Hampshire County, West Virginia.
—photo by Steve Fretwell

About the Author

George Constantz, a biologist and naturalist, founded Pine Cabin Run Ecological Laboratory, a nonprofit organization dedicated to preserving Appalachian rivers through science and education.

Born in Washington, D.C. in 1947, Constantz spent six years of his childhood in Barranquilla, Colombia, among the iguanas of the Magdalena River's floodplain, and in Chihuahua, Mexico, where he loved to chase roadrunners through the desert.

Since receiving a B.A. in biology from the University of Missouri-St. Louis and a Ph.D. in zoology from Arizona State University, Constantz has worked as a park naturalist, a college and high school teacher of biology and environmental science, a fish ecologist, a researcher, and a writer. Currently, he coordinates the West Virginia Watershed Conservation and Management Program.

Constantz lives with his wife, Nancy, and their daughter, Leah, in a pre-Civil War Appalachian log cabin nestled in a hollow off the Cacapon River in West Virginia.